O9-BTJ-622

The Macmillan Treasury of SPICES AND NATURAL FLAVORINGS

The Macmillan Treasury of

SPICES

AND NATURAL FLAVORINGS

A complete guide to the identification and uses of common and exotic spices and natural flavorings

JENNIFER MULHERIN

MACMILLAN PUBLISHING COMPANY
866 Third Avenue, New York, NY10022

Designed and produced by
Nicholas Enterprises Ltd,
70 Old Compton Street,
London W1V 5PA

Editor: Jacqueline Jackson
Art Director: Tom Deas
Illustrator: Ron Hayward
Photographer: Graham Young

The publishers would like to thank

Mike Clarke,
International Purchasing Co-Ordinator,
McCormick and Company Incorporated,
Dormer Road, Thame, Oxon, Great Britain.

for reviewing the information in this book.

Macmillan Publishing Company
866 Third Avenue, New York, N.Y. 10022
Collier Macmillan Canada, Inc

Library of Congress Cataloging-in-Publication Data

Mulherin, Jennifer.
The Macmillan treasury of spices and natural flavorings: a complete guide to the identification and uses of common and exotic spices and natural flavorings/Jennifer Mulherin.
p. cm.
Bibliography: P.
Includes index.
ISBN 0-02-587850-6
1. Spices—Dictionaries. 2.Herbs—Dictionaries. 3. Flavoring essences—Dictionaries. I. Title.
TX406.M85 1988
641.3'38'0321—dc19 88-16986
CIP

10 9 8 7 6 5 4 3 2 1

Printed in Belgium

Contents

Botanical (Latin) names of spices and plants

Notes on recipes Servings are for four people, unless otherwise stated. Measures are in metric and Imperial and include American cup measurements for larger volumes. For smaller measures, teaspoons or tablespoons are indicated for the greater convenience of the cook. Where old or traditional recipes are included, these are direct quotations, without conversions.

Introduction

There is something magical about the way spices and flavourings transform simple ingredients into exotic dishes which conjure up the aroma of Eastern bazaars and hint at oriental mystery. Even more fascinating are the history and legend that surround them. How spices were used in the past, and why, are aspects of social history often neglected by general historians. Recently too, there has been an upsurge of interest in the West in unusual spices as more people discover the delights of Thai, Vietnamese, Korean and Mexican cuisines (to name but a few), and as they want to reproduce these authentic flavours at home. Since all kinds of spices are becoming increasingly available, this is now not only possible but easy.

What spices and natural flavourings are and what criteria have dictated the choice of entries in this book can be defined by the following. Spices are usually the dried, aromatic parts of plants – generally, the seeds, berries, roots, pods and sometimes leaves and flesh – which mainly, but not invariably, grow in hot countries. Each one has its own characteristic flavour and bouquet which, when added to food, are unmistakable. Included too, are those flavourings which are also called herbs or vegetables such as oregano, bay and horseradish, onion and mushroom. These, in my opinion, warrant a whole entry to themselves because, like spices, they add their distinctive flavour to any dish in which they appear. Other natural flavourings included are nuts, honeys and syrups, strongly flavoured herbs, alcoholic flavourings, malt extracts, scented and milk flavourings. This selection is, I know, a fairly subjective one and covers only a number of ingredients which add their individual recognizable flavour, aroma and texture to food. Some, perhaps, like maple syrup or spirits, are hardly 'natural' by the time they reach the kitchen, having undergone refinements or industrial processes but they were – like condiments and ketchups – made at home and are, of course, a part of the history of flavourings in the kitchen.

The medicinal uses of spices in the past, like herbs, were often indistinguishable from their culinary uses, particularly so in medieval times, when apothecaries prescribed herbs and spices not merely for digestive problems, but for all types of ailments in a truly 'natural' form of medicine. Where spices and flavourings have had a long-standing, and even present-day, medicinal use, this has been noted in the text. The botanical and family names of plants are included where appropriate, as an aid to identification.

The reference section at the end of the book is principally a memory aid. Here, you will find a summary of the characteristics and uses of the spices and flavourings in different cuisines; a list of the botanical, common and foreign names for each spice (particularly useful for identifying Eastern flavourings); some further reading (including recipe books) and a list of useful addresses.

The way spices and flavouring can magically transform a dish was illustrated recently, when a friend described to me in exquisite detail a fish dish surprisingly flavoured, or rather delicately scented, with unsweetened vanilla – a novel, unorthodox and yet successful use of this fragrant spice, which is almost commonplace when used in ice creams and puddings but which, in the hands of a creative cook, can become innovative.

My aim has been to provide the reader with the essential facts about a number of common and unusual spices and flavourings, particularly how to identify them and use them in their time-honoured, traditional ways. This, however, is merely a starting point for the imaginative cook who, in rediscovering the extraordinary versatility of these simple but valuable substances, will be inspired to try new flavour combinations.

Spices in history

These provisions from the tomb of Tutankhamen were found recently and include many spices which are still used today.

Of the foods we eat, there are few which have had such a profound effect on our language and history as spices. In the quest for these simple, unassuming commodities, whole continents were discovered and subdued, and empires founded and destroyed for, at one time, spices were as precious and rare as gold and just as treasured. Nor is it an accident that so many spices were once regarded as aphrodisiacs. Associated with faraway, exotic lands, they colour the literature of the Bible and *The Arabian Nights*, hinting at sensuous pleasures and the mysterious East. Small wonder that the 17th century Puritans believed that spices inflamed the passions and banned their use – and that 'spice' or 'spicy' have an emotive as well as literal meaning, as something that adds piquancy or interest to, for instance, life or describes something that is racy or even risqué.

The use of spices predates recorded history. Archaeologists have found that caraway and sesame seeds were used by ancient civilizations; the Chinese knew of cassia and soy as long ago as 3000-2500 BC; and the ancient Egyptians used spices for embalming, while onions and garlic were staple foods for their slaves.

From Biblical to Roman times

The Queen of Sheba brought spices among other gifts to King Solomon who sang their praises, 'Awake, O north wind, and come thou south, blow upon my garden, that the spices thereof may flow out; let my beloved come into his garden and eat his pleasant fruits' (Song of Solomon 4:14,16). Solomon lived in about 1000 BC but even earlier cinnamon and cassia were part of the holy oil with which Moses anointed the Ark of the Covenant.

No one knew where these spices came from, although in 450 BC the great Greek historian, Herodotus recorded a curious and fabled account of the harvesting of cinnamon and cassia in Arabia. Neither grow in the Arabian peninsula but it was, of course, the Arabs who controlled the ancient spice trade. Precious spices came to Europe from China and India along the old caravan routes and particularly the Silk Route which wound south of the Gobi desert, north of the Himalayas and passed through Afghanistan and Persia before reaching eastern Europe. Arabian traders grew rich on the pleasure-loving Romans' insatiable appetite for highly seasoned and exotic food. Pliny the Elder, writing in AD 70, deplored the excessive amount of gold leaving the Empire's treasury, 'At the very lowest computation, India, the Seres and the Arabian Peninsula withdraw from our empire 100 million sesterces every year – so dearly do we pay for our luxury and our women.'

By this time, and probably even earlier, eastern spices were also being carried by Indonesian traders across vast tracts of open ocean to the east coast of Africa and the Arabian peninsula to be transported to Rome. Coriander, cloves, mustard, anise and caraway were all spices known and extensively used by the Romans in a cuisine which was as refined as any today. Throughout their campaigns in Europe and Britain, they introduced over 400 spices and herbs, many of which were lost in the Dark Ages, only to be rediscovered at the time of the Crusades.

Spices rediscovered

With the barbarian invasions following the fall of Rome, Europe sank back into its old ways, forgetting, it would seem,

Vasco da Gama (*c.* 1524)

Right An Italian 15th century fresco of the interior of a pharmacy.

all it had learnt from Roman civilization and it was not until the Normans conquered much of France (and Britain) that Europe began to emerge from its torpor. Some spices and herbs found their way to the West but it was not until the 11th century when the Crusades took European warriors to new lands that a passion for spices was awakened.

In Asia Minor and the Holy Land, the crusaders found new customs, new vices (sodomy and syphilis) – and spices such as cinnamon, nutmeg, mace and coriander. When the conquerors returned, they brought these with them, as well as rose and orange water and almonds. A thriving trade began with the East, centred on Venice, and silks, perfumes and oriental spices travelled their traditional routes to the West, transported, as before, by the enterprising Arabs. Venice, however, was the sole agent for the distribution of spices in Europe and gold was the currency in which she dealt. Before spices reached the kitchens of kings, princes and aspiring merchants, they had changed hands several times for fabulous sums of money. However, within a century or so, spices were common enough in Europe – although still expensive – to be casually mentioned by Geoffrey Chaucer (1340-1400) in *The Canterbury Tales*.

The herbs were springing in the vale:
Green ginger plants and liquorice pale
And cloves their sweetness offer,
With nutmegs, too, to put in ale
No matter whether fresh or stale,
Or else to keep in coffer.

Imperial and mercantile ambitions

For 300 years from the 16th century, a number of factors combined to produce an expansion of the hitherto known world to the furthest corners of the globe. New skills in navigation and shipbuilding coupled with imperial ambitions opened up exotic lands in the East and in the New World; most were not colonized peaceably but by force, for all these lands had a wealth of natural resources, particularly spices, which could be exploited by their conquerors – as well as a native population which could be enslaved or converted to Christianity.

In the 1480s, the Portuguese rounded Africa and in 1497 Vasco da Gama landed on Indian soil announcing, 'I have come for Christians and spices.' Like the Portuguese, the Spaniards also had territorial ambitions, and in 1492 Christopher Colombus sailed west and discovered the New World (and capsicum peppers), but not the eastern spices he was looking for. In the early years of the following century, the Portuguese established dominance in the Spice Islands (the Moluccas) and gained the monopoly of nutmeg, mace and cloves for nearly 100 years; in turn, in America and the West Indies, the Spaniards discovered the new spices of chilli, vanilla and allspice which found immediate favour in Europe.

The quest for spices was, in many ways, comparable to the search for oil and minerals in recent years, for the discovery of these valuable commodities created instant wealth and power – and stirred up envy and rivalries in other nations.

By the beginning of the 17th century, the French, English and Dutch were determined to get in on the act. With ruthless, single-minded efficiency, unhampered by the Christian zeal which partly influenced the Spanish and Portuguese, they achieved their aims, ousting the Spaniards from much of the New World and creating empires in the East which were to exist for the next three centuries.

The rise and fall of cloves

The story of an individual spice such as the clove illustrates imperial and mercantile ambitions in detail and gives a fascinating insight into the effect of colonial domination on an ancient tribal society.

Cultivated in the Moluccas for some ten centuries before the arrival of the Portuguese, Chinese records show that during the Han dynasty in the 3rd century BC, cloves were used as breath sweeteners and for the relief of toothache. A vigorous trade existed then and later between the Moluccas and the civilizations of China, India and Arabia – from which sources cloves entered Europe.

When the Portuguese conquered the Moluccas, cloves fetched three times the price of pepper in Europe, so their potential wealth was therefore substantial. Although the Portuguese built fortresses in the Moluccas, they were not strongly established in the islands and somewhat distanced themselves by largely buying their cloves from local traders at the port of Malacca (north of modern Singapore). With their missionary zeal, too, they were unpopular with the predominantly Muslim Moluccans who, at first, welcomed the Dutch conquest of the islands over a century later.

The Dutch East India Company, a joint capital venture, was set up with only one motive – profit. To this end, the Dutch imposed organization on to the cultivation and harvesting of the spice, as well as to its trade. So successful were they that

a glut of cloves flooded the European market, the spice was devalued and a ten-year supply, stored in Amsterdam warehouses, had to be officially burnt. In a desperate move to save their investment, the Company took drastic action and ordered the destruction of all clove trees in the Moluccas except for those on one island, Amboyna, where production was to be strictly controlled.

The Dutch policy of 'extirpation' was carried out with characteristic efficiency, so that in 1625 alone, 65,000 clove trees were cut down, with devastating effect on the local population who had traditionally traded cloves for rice. With one blow, a prosperous society was reduced to subsistence level, a traumatic experience, the memory of which still lingers in many local rituals surrounding clove cultivation.

In some areas, a religious leader must be present when cloves are planted and harvested; they must be planted when there is no new moon; and in Frazer's *The Golden Bough*, the author records, 'When the clove trees are in blossom, they are treated like pregnant women. No noise may be made near them; no light nor fire may be carried past them at night; no man may approach them with his hat on, all must uncover in their presence. These precautions are observed lest the trees should be alarmed and bear no fruit, or should drop its fruit too soon like the untimely delivery of a woman who has been frightened in her pregnancy.'

The Dutch East India Company went bankrupt in 1799, soon after the first batch of French cloves, grown from smuggled seedlings, were harvested in Mauritius in 1776, so ending the Dutch monopoly. Soon, cloves were no longer rare and today, like most other spices, they come from a number of sources, are reasonably priced, neatly packaged and available in supermarkets and grocery shops all over the world.

So despite the centuries of struggle among peoples who tried to control their trade, spices continued to be available to cooks who needed them. However, these once costly items, although common, are not commonplace. The vitality and magic of these age-old flavourings still remains and in modest kitchens everywhere they continue to add liveliness and 'spice' to lift simple dishes out of the ordinary.

Traditional uses of spices and flavourings

It is a common assumption that among the traditional uses of spices was their role in disguising food that was well past its best. While this may have been so of much medieval cooking, in Roman times, spices and flavourings were used in a cuisine as sophisticated and imaginative as any today. This is amply illustrated in a work *De Re Coquinaria* (On Cookery) by Apicius, a famous gourmet of the first century who, it is said, poisoned himself rather than give up his epicurean tastes. Apicius' recipes show that oriental spices and herbs (as well as perfumes, precious stones and silks) were part of a flourishing trade with the East which, as Pliny observed, created a severe strain on the Imperial treasury. One writer has even suggested that the Roman aristocracy's passion for expensive foreign spices over a period of four centuries contributed in no small way to the economic decline of the Empire.

Nowhere is the Roman's love of good living more evident than in Apicius' work where 90 percent of his recipes call for the use of imported spices, particularly pepper which was used as a universal flavouring in both sweet and savoury dishes to give pungency. Ginger, cinnamon, cardamom, nutmeg, cloves and asafoetida were also imported flavourings in the Roman kitchen, while European herbs and spices such as coriander, cumin, oregano, celery seed, bay, aniseed, mint, caraway and mustard seed appear regularly. Apicius, for example, cooked mushrooms in a wine and coriander sauce using a recipe similar to the popular *à la grecque* method today, offered tripe in a cinnamon-nutmeg sauce, stuffed chicken with almonds and ginger and made rose and violet wines.

Salt-pickled fish was a luxury food in Roman times but by the Middle Ages, salt was a major household item, the price of which was as regularly recorded in account books as that of grain. From such times until the age of canning and refrigeration, cured and brined products were among the most common types of meat and fish eaten by ordinary people since freshly slaughtered meat, even when it became available, was not particularly cheap. The hams, bacon, and salt beef and pork so popular today are great culinary legacies from past times, and although curing and salting are rarely carried out at home except in some farmhouse kitchens, interest in these traditional techniques is reviving. Many recipes for brines and pickling liquids can be found in old cook books; they are easily prepared and the results are particularly satisfying.

Pa'an spices on display for sale in New Delhi, India.

Green peppercorns growing in Brazil.

Spices for health

In Roman times and throughout the Middle Ages, herbs and spices were as much valued for their health-giving properties as for their flavour and it is rare to find a flavouring used solely for its taste. Hot spices like pepper were regarded as an appetite stimulant and a digestive aid; asafoetida, now known only in Indian cookery, was used by the Romans as a healing ointment, an antidote for snakebites and as a cure for gout, cramps, pleurisy and tetanus; spiced salts were made with ginger, pepper, cumin, thyme and celery seed which, according to Apicius, were good for the digestion, for promoting regularity and preventing all sorts of illnesses, plagues and chills; and citron seeds were given to pregnant women to relieve nausea. Roman and medieval writers believed that fennel helped to promote and restore good vision and it was at one time a cure for obesity. Almost every food flavouring has some attributed property, the most curious perhaps attaching to sugar, today regarded as a major contributor to many diseases.

Sugar and spice . . .

Although the Romans knew of sugar, it was used not in the kitchen where honey was the accepted sweetener, but as a medicine; an idea inherited from the Arabs who used it as a tonic. Rediscovered again by the first crusaders who 'beheld with astonishment and tasted with delight, as a thing unknown, the cane growing in the plains of Tripoli', sugar found its way into western Europe. Rare and very expensive at first, only royal households and apothecaries had it, for its principal use was as a remedy for colds and consumption. Little twists of sugar (like barley sugar) called *penidia* became a famous protection against the common cold throughout Europe and were given to delicate children and nursing mothers to improve their health.

It cannot be said that sugar was used with discrimination in rich medieval housholds for it flavoured fish and meat dishes as well as the popular digestive 'comfits'. These were a most interesting use of spices, similar to the *pa'an* served at the end of an Indian meal today. Seeds such as caraway or aniseed were encased in up to ten coats of molten sugar and served on elegant silver platters as a final course at banquets. The practice was known in Europe as *voidée* and the idea was to relax the diner and aid digestion; an identical practice existed in Moghul courts at the same time. A recipe book of the 1630s also shows that sugar was sprinkled over trout cooked in wine, herbs and mace, over minced lamb and over a leg of lamb stuffed with cloves, mace, nutmeg, rose water, caraway seeds and dried fruit.

Although refined to varying degrees of whiteness, sugar was undoubtedly healthier for being less refined than now and the craving for its concentrated sweetness caught on. Despite its expense, it became increasingly used in the kitchen until by the end of the 18th century even the poorest families could not do without a few ounces each week. Interestingly, its medicinal reputation was still high and cough syrups were made with sugar, liquorice and coriander seeds, a rose and sugar syrup was recommended for melancholy, and a violet syrup for fever.

Preserved and dried vegetables and dried and salted fish.

The beginning of taste

Even before the popularity of sugar, the combination of sweet and savoury flavours in a prepared dish was commonplace. This was largely due to limited cooking methods before the introduction of the kitchen range in the 18th century. Generally, food was either roasted on a spit or boiled in a single cauldron over an open fire. Meat, vegetables and puddings were all therefore cooked in the same broth. Before methods of feeding livestock over winter were introduced, spices undoubtedly helped to conceal frequently rancid meat but even when freshly slaughtered meat was available, at least in the households of the rich, regular spicing was habitual. Palates had simply become accustomed to strong aromatic flavours and without them, food tasted insipid.

Pottages (various mixes of powdered grain combined with chicken, pork or veal flesh) were the standard fare for rich and poor alike. While locally grown herbs and flavourings may have added interest to the often meatless pottages of the poor, in aristocratic households exotic spices enhanced this basic dish. Fanciful combinations such as *blanc dessore* graced the banquets of the rich, along with brightly coloured jellies sculptured into fantastic shapes which were more for show than for eating. *Blanc dessore* consisted of pounded chicken flesh amalgamated with broth, breadcrumbs, egg yolks, ground almonds and spices and was sometimes coloured gold with saffron. A beef stew, too, in the late Middle Ages would have contained cinnamon, cloves, mace, grains of paradise, cubeb, minced onions, parsley, sage and saffron; and although such combinations seem curious, perhaps they are not so very far removed from many of the amalgams of sweet fruits or vinegars and meat which appear on gourmet menus in 'designer' restaurants today.

More discriminate flavouring

It was not until the middle of the 17th century that a more discriminate use of spices and flavourings is discernable. This was because of the increasing availability and relative cheapness of imported spices due, at least in Britain, to the East India trade and the importation of sugar and spices from colonial possessions in the West Indies and Americas. As exotically spiced food became less associated with the wealth and status of its presenter, it became more subjective or a matter of 'taste'. Increasingly, women turned to cookery (chefs in royal households had always been men) bringing a practical and pragmatic approach to the everyday fare of a now prosperous and influential middle class.

Conserves and preserves became fashionable with the general availability of sugar, and spices such as cinnamon and vanilla became increasingly used specifically for sweet dishes and puddings (which could now be prepared in separate pots), while pungent spices flavoured savoury dishes including the Anglo-Indian food which had been introduced from the East. Oddly, colonial influences were more apparent in British food than in most European food; highly spiced Creole and Indo-chinese cookery, for example, had little impact on traditional French cuisine and to this day have never been absorbed into it.

Pickles and sauces

Along with the vogue for sweet jams and preserves came the introduction of hot pickles and chutneys, stimulated by the East India commerce. Pickles made from exotic vegetables such as mangoes, squashes and limes reached England in the late 17th century and were copied using local ingredients such as cucumbers, melons and onions. Piccalilli, with ginger, garlic, pepper, mustard seed and turmeric, made its appearance at this time and has been successfully produced in British kitchens ever since.

The spicy bottled sauces and ketchups which are a part of everyday cuisine in English-speaking countries, developed from chutneys and pickles, when cooks and housewives found that the liquor in which, say, mushrooms were pickled was more piquant than the pickled vegetables themselves. So where spices were once added directly to food, now long-lasting sauces were produced to season ready-made food according to the preference of the individual diner. Harvey's sauce was one of the most famous, requiring anchovies, walnut pickles, soy, shallots, an ounce of cayenne, three heads of garlic and a gallon of vinegar. This was mixed together, stirred every day for a fortnight and then bottled. Like Worcester sauce, Harvey's sauce was soon produced commercially, as was tomato ketchup (a fiery blend which included large quantities of chillies plus other spices); although all continued to be made in the kitchen until the 1900s. (*See* Condiments, sauces and chutneys, pages 132-5.)

Nowadays cooks are rediscovering these traditional uses for spices and, while some of the recipes in this chapter are merely of historical interest, others are refreshingly different, even imaginative, and could well be tried today.

Canned and bottled foods (*c*.1897).

Left The vogue for sauces, pickles and extracts began in the 18th and 19th centuries as colonial influences grew.

RECIPES

Broccoli in coriander and wine sauce
Boil the stalks and put them in a saucepan with some stock, oil, wine and cumin. Sprinkle with pepper, and chop chives, cumin and green coriander over it.
Apicius, 1st century AD

Dark sauce for roasted capons
Take the liver of capons and roast it whole. Take anise and grains of Paris [cardamom], ginger, canel [cinnamon] and a little crust of bread and grind it small; and grind it with verjuice [brandy] and with chicken juices. Boil it and serve it forth.
The Forme of Cury, c1390

Knot biscuits
To make Knots or Gumballs: Take 12 yolks of eggs and 5 whites, a pound of searced [granulated] sugar, half a pound of butter washed in rose water, 3 quarters of an ounce of mace finely beaten, a little salt dissolved in rose water, half an ounce of caraway seeds; mingle all these together with as much flour as will work it up in paste, and so make it into knots or rings or what fashion you please. Bake them as biscuit bread, but upon pie-plates.
Henry Fairfax, *Arcana Fairfaxiana*, 18th century

Dutch pudding
Take a pound and a half of fresh beef, all lean, take a pound and a quarter of beef suet, sliced both very small; then take a half-penny stale loaf and grate it, a handful of sage and a little winter savoury, a little thyme, shred these very small; take 4 eggs, half a pint of cream, a few cloves, nutmegs, mace and pepper, finely beaten, mingle them all together very well, with a little salt; roll it all up together in a green colwort [cabbage] leaf, and then tie it up hard in a linen cloth. [Simmer about 2 hours]. Garnish your dish with grated bread and serve it up with mustard in saucers.
Elizabeth Cromwell, 18th century

Basil vinegar or wine
Fill a wide mouthed bottle with fresh green leaves of basil and cover them with vinegar or wine, and let them steep for 10 days; if you wish a very strong essence, strain the liquor, put it on some fresh leaves and let it steep 14 days longer.'
Richard Dolby Cook's *Dictionary and Housekeeper's Directory*, 1832
[Another early 19th century cookery writer observes of basil vinegar, 'the French add cloves and lemon rind: we admire this addition.']

Tapp's sauce
Take of green sliced mangoes, salt, sugar and raisins each 8 ounces; red chillies and garlic each 4 ounces; green ginger 6 ounces; vinegar 3 bottles; lime juice 1 pint. Pound several ingredients well; then add the vinegar and lime juice; stop the vessel close, and expose it to the sun a whole month, stirring and shaking it well daily; then strain it through a cloth, bottle and cork it tight. The residue makes an excellent chutney.
Indian Domestic Economy, 1850

Cumberland sauce
Cut the rind, free from pith, of two Seville oranges into very thin strips half an inch in length, which blanch in boiling water, drain them upon a sieve and put them into a basin, with a spoonful of mixed English mustard, four of currant jelly, a little pepper, salt (mix well together) and half a pint of good port wine.
Alexis Soyer, *Gastronomic Regenerator*, 1853

To make stewed steaks
Take a piece of mutton, and cut it into pieces, and wash it very clean and put it in a fair pot with ale, or with half wine; then make it boil, and skim it clean and put into your pot a faggot of rosemary and thyme; then some parsley picked fine and some onions cut round and let them all boil together; and season it with cinnamon and ginger, nutmegs, two or three cloves and salt; and so serve it on plates and garnish it with fruit.
Thomas Dawson, *The Good Huswifes Jewell*, 1596

The right way to make coffee
. . . is to heat the berries in a fire shovel till they sweat a little; and then grind them, and put the coffee pot over the fire with water; when hot, throw the water away, and dry the pot by the fire, then put the powder into it, and boiling water immediately over the same; let it stand three or four minutes, and pour off the clear. By this means the hot water meets the spirit of the coffee; whereas if you boil coffee, as the common way is, the spirit goes away, so that it will not be so strong or quick to the taste.
William Ellis, mid-18th century

Unusual spices and flavourings

There are some spices and flavourings which are rarely found outside their countries of origin or which have only limited use in special cuisines. Travellers abroad or cooks coming across them in ethnic grocery shops or even cookery books may be puzzled by what they are and how they are used. The following includes some of these unusual ingredients and, where possible, substitutes that can be used in the Western kitchen.

Ajowan (*Carum ajowan*), a member of the parsley family, is used in Middle Eastern and Indian cookery for its seeds which look rather like large celery seeds. In Indian cookery books, it is sometimes called 'lovage', has a strong, pungent flavour of thyme and is added to lentil dishes (*dhals*), savouries, breads and sometimes to curry mixes. In the Middle East, ajowan water is often used for diarrhoea and wind and in India the seeds are a home remedy for indigestion and asthma. It is probable in India that ajowan is used as much for its medicinal properties as for its flavouring. It is available in the West in Indian grocery shops.

Amchoor (*Mangifera indica*), an important flavouring in Indian curries, chutneys and pickles, is unripe, leathery mango slices dried to a light brown. Also available in powdered form, it is used as a souring or tenderizing agent and to add an agreeable piquancy to mainly vegetarian curries. Unlike tamarind (*see* page 92), which is similarly used, it needs no preparation and can, if necessary, be substituted for it. It is generally stocked by most Indian grocery shops.

Annatto (*Bixa orellana*), native to the West Indies and tropical Americas, is grown for its orangey-red seeds which colour and give a slight peppery flavour to various soups, stews and fish dishes in Caribbean and Latin American cookery. It is an ingredient in the spicy sauce which is served with the Jamaican national dish, ackee and salt cod, and was introduced to the Phillipines by the Spaniards where it features in such dishes as *ukoy* (shrimp and potato cakes) and *pipian* (a chicken and pork dish). In the West, it is principally used as a colouring for cheeses such as Leicester and Red Cheshire and in confectionery. Although rarely available in grocery stores, one may come across it under its Spanish name '*achiote*' or as '*roucou*', its name in former French and Dutch colonies. If called for in a recipe, turmeric can be substituted.

Carob (*Ceratonia siliqua*) is the sweet-flavoured, fragrant seed of a tree which grows around the Mediterranean, in the Middle East and in India. Available commercially in powdered form (and in bars for eating) from health-food shops, it is mainly used in cooking as a chocolate substitute since it does not induce the allergies associated with chocolate which some people experience.

Cubeb (*Piper cubeba*), the dried unripe berry of a climbing plant native to Java, has a pungent, spicy flavour similar to allspice but more peppery. A popular spice in the West in Roman and medieval times, its use is now mainly confined to Indonesia where it flavours a number of curries. It is not commonly available outside Indonesia but should you find it, it can be used to good effect as an interesting substitute for allspice in conventional recipes.

Galangals are spicy, ginger-like roots used extensively in south-east Asian cookery. There are two varieties: greater (*Alpinia galanga*), better known as *laos* (Indonesia) or *leugkuas* (Malay); and lesser (*Alpinia officinarum*), often called *kenchur* (Indonesia). Both have a peppery ginger flavour, although *kenchur* is more pungent than greater galangal. Like ginger, the roots are sometimes available fresh in oriental shops but are more common in powdered form. Once well known in Europe (Chaucer mentions them) and used for their stimulating and tonic qualities by the Arabs, the galangals are important flavourings in all south-east Asian cookery (except in Chinese-influenced dishes), with *laos* being the most significant. They feature in fish dishes particularly, but *laos* also adds its distinctive flavour to delicately spiced food, as well as soups, *satés* and pungent curries of all kinds. Ginger with a little pepper makes an acceptable substitute.

Grains of Paradise (*Aframomum* or *Amomum melegueta*), also known as Melegueta pepper, are the small, red-brown seeds of a cardamom-like plant found on the coast and islands of tropical West Africa. They have a peppery flavour with overtones of ginger and cardamom. A popular spice in Europe from the time of Elizabeth I (who is said to have been especially fond of them) until the beginning of the 19th century, they appear frequently in old recipes and were used as a pepper substitute in the reign of George III. Their use nowadays is principally in West African cookery, although they are sometimes added to beer, wines and spirits, notably in Scandinavia where they flavour akvavit. An interesting spice, they are not readily available, although some pharmacists can obtain them. Pepper mixed with a little ginger and cardamom can be substituted for them in old recipes.

Mastic (*Pistacia lentiscus*), a common ingredient in Middle Eastern cookery, is the hard resin of an acacia tree, with a slightly piney flavour. It is pulverized before use in milk puddings and in a famous Turkish ice cream '*dondurma kaymak*' where it is combined with vanilla. In Cyprus, where the best mastic comes from, it flavours breads and is an ingredient in the traditional marinade for '*shawirmah*', the spit-roasted doner kebab-like slices of lamb from Damascus. It can be found in Greek Cypriot or Middle Eastern food stores.

Monosodium glutamate (MSG) is the salt of glutamic acid, one of the amino acid food proteins. Although not particularly unusual, since it is found in the West in a wide number of processed foods, it is an important ingredient in Chinese and Japanese cookery. Sold in Chinese or Japanese grocery stores under names such as Ve-tsin, Taste Powder, Ajinomoto and P'sst, it has no flavour itself but brings out the flavour of other food. Used in very small quantities, it enhances meat or salty tastes in oriental cookery. It is a relatively harmless additive, except when used to excess over long periods when it is thought to cause liver damage. For this reason, it is avoided by many people and has been removed from much processed food.

Right Ripe mangoes on sale.

Below *Carica papaya* or pawpaws on the tree.

Bottom Papaya seeds are often used in salads and the milky juice (*papain*), found in the seeds and skin, has tenderizing properties.

Nasturtium (*Tropaeolum majus*), a common garden plant, produces buds, flowers and seeds which can be used, pickled in vinegar, as an excellent substitute for capers. Nasturtium leaves are well known for their cress-like flavour in salads or sandwiches; the dried seeds, too, have this taste and can be used to good effect in a peppermill as a slightly unusual pepper.

Papaya (*Carica papava*), a small tree widely grown throughout the tropics, bears a fleshy fruit, the seeds of which are frequently used as a spice. The ripe seeds, similar in appearance to large caviar, are black or grey and gelatinous. Fresh, they are mildly pungent, with a flavour resembling cress, and in countries where papayas grow, the seeds add a pleasant piquancy to salads and meat, the latter often rubbed or marinated with the seeds which also act as a tenderizer. Commercial tenderizing powders, in fact, contain *papain*, a milky substance from this tree which also occurs in the seeds and skin of the fruit. It is worth experimenting with papaya's many uses since it is widely available nowadays. Most people are familiar with its aromatic and delicately flavoured flesh and use it in fruit salads. In the tropics, it makes one of the most refreshing breakfasts imaginable, simply served with orange juice or a squeeze of lime.

Pomegranate (*Punica granatum*), it is claimed, was the 'apple' in the Garden of Eden, and its striking vermilion flowers make it a decorative plant in the Mediterranean, Middle East and similar warm dry climates. Like the pomegranate fruit widely used in Middle Eastern cookery, the seeds have a pleasant sweet-sour fruity taste. Mostly used fresh when a juicy, shiny pink, the seeds are sprinkled on salads, over tahini sauce for fish and on *hummus*. In India, the dried seeds flavour breads, fritters and some curries. Pomegranate syrup or paste, made from the juice of sour rather than sweeter fruits, is much used in Iranian cookery. It is the base for a refreshing Middle Eastern drink and also flavours the syrup, grenadine. Although fairly uncommon in Britain and northern Europe, pomegranate syrup can be found in shops specializing in Middle Eastern food.

Sandalwood (*Santalum album*) is a small Indian tree, small chips of which sometimes perfume milk custards and such fruit jellies as crabapples. Its use is mainly historical and sandalwood is now associated with soaps, perfumes and cosmetics but, in the Middle Ages, it added fragrance to many exotically spiced dishes, including chicken and meat dishes. In Indian cookery, it is often added to festive *pilaus* and Danish recipes for salted herrings sometimes include it.

Screwpine, a tropical tree of which there are two varieties, yields a scented sweet spice which has application in Indian and south-east Asian cookery. *Pandanus odoratissimus*, the larger tree, produces *kewra* essence or water, used in Indian cookery in milk puddings and ice creams in a similar way to vanilla in the West. *Pandanus odorus*, the smaller tree, has sharp, sword-like leaves which flavour and colour rice and puddings in Indonesia and Malaysia. *Kewra* essence or water is obtainable from Indian grocery stores, while *pandan* leaves (called *daun pandan*) can sometimes be found in Chinese food shops.

Curries and spice mixtures around the world

A spice shop in Jaipur, India.

Right Curry spices.

In the word association tests beloved of psychologists, say 'spicy' and the response will be 'curry'. Assuredly you are perfectly normal for no other food is so inextricably linked with the aroma and flavour of exotic spices than this inviting preparation, the smell of which excites the taste buds in a unique and inimitable way. To define 'curry', however, is another matter; the millions of people who have subsisted on this very dish for centuries do not know the meaning of this word which has no direct translation into any of India's fifteen languages. English in origin, it usually describes a limited combination of spices used to flavour food in the Indian manner.

Curry powders

'Curry' powder has been known and used in Britain and Europe since the 18th century and has become an integral part of many traditional cuisines. An interesting cream sauce, flavoured with a little curry powder, has existed in the French repertoire for at least a century and in English-speaking countries all over the world, leftover beef or mutton was (and probably still is) combined with curry powder, apples and sultanas to produce a pleasantly piquant, faintly exotic dish which made an agreeable change from the everyday fare of meat and two vegetables.

Anglo-Indian tradition

The British love affair with Indian food goes back to the early 17th century. Edward Terry, secretary to an East India Company official and one of the first Englishmen to taste Indian food observed, '. . . they stew all their flesh . . . cut into snippets or slices or small parts, to which they put onions and herbs and ginger (which they take green out of the earth) and other spices, with some butter, which ingredients when they are well proportioned, make a food that is exceedingly pleasing to all palates, at their first tasting thereof most savoury meat, happily that very dish which Jacob made for

his father Isaac, when he got the blessing.'

British administrators in India in these early years took to curry; after all, their cooks knew how to prepare little else and colonial gentlemen were ill-equipped to instruct them in the ways of British cooking. Once returned to England's green and pleasant land, they longed not only for the warmth of India but also for its food – so cooks and friends duly sent back their own particular curry mixes. By the 1780s, recipes for curry powder had found their way into English cookery books. One recipe, dated 1831, includes one ounce each of turmeric, coriander seed, ginger, nutmeg, mace and cayenne pepper, instructing 'pound all together, and pass them through a fine sieve; bottle and cork it well – one teaspoonful is sufficient to season any made dish'; an interesting fragrant mix that could well be tried today.

By this time, however, and throughout the Victorian era, the wives and families of officers took up residence in India and adapted curries to English ways. Many a *memsahib* became an expert in Indian cookery and, returning to suburban villas in southern England, wrote instructional works with titles such as *Anglo-Indian Cookery at Home, A Short Treatise for Returned Exiles by The Wife of a Retired Indian Officer* (by Mrs Henrietta Harvey of Hammersmith, 1895). This style of cookery is enshrined in many late 19th-century cookery books including Mrs Beeton's *Book of Household Management* and remained prevalent throughout the British Commonwealth until the 1950s when, as a result of immigration, Indian and Pakistani restaurants sprang up in England to provide the genuine tastes of the East to a homesick section of the population.

Styles of Indian curries

There are almost as many curry mixes in India as there are people, for no Indian would dream of using curry powder – except for *garam masalas* – which as experts point out are not curry powders (and should never be used as such), but simply 'hot spice mixes' which are used to enliven a curry in its last stages of cooking.

The spices in which curries are cooked are carefully chosen, according to regional preferences or traditions; the dishes themselves are balanced in such a way as to provide contrast between mild and pungently spiced food, and dry and moist textures. Vegetables, meat and pulses, along with the rice, relishes and chutneys served at an Indian meal all conform to a harmonious system, as old and venerable as India herself.

Only a mere handful of regional styles can be touched on here, each with an idiosyncratic mixture of spices and ingredients, largely dictated by geographical factors such as proximity to the sea and the produce of the particular terrain.

Kashmiri and northern Indian cookery produces the haute cuisine of curries, for this is essentially Moghul food where the use of spices is as refined as the culture from which it sprang. *Birianis, tandooris, pilaus, korma* and *rhogan gosht* as well as numerous other dishes originated here. *Korma* curries, for example, are mild and delicately spiced rather than hot. Usually creamy white, they traditionally contain nuts, cream and aromatic spices such as cardamom, mace, nutmeg, cinnamon and cloves, while festive *kormas* are often decorated with gold or silver leaf. Kashmiri cooking, similar in style, sometimes contains lotus roots or lychees, reflecting its proximity to neighbouring China.

The *tandoori* style of cooking comes from the north-west frontier (nowadays Pakistan) and is so-called because of the clay oven, the *tandoor*, in which meat, chicken and fish are cooked. All the meats are marinaded in a complex mixture of spices and yogurt before being cooked, and are often tenderized with crushed papaya; the characteristic orange

Left 'Curry powder' as such does not exist in India – each dish is flavoured with its own unique blend of spices, which is ground and mixed just before use.

Above A nutmeg grading station in Grenville and **(right)** a typical spice market in Bali.

colour of *tandoori* food (now usually charcoal-grilled) comes from a vegetable dye. *Rhogan gosht* is another Moghul dish with a thick, dark, nutty sauce made with almonds, roasted cumin, coriander and coconut. Yogurt and tomatoes (unusual in Indian curries) are additional ingredients.

All these are relatively mild, fragrantly aromatic dishes, but further south, the food becomes more highly seasoned and pungent. Madras-style curries invariably contain chillies, fenugreek, turmeric, mustard seeds and tamarind, as well as other ingredients. *Vindaloo*, like the Portuguese curries from Goa, is usually a fiery blend of hot spices and vinegar – and a highly regarded dish in and around Bombay. On the Kerala coast of southern India and in Sri Lanka, hot, richly spiced seafood curries abound, flavoured differently again with coconut, curry leaves, asafoetida and tamarind.

South-east Asian and Caribbean curries

In India, there are literally thousands of spice combinations for wherever Indians went, so too went curry, to be adapted and transformed by local ingredients into yet another aromatic blend, uniquely suited to the region's produce and the tastes of the inhabitants. In Sri Lanka, throughout south-east Asia and in the Caribbean islands, endless versions of curry exist, all 'authentic', yet all different.

South-east Asian cookery is essentially derived from the two great cuisines of the East – Indian and Chinese, although it is also influenced by early Arab traders, as well as by colonial invaders, the Dutch, Portuguese, English and French. Yet with the exception of Vietnam and Cambodia, nearly all countries produce curries in the Indian manner. Less hot and spicy and with a predominance of local ingredients, these nonetheless follow the same methods and style of cooking as the sub-continent from which they are obviously derived.

Left In Mombasa market, coconut is sold mixed with spices.
Right Spices on sale in Qing Ping Market, Canton, China.

The *gulehs* of Indonesia and Burma are highly seasoned dishes flavoured with coconut, curry leaves and tamarind in a similar way to southern Indian cuisine. The relishes and chutneys, called *sambals* in Indonesia, are likewise hot, piquant mixtures with chillies, while *satés* are obviously related to Indian kebabs, except for the spicy peanut-based sauces that accompany them.

In Malaysia, the *rendangs* resemble Indian dry curries but are less hot and made sweeter by the addition of *jaggery* (raw sugar, a local product) and sweet fruits. Freshly-ground curry pastes, rather than dry powders, are the norm in Thailand, for example, and can be differentiated by their colours. The searingly hot red curry paste takes its name from the quantities of dried red chillies in it, which flavours and colours mainly beef dishes. Green curry paste, also fairly hot, takes its colour from green herbs and green chillies, while orange curry paste combines red chillies, onions, shrimp paste and citrus juice. Add to these derivative curries the special spices and flavourings of these lands such as lemon grass, *galangal, daun pandan* and the fish pastes and sauces and the result is a variety of cuisines in which spices and natural flavourings are used in novel and inspired ways.

In the West Indies, where there is a substantial population of Indian origin, curries have undergone yet further transformations. Local fruits such as mangoes and bananas frequently appear in curries, as does allspice, (the Jamaican berry known principally in Europe as a pickling spice) and dishes here are often sweetly aromatic, for sugar cane is readily available. Pork, fish and chicken, and a wide variety of local vegetables are all seasoned and 'curried', as is goat in a famous and traditional Jamaican recipe.

This pinpoints the difficulty in defining what a curry is and, in conclusion, one can only say, perhaps, that it is a highly seasoned dish of Indian derivation. Today, in Japan and North America, curries are eaten regularly and soon, no doubt, there will be more variations on this versatile dish. To curry enthusiasts, this can only be a good thing.

Spice mixtures around the world

The art of blending spices is a subtle one, as refined as blending perfumes, or tea, so that over the centuries a number of regional or national mixtures have become recognized and established. Some of the best known are discussed here.

Quatre épices (literally four spices) is the French blend of pepper, cloves, nutmeg and either cinnamon or ginger, used in *charcuterie* cooking to flavour sausages, patés, black and white puddings (*boudins noirs, boudins blancs*) and trotters. The blended powder can be bought in France but it is far better to make your own from freshly ground spices. Proportions can vary according to manufacturer, or taste, but *Larousse Gastronomique* gives this recipe, which should be ground to a fine powder: 125g/1⅛ cups white peppercorns, powdered, 10g/½ tbsp cloves, 30g/4 tbsp ginger, grated, 35g/4 tbsp nutmeg.

English pickling spice varies according to the spice manufacturer and individual recipes but generally consists of mustard seeds, coriander, allspice, a small portion of red chillies, sometimes bay leaves, and dry ginger. The spices are added whole, tied in a small muslin bag, to pickle fruits and vegetables and to spice chutneys.

One of the best-known oriental blends is the Chinese five-spice powder, which can be bought already ground at Chinese supermarkets and which is used in a wide variety of dishes but particularly with pork and chicken. A cocoa-coloured combination of dried anise, anise pepper, fennel seeds, cloves and cinnamon, it is always used sparingly since its flavour is strong and aromatic. Another is *shichimi togarashi*, a favourite table condiment in Japan, used as a garnish and also sprinkled on soups, noodles or rice for flavouring. It is a seven-flavoured spice consisting of ground anise pepper leaves (*sansho* spice), sesame seed, rape seed, hemp seed, poppy seed, dried tangerine peel and ground chillies; it is available in cans or bottles and ranges in flavour from mild to very hot.

In the Middle East and North Africa, classic spice mixtures usually include four spices. In Egypt, this blend is the same as the French *quatre épices*, but in Tunisia and elsewhere, cinnamon, pepper, rose buds and paprika may be combined. *Ras el hanout* is another famous mixture which is widely used in Morocco to flavour soups and stews and renowned for its alleged aphrodisiac qualities. It can contain more than twenty aromatics (presumably to leave nothing to chance) but the basic blend generally contains cinnamon, nutmeg, dried rose buds, dried ginger, cloves, cubebs and various hot peppers.

The Bengali *panch poron* (literally five seeds) is a spicy chilli-free seasoning common in southern Indian vegetarian cooking which gives zest to relatively bland ingredients. It can be bought already ground from Indian shops and is a mixture of cumin, fennel, fenugreek, black mustard seeds and nigella (*kalonji*). *Pa'an*, the Indian digestive, is sold on every street corner and also acts as a breath sweetener. Many varieties exist, all seasoned differently but the basic ingredients include chopped betel nuts, betel leaves and a mixture of spices (lime paste, cardamom and aniseed are popular). The nut and spice mixture is placed in the betel leaf (sometimes silvered) which is folded and fastened with a clove. The *pa'an* is mildly stimulating and leaves a clean refreshing taste but also turns the mouth bright red for a time.

Sorting the tiny stones from spices is done by hand in India.

RECIPES

Ingredients for curry powder
'Coriander seeds (to be well roasted, pounded) (1lb); turmeric (1lb 2oz); fenugreek (4oz); ginger, dried (1lb); black pepper (1lb); dried chillies (12oz); cardamoms (8oz); cinnamon (8oz). Salt in proportion to be added when using the curry stuff. The whole to be cleaned, dried, pounded, and sifted; then properly mixed together and put into bottles, well corked. A tablespoonful is sufficient for a chicken or fowl curry.'
Indian Domestic Economy, Madras 1850 (Elizabeth David's *Spices, Salt and Aromatics in the English Kitchen*, Penguin)

Thai orange curry paste
6 dried red chillies, seeded, soaked in warm water, finely chopped
1 tsp salt
1 medium onion, chopped
1 tbsp blachan *(shrimp paste)*
1 tsp lime, lemon juice or wine vinegar
In a spice blender or mortar, grind the chillies and salt to a paste. Add the remaining ingredients and grind until smooth.

Portuguese curry (Vindaloo or Bindaloo)
This well-known Portuguese curry can be made properly of beef, pork or duck. The following is a recipe for the vindaloo in general use: 'Six ounces of ghee or lard, one tablespoonful of bruised garlic, one tablespoonful of ground garlic, one tablespoonful of ground ginger, two teaspoonfuls of ground chillies, one teaspoonful of roasted and ground coriander seed, two or three bay leaves, a few peppercorns, four or five cloves roasted and ground, four or five cardamoms roasted and ground, with a half a cup of good vinegar, to two pounds of pork or beef or a duck.
N.B. The best vindaloo is that prepared with mustard oil.'
The Indian Cookery Book by a Thirty-five Years' Resident, Calcutta 1869 (Elizabeth David's *Spices, Salt and Aromatics in the English Kitchen*, Penguin)

Madhur Jaffrey's garam masala
To make 3 tablespoons:
1 tbsp cardamom seeds
1 5cm/2in stick cinnamon
1 tsp black peppercorns
1 tsp black cumin seeds
1 tsp whole cloves
1/4 of an average sized nutmeg
Combine all the ingredients and grind very fine, in a coffee grinder reserved for spices. (If you want to make your *garam masala* less hot, decrease the amount of black peppercorns and increase the cumin proportionately.) Store in a tightly covered container, away from sunlight and dampness. If carefully stored, this *garam masala* can be kept for a couple of months.
From *An Invitation to Indian Cooking* (Jonathan Cape)

Lamb korma
75g/3oz almonds
a 2.5cm/1in piece of ginger, finely chopped
2-3 cloves garlic, finely chopped
2 green chillies, seeded and finely chopped (optional)
75ml/3fl oz/6tbsp plain yogurt
2 whole cardamom pods
2.5cm/1in cinnamon stick
3 cloves
3 tbsp vegetable oil
1 large onion, chopped
750g/1 1/2lb boneless lamb, cut into cubes
1 tsp ground coriander
1 tsp ground cumin
75ml/3fl oz/6 tbsp double [heavy] cream
salt to taste
chopped fresh coriander leaves, to garnish
In a spice (or coffee) grinder combine the nuts, ginger, garlic, chillies and yogurt and blend to a stiff paste. Heat the oil and sauté the cardamom, cinnamon and cloves for about 5 minutes. Add the onions and cook, stirring, for a further 5 minutes. Add the lamb and brown the pieces, removing them with a slotted spoon as they cook. Add the coriander and cumin to the juices in the pan and cook for about 5 minutes before adding the paste and returning the lamb to the pan. Add enough water to barely cover the lamb and simmer for about 1 hour, stirring once or twice. Add the cream and salt about 10 minutes before the end of cooking. Garnish with coriander.

Allspice

(*Pimenta dioica,* syn. *P. officinalis*) MYRTACEAE

Allspice is so-called because its flavour is like a combination of cloves, cinnamon and nutmeg. However, it is one spice with berries the size of large peppercorns which grow onto the evergreen allspice tree of the myrtle family. It should not be confused with 'mixed spice' or with *pimiento*, the Spanish name for chillies and sweet peppers, to which its popular name (pimento) bears a resemblance.

Allspice is one of the few spices native to the Western hemisphere, unlike most which are from the East. Although it grows profusely in Jamaica and to a lesser extent in other parts of the Caribbean and South America, it has never been successfully cultivated on a large scale in other tropical lands, despite attempts. It was brought to Europe soon after the discovery of the New World. Since then, in spite of its versatility in both sweet and savoury dishes, it has never been an essential spice in the kitchen except perhaps in northern and eastern Europe, where it is widely used when pickling and preserving fish and meat. In Britain, it enjoyed a brief period of popularity in Edwardian times when it appeared in many recipe books.

A useful but somewhat neglected spice, it is worth experimenting with allspice. Try adding a few berries to soups and stews, as the Jamaicans do, or add a pinch of ground allspice to puréed root vegetables. It is often added to sauerkraut, game, ham, veal, pork and beef and is one of the essential ingredients in the traditional English spiced beef.

Cultivation Pimento trees, which can live up to 100 years, are mainly grown on tropical plantations along hillsides and once established need little attention. Allspice berries are picked by hand while still green and then sun-dried in their countries of origin.

IDENTIFICATION

Dark, reddish-brown berries similar to large peppercorns in size; they are the fruit of the tropical evergreen pimento tree, picked when fully grown but still green, and dried in the sun. **Plant** Grows to about 9m (30ft) with thick leathery leaves and in mid-summer, small white aromatic flowers in clusters. Ripe berries are dark purple.

ESSENTIAL FACTS

Countries of origin West Indies, Central and South America; these produce 100 per cent of the world's allspice exports, most of which comes from Jamaica and Mexico.
Preparation and storage Available whole or ground. For preference, buy whole berries and store for an indefinite period in an airtight jar; grind in a mortar or special pepper mill as necessary. Ground allspice quickly loses aroma and flavour.
Culinary uses In European cooking, it is commonly used as a pickling spice for fish, notably Scandinavian raw herrings, beef and pork and in marinades, patés, sausages and terrines. Ground allspice is used in baking, fruit desserts and pies and in puddings, especially Christmas pudding. It is popular in the Middle East and the Levant where it is used to flavour rice and meat dishes. In Jamaica, it is popular in local dishes, such as Jerk pork; (*see below*), it is used in pickles; marinades, soups and stews and for a Jamaican liqueur known as *pimento dram*.

RECIPE

Jerk Pork
This is a traditional Jamaican dish which is barbecued on roadside stalls throughout the country. 'Jerk', according to one expert, is the English version of a Spanish word meaning to prepare pork in the manner of the Quichua Indians.

25g/1oz/¼ cup allspice berries
3 spring onions, chopped
1-2 fresh red or green chillies, seeded and chopped
2 bay leaves
salt and freshly ground pepper
4 pork chops or pieces of boneless loin, approx 225g/8oz each

Heat the allspice berries in a small pan over a medium heat, stirring for about 3-5 minutes. Combine them in a blender with the spring onion, chillies, bay leaves and seasoning. Work to a thick paste. Rub the paste into the pork and leave for at least 2 hours, preferably overnight in the refrigerator. Slowly grill the chops (over charcoal if possible) for about 40-60 minutes, turning them after half the cooking time. To give the meat an authentic aroma, throw allspice berries on the charcoal.

Ground allspice

Whole allspice

Aniseed

Aniseed is one of the oldest cultivated spices, enjoyed by the early Egyptians, Greeks and especially the Romans who used it to flavour chicken, pork and vegetables and in small spicy cakes which were served as a digestive. Known in England since the 14th century, anise was principally used to flavour cakes, breads and sweetmeats including the popular gingerbreads sold in town and country fairs right up to Elizabethan times. As in Roman times, aniseed 'comfits' (sugar-coated seeds) were chewed after sumptuous medieval banquets to aid digestion, a use to which this spice is still put in India.

Aniseed's sweet, mildly liquorice taste is familiar in children's sweets such as aniseed drops and in the refreshing, fragrant alcoholic drinks of Pernod, *pastis* and *ouzo*, so popular in sun-drenched Mediterranean lands. The aniseed plant, which is native to the Middle East, has always been extensively cultivated throughout Mediterranean regions and since classical times has been associated in the kitchen with fish and seafood. Dioscorides, the Greek physician living in Rome in the 1st century AD recommended that *racasse*, a spiny, beautiful scorpion fish found only in Mediterranean waters, be cooked 'with nothing else but water and oyle and Annise'; many centuries later Alexandre Dumas recorded a delicious anise-flavoured dressing for lobster and other shellfish (see right) and today lobster flambéed in *pastis* is a justifiably popular dish in the south of France, while Pernod is an essential flavouring in that most celebrated American *hors d'oeuvres* Oysters Rockfeller to which it adds a distinctive classic touch.

Cultivation Anise needs a long hot summer for its seeds to ripen. Sow in early spring in a sheltered, sunny position. Thin the seedlings to 20cm (8in) and keep carefully weeded. Harvest the seedheads when the seeds change colour and hang them to dry in paper bags in a warm, dry place.

ESSENTIAL FACTS

Countries of origin Warm temperate and Mediterranean-type climates worldwide, especially Spain, Greece, Egypt, Mexico and India.

Preparation and storage Available whole or ground; buy whole for preference; store in airtight containers away from sunlight; note that seeds turn brown as they get stale; ground aniseed quickly loses its flavour and aroma.

Culinary uses Used to flavour sweets, creams, cakes and breads; also widely used to flavour fish and, like fennel, added to soups, sauces, poultry, pork and vegetables; notable as a flavouring in various alcoholic liqueurs and cordials such as *pastis*, Pernod, Ricard, *ouzo*, *raki* and *arrak*.

RECIPE

Dumas's anise dressing (for shellfish)

75ml/5 tbsp/7¼ tbsp olive oil
1 tbsp Dijon mustard
a bunch each of parsley, tarragon and chives, chopped
1 tbsp shallots, finely chopped
12 drops soy sauce
freshly ground pepper
a small glass of pastis *or Pernod*

Combine all the ingredients and add to cooked prawns [shrimp], crab or other shellfish and mix well.

(*Pimpinella anisum*)
UMBELLIFERAE

IDENTIFICATION

Small, grey-green seeds of anise plant which grows to about 60cm (2ft). **Plant** Annual with yellow-white flowers in clusters with small fruit which splits into two seeds.

Aniseed balls

Aniseed

Ground aniseed

(*Xanthoxylum piperitum*)
RUTACEAE

Anise pepper

IDENTIFICATION

Dried red berries of a small feathery-leaved prickly ash plant, various species of which are grown in the USA as well as Asia.
Plant Small deciduous tree, the branches of which bear berries in clusters.

ESSENTIAL FACTS

Countries of origin Temperate regions of China, especially Sichuan province, Japan, Tibet and North America.
Preparation and storage Available whole or ground; dried leaves of plant (*sansho* spice) or pickled leaves (*kimone*) are Japanese spices. Store in airtight containers away from light; ground berries or leaves quickly lose flavour and aroma.
Culinary uses Important in Chinese (notably Sichuan) cuisine; ingredient in Chinese five-spice powder; dried or pickled leaves used in Japanese cooking.

This hot, peppery spice is derived from the crushed, dried red berries of a prickly ash plant and is one of the principal sources of the zest and piquancy associated with Chinese Sichuan cuisine. Little known in the West, it is called Sichuan pepper, or labelled *farchiew* spice in many Chinese grocery stores and, in China, where it is known as the 'great spice', it is widely used throughout the country. It is one of the ingredients of the ubiquitous Chinese five-spice powder, the exotic aroma of which permeates Chinese food stores and restaurants.

It is used in Sichuan to add pungency and aroma to duck and chicken dishes and it imparts its unique bitter-sweet hotness either in the cooking process or, more commonly, in accompanying sauces where it is frequently combined with ginger, chillies and sesame oil or paste. It is worth seeking out this inimitable spice if you want to capture the authentic flavour of Sichuan food. Note that it does not look particularly berry-like because the husks are also part of the spice.

To bring out the flavour, heat the peppercorns in a dry frying pan, grind them and mix with salt. Anise pepper will enliven any bland oriental dish and, along with chilli sauce, makes an excellent spicy condiment at a home-cooked Chinese dinner.

Sansho spice, produced from the dried leaves of the anise-pepper plant, is only mildly hot and is a popular additive, in Japanese cooking, to soup and noodle dishes. The leaves also make one of the many pickles used by the Japanese to flavour rice.

Cultivation Deciduous varieties of this plant generally grow wild in temperate regions, especially on hill slopes in China and the Himalayas. In North America, where it is cultivated as a herbal remedy, it needs little attention.

RECIPE

Sichuan chicken with hot pepper sauce

small iceberg lettuce, shredded
225g/8oz/1 cup parboiled beansprouts, cooled
700g/1½lbs/3 cups cooked chicken, sliced
2 tsp freshly ground anise pepper
2 tbsp spring onion, finely chopped
2 tsp ginger root, finely diced
30ml/2 tbsp soy sauce
30ml/2 tbsp sesame seed oil
1 tbsp chicken stock
1 tsp wine vinegar
1 tsp sugar
1 tbsp sesame seeds, lightly toasted

Combine the lettuce and beansprouts in a serving bowl. Arrange the chicken slices on top. Mix together the remaining ingredients, except the sesame seeds, and pour the sauce over the chicken. Sprinkle toasted sesame seeds over the chicken and sauce.

Anise pepper

Asafoetida

(*Ferula asafoetida*)
UMBELLIFERAE

This unusual spice comes from the hardened sap of giant fennel plants which grow in Asia. Its name gives the clue to its most notable characteristic – a nauseous smell which is reminiscent of rotten garlic. Do not, however, allow this to deter you. The odour disappears in cooking and asafoetida has been highly regarded since ancient times for the delicate onion-like flavour it imparts. A most powerful seasoning, it is only ever used in the tiniest quantities – a pinch or a small sliver at a time – and is extremely unpleasant if tasted on its own.

Yet asafoetida has almost magical properties when combined with other spices and ingredients. The Persians call it the 'food of the gods' and so popular was it in ancient Rome that it was depicted on coins. It was introduced to Britain by the Romans and was still in evidence in 18th-century England as a favourite spice of playwright and novelist, Oliver Goldsmith. Although it has now virtually disappeared from Western cooking, there is no reason why the intrepid cook should not use it to enhance fish, vegetable soups, sauces and vegetarian dishes such as Indian *dhals* (purées of lentils, chick peas or split peas) or spicy potato and aubergine [eggplant] dishes. Mashed potatoes added to sautéed onions cooked in a spicy mixture of asafoetida, cumin, chilli powder and turmeric is one of the simplest and most satisfying dishes imaginable and, like the recipe below, can make a perfect introduction to a flavouring largely overlooked as yet by most Westerners.

Cultivation The plant generally grows wild in western Asia and thrives in continental climates with extremes of temperature.

ESSENTIAL FACTS

Countries of origin Principally western Asia, especially Iran and Afghanistan, also southern Europe and North Africa.

Preparation and storage Available in wax-like blocks, pieces or powdered; block variety is purest but powdered most convenient; to avoid its powerful foetid smell permeating its surroundings, keep it in a firmly closed, airtight container.

Culinary uses Widely used in minute quantities in Indian cooking, particularly vegetarian food, and as a delicate flavour in fresh and salted fish dishes; its nauseous smell disappears in cooking.

IDENTIFICATION

The milky sap from roots and stem of certain odiferous species of giant fennel which hardens into a resin-like substance, darkening with age to deep brown. **Plant** Grows to 3m (10ft) with soft-centred finely-reeded stems, toothed leaves and yellow flowers in clusters in summer; all plant parts have an unpleasant odour.

Ground asafoetida

RECIPE

Spicy mushrooms with tomatoes

700g/1½lb button mushrooms
30ml/2 tbsp corn or safflower oil
pinch ground asafoetida
½ tsp cumin seeds
3 fresh green chillies (seeded for greater mildness, if preferred) or *1-2 dried chillies*
¼ tsp turmeric
450g/1lb can peeled tomatoes
1 tsp salt
¼ tsp sugar

Wipe the mushrooms clean with a damp cloth and remove any coarse stems. Heat the oil in a saucepan over a medium heat. Add the spices in the order above, allowing a few seconds to elapse between additions. Stir in the mushrooms and cook, stirring for about 1 minute before adding the tomatoes, salt and sugar. Lower the heat, stirring to break up the tomatoes and cook gently for about 20 minutes. Serve immediately, or, even better, remove from the heat and leave for 1-2 hours to develop the flavours. Re-heat gently before serving.

(*Laurus nobilis*)
LAURACEAE

Bay leaf

IDENTIFICATION

Shiny, leathery green leaves of small shrub or tree growing to an average 7.5m (25ft) or in cool temperate conditions 4.5m (15ft).
Plant Bears tiny, insignificant yellow flowers in spring and fruit in the form of purple-black berries.
Countries of origin Indigenous to Asia Minor, widely grown in Mediterranean climates and cool temperate regions.
Preparation and storage Available fresh and dried whole or ground; fresh leaves have a strong aroma and slightly bitter flavour; dry a branch at home for preference or buy olive green (not brown) whole dried leaves; ground leaves quickly lose flavour and aroma.
Culinary uses Used worldwide, but particularly in French and Mediterranean cooking; an essential ingredient in *bouquet garni*; used in marinades, pickles and to flavour all types of savoury dishes, soups and sauces and occasionally in sweet creams and custards.

History and legend surround this robust, full-flavoured herb whose botanical name points to its distinguished provenance. Also known as sweet bay, the laurel was venerated by the Greeks and Romans, and made sacred by Apollo in the enchanting legend of the beautiful nymph, Daphne. She was turned into a laurel tree to protect her honour, and the tree became a symbol of honour in her memory. Thereafter, heroes, poets and emperors were rewarded with leafy crowns of laurel and today the term 'bachelor' for academic honours is derived from the Latin *bacca lauri*, laurel berry.

Strongly aromatic, bay is an indispensable herb, used in almost every cuisine in the world but to best effect, perhaps, in French Mediterranean cooking. It is an essential ingredient in the *bouquet garni* and flavours marinades, stocks, soups and sauces, as well as pickles and brines, in all European cooking. A bay leaf simmered with the milk for *béchamel* sauce, for example, makes an incomparable difference to its flavour.

The leaves when fresh are more sharply flavoured than when allowed to dry for a few days, so use them with discretion. Buy olive green leaves rather than the elderly brown leaves seen in many shops, or even worse, commercially produced ground bay leaves which soon acquire an acrid, stale flavour that ruins, rather than enhances, any dish. The bay tree is easy to grow either in the garden or as an ornamental plant in tubs, thus providing a fresh supply throughout the year.

Cultivation Plants can be propagated from heal cuttings or young trees bought from garden centres. Plant trees out in sunny sheltered places in well-drained soil. No particular care is needed except to protect young plants in severe winters.

RECIPE

Boeuf en daube Provençal

900g/2lb chuck steak, cut into large cubes
2-3 onions, sliced
3 carrots, sliced
1 strip of orange peel
3 bay leaves
4-5 peppercorns
300ml/½ pint/1¼ cups red wine
30ml/2 tbsp olive oil
3 cloves garlic, finely chopped
6 well-flavoured tomatoes or *450g/1lb can of peeled tomatoes*
3 tbsp brandy or grappa
salt and pepper to taste
100g/4oz/1 cup stoned black olives
parsley to garnish

Serves 4-6

Marinate the beef with the next six ingredients for 6-8 hours or overnight. Remove the meat and vegetables from the marinade; pat dry with paper towels, reserving the marinade. Heat the oil in a casserole and brown and seal the meat. Lower the heat and add garlic, tomatoes and brandy, plus marinade vegetables, 1 bay leaf and orange peel, discarding remaining spices. Pour in the marinade liquid, adding enough water or stock to just cover the meat. Add seasoning then bring casserole to the boil, and place in a slow oven (160°C/325°F/gas mark 3) for 2-2 ½ hours. Add the olives for the last 30 minutes of cooking. Sprinkle a little chopped parsley on top and serve straight from the casserole.

Dried bay leaves

Fresh bay leaves

Bouquet garni

Ground bay leaves

Caper

(*Capparis spinosa* 'inermis')
CAPPARIDACEAE

The caper is the small, heart-shaped bud of the unopened flower of a beautiful perennial shrub. Growing wild in profusion on stony ground and in ruins and walls in hot Mediterranean countries, its pretty pink and white flowers, similar in size to a wild rose, have only the shortest life; they open in the morning but are dead by noon, suggesting to one writer that they could be the flower referred to in the Bible (Ecclesiastes), 'The flower shall wither, beauty shall fade away'. In fact, capers have been an important flavouring in the Holy Land and all over the Mediterranean region since ancient times.

Nowadays, the finest capers come from Provence and, in France, they are graded according to size. *Nonpareilles*, the smallest and best, are about 3mm (⅛in) in size, while the largest, the *capote*, is about five times larger. Manual labour is required to gather capers, for the buds must be picked each morning just as they reach the proper size. The larger, coarser buds are also harvested and you will see them packed in salt on market stalls in areas where capers are plentiful. These can taste good but are often of inferior quality, and can turn rancid quickly.

The flavour of capers is acidic with faint overtones of goats' cheese. They add an appetizing and tonic lift to a wide variety of dishes and sauces. It is worth seeking out (and paying extra for) the *nonpareilles* because their flavour is much finer. They are used in dishes such as skate with black butter and the English caper sauce eaten with boiled mutton.

Cultivation In Mediterranean regions, the caper plant grows wild or is cultivated in plantations. It is a greenhouse plant in north temperate zones and can be propagated from cuttings.

RECIPE

Tapénade

Tapéno is Provençal for capers. This sauce goes well with hard-boiled eggs, cold fish and beef salads.

2 tbsp capers, drained
4 anchovy fillets
4-5 black olives, stoned
approx 200ml/⅓ pint/1 cup olive oil
lemon juice
black pepper

Pound the capers, anchovies and olives in a mortar to form a paste. Gradually add the oil as for mayonnaise until blended. Add a little lemon juice and ground black pepper to taste.

IDENTIFICATION

Unopened green flower buds of wild and cultivated caper shrub, which grows to 1-2m (3-6ft).

Plant Stems carry thick shiny leaves, prickly in the wild variety; flowers on stalks are followed by small pear-shaped fruits.

ESSENTIAL FACTS

Countries of Origin Grows mainly in Mediterranean countries, notably southern France, Italy and Algeria; also California and other Mediterranean-type climates.

Preparation and storage Characteristic flavour develops only when the buds are pickled in wine vinegar; available pickled and bottled or, where plentiful, dry-salted and sold loose; will keep indefinitely in jars as long as covered by pickling liquid; carefully remove capers from liquid and chop or pound as required.

Culinary uses Used in a wide variety of cold sauces eg *tartare, rémoulade, ravigote, gribiche*; in Provençal *tapénade*, in Italian *salsa verde*; often combined with anchovies in *antipasti*, pizzas etc; in hot fish and meat sauces; in fish sauces in Britain and northern Europe; in steak *tartare*; can be added to beef casseroles for an interesting flavour.

Small capers (*Nonpareilles*)

Large capers

(*Carum carvi*)
UMBELLIFEREAE

Caraway

IDENTIFICATION

Light to dark brown seeds, 3-6mm (1/8-1/4in) long, of wild and cultivated plant growing to over 60cm (2ft) in temperate regions. **Plant** Has feathery, light green leaves with tiny white to pink flowers appearing in clusters in summer.

ESSENTIAL FACTS

Countries of origin Grows wild and cultivated in Europe, especially Holland, Germany and Soviet Union; also India, North Africa, Turkey, the USA and Canada.
Preparation and storage Available whole; if desired, grind or pound before using; keep in airtight containers away from light.
Culinary uses Important in German and Austrian cooking; also in the Soviet Union, eastern Europe and Scandinavia where it is added to vegetables, soups, goulash, dumplings etc; ingredient in rye bread, in liqueurs eg Kümmel and Akvavit; in sweet cakes and biscuits, notably English seed cake.

The popularity of this aromatic seed in Europe, where it grows wild, can be traced back to prehistoric times. In Elizabethan England, the seeds were used as extensively as they are today in Germany and Austria. Shakespeare's Falstaff, for example, is invited to eat a dish of roast apples with caraway seeds in *Henry IV, Part 2*.

Caraway seeds have a sweetish, sharp flavour reminiscent of aniseed and in present-day German and eastern European cooking, they flavour all kinds of vegetables, pork, goose, goulash and cheese. They are also added to cakes, biscuits, breads and dumplings.

In Great Britain, however, English seed cake (not one of Britain's gastronomic triumphs) has given caraway a bad name but it is an interesting spice when used infrequently and in small quantities. Freshly ground and added in no more than a teaspoonful to carrot, potato and cabbage dishes, it can distinctly enhance their flavour. Moreover, the characteristic taste of rye bread – the perfect accompaniment to salt beef and liver-sausage spreads – is due to caraway seeds. The fiery liqueurs, Kümmel and Akvavit, are also based on caraway.

Cultivation The biennial caraway plant is easily grown in temperate climates. Sow the seeds in early autumn or spring, thinning the seedlings to about 20cm (8in) apart. Cut the seedheads in mid- to late summer just before the seeds are fully ripe and hang them in a paper bag in a dry airy place.

RECIPE

Borsch

4-5 large raw beetroots, peeled and coarsely grated
2 onions, sliced
1.7 litres/3 pints/7½ cups water or chicken stock
4 medium potatoes, peeled and quartered
30ml/2 tbsp tomato purée
15ml/1 tbsp lemon juice
1 tsp caraway seeds
salt and pepper to taste
1 tsp sugar
300ml/½ pint/1¼ cups sour cream

Put the beetroot, onions and stock or water in a large pot. Bring to the boil, then simmer for 40 minutes. Add the potatoes, tomato purée, lemon juice, caraway seeds, seasoning and sugar. Cover and simmer for about 1 hour. Stir in the sour cream just before serving.

Caraway seeds

Akvavit

Cardamom

Cardamom is an old and exotic spice. A native of the tropical forests of the East, it is said to have grown in the fabulous Hanging Gardens of Babylon and was, without doubt, brought from the East to Greece and Rome where it was used in perfume. Its reputed aphrodisiac qualities are celebrated in *The Arabian Nights* and certainly its delightful, heady scent conjures up all kinds of Eastern promise.

Cardamom is one of the most expensive spices in the world, although in northern India it is used extensively in festive rice dishes such as *biryanis* and *pilaus*, often in combination with almonds, saffron and other spices, as well as in elegant Mogul dishes such as *murg mussallum* (marinated whole chicken with almonds and cream), which are fragrantly spiced rather than hot. *Garam masala*, the spice mixture used all over the Indian sub-continent, also includes cardamom.

Cardamom also features in many Persian and Middle-Eastern dishes, usually along with fruit and nuts. It is the distinctive ingredient in Arab coffee served throughout the Mediterranean and near East. To savour this exotic brew at home, add half a teaspoon of cardamom seeds to a potful of strong, high-roast coffee.

There are a number of cardamom-related plants, the seeds of which are inferior to the true cardamom, and have a strong camphor flavour. These are often sold as cardamom and frequently added to ground cardamom mixtures. For this reason always buy the green or brown (which are natural colours) or white (which are bleached) cardamom pods and use whole, or extract the black seeds which contain the aroma and taste and grind as required.

Cultivation Cardamom grows wild or in cleared plantations in tropical rain forests. It is propagated by roots or seed and the pods are harvested in late autumn just before they ripen.

RECIPE

Sultan's pilaff

450g/1lb/2 cups long-grain rice
60ml/4 tbsp vegetable oil
2 large onions, sliced
2 cloves garlic, finely chopped
6 cardamom pods, split
2 cloves
2.5 cm/1in cinnamon stick
1 sachet powdered saffron
225g/½lb lamb fillet, cubed
50g/2oz raisins or sultanas
salt and pepper
1.1 litre/2 pints/5 cups chicken stock
50g/2oz/2 tbsp blanched almonds, lightly toasted

Soak the rice for 20 minutes in cold water. Meanwhile, in a heavy-based saucepan, sauté the onions and garlic until lightly coloured. Increase the heat, add spices and sauté for a few minutes. Transfer the onion and spice mixture to a dish; quickly brown and seal the meat in the remaining oil in the pan. Return the onions and spices to the pan, add the rice (carefully drained under running water) and cook, stirring for about 5 minutes, before adding stock, raisins and seasoning. Bring to the boil then lower the heat, cover the pan tightly and simmer gently for about 20 minutes without lifting the lid. When all the stock is absorbed, stir in the almonds and transfer to a serving platter, garnishing with a few coriander leaves if desired.

(Elettaria cardamomum)
ZINGIBERACEAE

IDENTIFICATION

White, brown or green pods containing brown-black, sticky seeds of ginger-type plant growing to 2-5m (6-16ft); stalks bearing pods sprawl flat on ground from base of plant. **Plant** Has long tuberous roots, long green leaves and green flowers with white purple-veined tip.

ESSENTIAL FACTS

Countries of origin Grows wild and cultivated above 3000 ft mainly in southern India, Sri Lanka Thailand, Tanzania and Central America.
Preparation and storage Available as whole dried pods, loose seeds or ground seeds; for preference, buy whole pods and use split or extract seeds from pods then crush or grind as required; loose and ground seeds quickly lose their flavour and aroma.
Culinary uses Widely used in Arab countries to flavour sweet and savoury dishes as well as coffee; essential spice in rice dishes of northern India and Pakistan; important flavour in Scandinavian cakes and pastries; also used in pickles, punches and spiced wine.

White cardamom

Green cardamom

Ground cardamom

Brown cardamom

(*Capsicum frutescens*)
SOLANACEAE

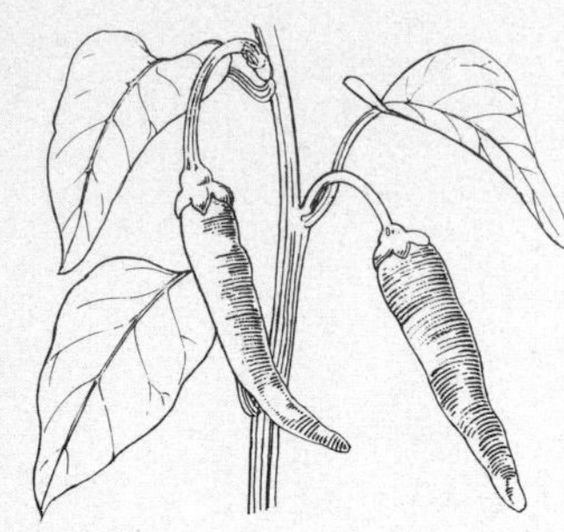

Cayenne

The red powder sold commercially as cayenne pepper is a blend of the ground dried fruits of the many pungent small-fruited varieties of chilli, *Capsicum frutescens*, grown in East Africa, Japan, India, Mexico and the USA. The distinction between cayenne and other chilli powders is not great; all are equally fiery but cayenne is more finely ground and it is traditionally used at table as a condiment in the same way as salt and pepper. However, finely sieved chilli powder can be substituted for cayenne.

Cayenne has been an important hot spice in Western countries since the 18th century, and was widely used to pep up sauces and fish dishes, and to add heat to many Anglo-Indian dishes such as kedgeree and to the devilled kidneys, cutlets and chicken legs popular on Victorian and Edwardian breakfast menus. Its use has somewhat declined in recent years with the widespread availability of fresh and dried chillies.

Cayenne is an attractive spice, however, adding piquancy and a light pink blush to fish sauces and pastes in particular. It is also a notable ingredient in the spicy Creole and Cajun dishes from the southern states of America, many of which combine Spanish or French and West African cooking.

Cultivation *Capsicum frutescens* is a perennial shrub propagated from seed in nurseries, which needs a tropical climate and a long growing season to mature the fruits.

IDENTIFICATION

Blended finely ground powder of dried fruits of pungent varieties of red chilli. **Plant** *C. frutescens* grows to 2m (6½ft) has densely branching stems; pod-like fruits are usually small, slender, green and yellow when immature, turning red when ripe.

ESSENTIAL FACTS

Countries of origin Possibly named from Cayenne, French Guiana; now widely grown in Africa, Mexico, the USA, India and Japan and other tropical and sub-tropical regions.
Preparation and storage Beware of sprinkling too much on food; it tends to clog and them comes out in a lump; buy in small quantities since the flavour deteriorates with time; store away from light in airtight containers.
Culinary uses Important in the West as a source of spicy heat before other types of chilli were widely available; now used principally as a condiment at table with seafood, in fish pastes; to flavour cheese dishes, soups etc; sometimes in cooking eg, kedgeree, devilled sauces.

RECIPE

Jambalaya

This is an easy version of a traditional Creole dish. Chicken, ham or sausage can be used to replace the prawns [shrimp] and bacon if preferred.

175g/6oz streaky bacon, diced
8 spring onions, chopped
2 cloves of garlic, minced
500g/1lb canned, peeled tomatoes
¼ tsp cayenne pepper
salt and freshly ground black pepper to taste
500g/1lb/2 cups cooked rice
500g/1lb cooked prawns [shrimp], peeled
finely chopped parsley to garnish

Serves 4-6.

Gently sauté the bacon in a large pan until the fat becomes translucent. Add the spring onions and garlic and cook for a few minutes or until lightly coloured. Add the tomatoes and cayenne pepper and simmer for about 15-20 minutes or until reduced and thickened. Stir in the cooked rice and prawns [shrimp], season to taste and cook on a low heat for a further 10 minutes or until the mixture is heated through. Sprinkle with chopped parsley just before serving.

Cayenne pepper

Celery seed

(*Apium graveolens* 'dulce')
UMBELLIFERAE

Celery seed is a Western spice and a relative newcomer to the kitchen, as is the cultivated vegetable which became widely used in Europe, England and America only in the 19th century thanks to the breeding of the white-stalked variety in Italy during the previous century.

Dried celery seeds are not readily available and unless you grow your own celery, you may need to go to a specialist [gourmet] shop. Celery salt and celery seasoning can, however, be found in almost all supermarkets and grocery stores and it is in these forms that celery seed is most commonly used.

The seeds themselves are rather bitter with a concentrated celery flavour. They can be crushed and added where this flavour is needed but when the use of the vegetable itself would be inappropriate. Pastry, savoury biscuits and breads can, for example, be enhanced with celery seeds. They can also add zest and pungency to cheese dips, fish pastes and salad dressings, and in particular to sauces made with tomato, with which celery has a natural affinity. Celery salt's most celebrated use is in the Bloody Mary cocktail, while celery seasoning is often added to barbeque marinades.

Cultivation Sow seeds under cover in early spring or outdoors in late spring in rich moist soil. Thin self-blanching seedlings to 23cm (9in) apart. Stems are usually harvested in autumn but for seeds, allow the plants to continue into the following year. Dry the seedheads in paper bags in an airy place.

RECIPE

Cheese sablés

Eat these tiny savoury biscuits with drinks.

100g/4oz/1 cup plain flour
1/4 tsp celery salt
pinch cayenne pepper
50g/2oz/4 tbsp butter
50g/2oz/1/2 cup grated Parmesan cheese
1 egg yolk, beaten

Sift the flour with the celery salt and cayenne, and rub the butter into the flour until the mixture resembles fine breadcrumbs. Add the cheese and egg and mix to a firm dough, adding a little water if necessary. Roll out fairly thinly and cut into 5cm (2in) strips. Cut each strip into triangles. Bake on greased baking trays for about 10 minutes in a moderate oven (190°C/375°F/gas mark 5) until golden brown.

IDENTIFICATION

Tiny green to brown seeds of garden celery plant. **Plant** Biennial growing to 30-60cm (1-2ft) with bunched, grooved stems and jagged leaves; stems and leaves provide edible vegetable; garden varieties are blanched or self-blanching.

ESSENTIAL FACTS

Countries of origin Europe, the USA, the Near East and other temperate regions worldwide.
Storage and preparation Available whole dried or (commonly) ground with salt (celery salt) or other herbs (celery seasoning); use ground forms quickly to avoid loss of flavour and aroma.
Culinary uses Used as a celery substitute, to flavour soups, dips, sauces, salad dressings, tomato dishes, savoury breads and biscuits; a notable ingredient in the Bloody Mary cocktail.

Celery seed

Celery seasoning

Celery salt

Chilli peppers

With the exception of, perhaps, garlic, chilli peppers are arguably the world's most popular flavouring. Chillies were 'discovered' in the New World by the Spanish in the 16th century. They had come seeking one spice, pepper, but instead found not only chillies but potatoes, tobacco, tomatoes, (all, interestingly, belonging to the same Solanaceae family), as well as vanilla and chocolate and a number of other foodstuffs which are now part of everyday fare. Chilli peppers are, in fact ,an ancient spice, found in Aztec and Mayan remains and used since time immemorial in Central and South America. The Spaniards took the plant home where it thrived in the hot, humid conditions of the Mediterranean basin. Soon after, it was carried by Spanish and Portugese traders to Africa, India and the East where, at least in India, it was so widely adopted that an entire cuisine was based on it. It is fundamental, too, to South-eastern Asian cooking where chilli *sambals* (sauces) are served at every meal.

Chilli peppers are the fruits of pungent types of the Capsicum species. Capsicums are also known as sweet, or bell, peppers, paprika (*see* page 73), pimiento, red or green, cayenne (*see* page 32), or bird pepper (depending on which cultivar it comes from and how it is used) and should not be confused with black and white pepper from *Piper nigrum* (*see* pages 74-6).

Generally speaking, chillies come from the small but hot fruits of *C. frutescens*, also known as bird chillies, grown in many tropical countries. However, there are so many kinds of chillies that they defy cataloguing. Not all are blisteringly hot; some Mexican types, for example, have an almost sweet, richly-flavoured but mild pungency which adds subtle distinction to the dishes in which they are used. Fresh green, unripe chillies are often less hot than ripe chillies which, depending on the variety, can be coloured red, orange, yellow, brown, purple or black. For a less hot flavour, remove the seeds from chillies.

It is worth experimenting with fresh chillies, and with different varieties in small or larger quantities to add varying degrees of heat. Chilli powder and other commercial chilli products are useful culinary aids but are no substitute for the fresh spice or for home-made mixes and sauces which can be subtly blended according to personal taste. Tabasco sauce, made from Louisiana chillies, is perhaps a notable exception; no other chilli sauce can really replace it in the famous Bloody Mary cocktail.

Cultivation Capsicum species are grown from seed in heated nurseries, then transplanted outdoors. They can be killed by frost. *Capsicum frutescens* is a perennial which needs tropical climates or artificial heat for a long period to ripen the peppers.

Jalepeño chillies

Crushed red chillies

Dried Mulato chilli

Mexican whole dried chillies

(*Capsicum frutescens*)
SOLANACEAE

IDENTIFICATION

Chillies are berry-like fruits with the shiny outer skin and flesh enclosing ridges of small white seeds; they vary enormously in size, shape, colour and pungency: ranging from green when unripe to red, yellow, brown and purplish-black, and from tiny to extremely large; in pungency, they vary from mild to blistering, which distinguishes them from their larger, very mild cousins, sweet or bell peppers, which are a vegetable rather than a spice.
Plant *C. frutescens* is a shrub-like perennial growing to 2m (6½ ft) with quite small, shiny green leaves and tiny white flowers. Fruits are usually small and narrow.

ESSENTIAL FACTS

Countries of origin Native to Central and South America, chillies are now widely grown throughout sub-tropical and tropical regions; principal producers are China (the world's largest grower and exporter), India, Mexico, the USA, West Indies and East and West Africa.
Varieties of chilli There is an astonishing range of chilli varieties, all of which are considered the best in their country of origin. Among the major Mexican types are *Ancho*, a mild, dark chilli, usually dried; *Jalepeño,* dark green, very hot, usually fresh or canned; *Mulato,* brown, hot, usually dried; *Pasilla*, long, thin, brown, hot rich flavour; *Serrano*, small, green, very hot, usually fresh or canned. The hottest chillies of all are *Uganda* or *Mombasa* chillies; other notable hot chillies include *Hontaka* and *Santaka*(*Capsicums*) from Japan, *Péquin*, *Tabasco* and *Louisiana Sport* peppers.
Preparation and storage Chillies are available fresh, dried, canned, dried and flaked or processed (*see also* chilli products below). Take care when handling chillies (some varieties can literally burn the skin) and always wash hands after seeding and chopping; seeds particularly can cause an unpleasant burning sensation on the skin, especially on sensitive areas such as mouth, eyes and face. Discard seeds for a less pungent flavour. Add chopped fresh or ground chillies sparingly to dishes; use whole chillies to flavour food then extract

Chilli peppers

Continued from page 35

and discard when the desired pungency is reached. Use fresh or dried whole chillies in preference to powder; store dried chillies in airtight jars away from sunlight. Remedies for chilli burns in the mouth are milk, yogurt and ice cream.

Chilli products

Chilli powder in India, China and other tropical countries is the powder ground from small, hot chillies; buy in small quantities and use quickly for, like all spices, if stored for long periods, it can lose flavour and aroma. Better still, make your own chilli powder (*see* pages 20-23).

Chili powder in the USA and Mexico is a blend of spices, such as garlic, cumin and oregano in which chilli predominates. It is not quite as fierce as chilli powder and is used in Mexican dishes and in *chilli con carne*, chillied beans etc.

Nepal pepper is a relatively mild yellow powder produced from an Indian species of chilli and is much used in Indian cooking.

Chilli seasoning is a mixture of salt, spices and chilli usually added to grilled or barbequed meat after cooking or used as salt to add pungency to salad dressings etc.

Chilli sauce is usually a thick dipping sauce, varying in pungency from 'sweet' to hot, made from pulped chillies flavoured with vinegar, garlic and other spices. It is used as a condiment in Chinese cooking and can be home-made (*see* pages 132-5).

Hot pepper sauce from the West Indies is a fiery blend of pulped chillies, onions, vinegar and Caribbean spices.

Chilli oil, used in Chinese cooking, is produced by frying chopped fresh or dried chillies, then straining the oil; it can be home-made.

Tabasco sauce is commercially made in Louisiana from pulped Tabasco chillies matured in wood for three years before being mixed with distilled vinegar.

Culinary uses Chillies are principally associated with Indian cooking where they are an essential ingredient in curry blends and with Mexican food, where they are used in a wide variety of dishes, the best known of which is *chilli con carne*. They are, however, extensively grown and used in South-eastern Asia in Indonesian, Malay and Thai cuisines and in the Chinese province of Sichuan (the cooking style of which has been successfully exported to the West); in Japan, ground chilli is an ingredient of the much used seven-spice mixture. In European cuisine, chillies are found principally in the Mediterannean region where they are used to flavour fish soups and add pungency to meat dishes. *Rouille*, the chilli-based sauce from France, which traditionally accompanies *bouillabaisse*, is similar to *romesco* sauce in Spain and *harissa*, the fiery sauce served with *couscous* in North Africa. Chillies are imported in huge quantities in Northern Europe and North America and are now a common household spice.

Fresh prawns [shrimp] in rich chilli sauce (*Udang sambal*)

This quickly-cooked dish of prawns [shrimp] and chilli is found, with variations, throughout South-eastern Asia. This Indonesian version uses tamarind juice (available from Chinese food shops) to give it its special flavour. Curry leaves are also available from Indian and Chinese grocers. If difficult to find, leave them out.

4 fresh or dried hot red chillies
1 large onion, sliced
3 cloves garlic, chopped
2.5cm/1in piece fresh root ginger
15ml/1tbsp peanut or soya oil
30ml/2tbsp tamarind juice or *15ml/1tbsp lemon juice*
2 curry leaves (optional)
450g/1lb raw peeled prawns [shrimp]
100ml/4floz/8 tbsp thick coconut milk (to make, soak 90g/3½ oz/6 tbsp creamed coconut in 100ml/4 floz/8 tbsp water. Stir until dissolved.)
salt to taste

If desired, seed the chillies for a milder flavour. Using a mortar and pestle or spice grinder, pulp the chillies, then add garlic and ginger. Grind to a coarse paste. Heat the oil in a heavy frying pan or wok and fry the spice mixture and onions until coloured and aromatic. Add the prawns [shrimp] and stir-fry for about 3 minutes or until just pink. Add the tamarind or lemon juice, coconut milk, curry leaves and salt. Allow to boil and cook stirring until the sauce is thick. Do not overcook or the prawns will toughen. Serve immediately with boiled rice.

Chilli oil

Sweet chilli sauce

Fresh prawns (shrimp) in rich chilli sauce

Mexican chilli con carne

1 ancho chilli or 1tbsp mild chilli powder
6 dried red chillies, seeded and chopped, or 1 tbsp hot chilli powder
30ml/2tbsp vegetable oil
350g/12oz/1½ cups onions, chopped
3 cloves garlic, finely chopped
1kg/2lb chuck steak, cubed
½ tsp ground cumin
1 bay leaf
½ tsp dried oregano
½ tsp dried marjoram
salt to taste
750g/1½lb can Italian peeled tomatoes with juice
500g/1lb red kidney beans, cooked

Cover the chillies with warm water and soak for 30 minutes. Drain them, reserving the liquid. Grind the chillies to a paste in a liquidizer or mortar and pestle, adding a little soaking liquid if necessary. Set this aside. Heat the oil in a large saucepan, add the onions, garlic meat and cook over moderate heat until the cubes are lightly browned. Add the chilli paste and soaking liquid (or powder), cumin, herbs and salt and cook for a few minutes before adding the tomatoes. Bring to the boil and simmer for about 1 hour or until the meat is tender, adding the cooked beans for the last 30 minutes of cooking time.

Chinese chilli paste

Tabasco sauce

Indonesian *Sambal*

Taco sauce

Harissa

Chilli powder

Mexican chilli seasoning

Ground Ancho chilli

West Indian hot pepper sauce

(*Theobroma cacao*)
STERCULIACEAE

Chocolate & cocoa

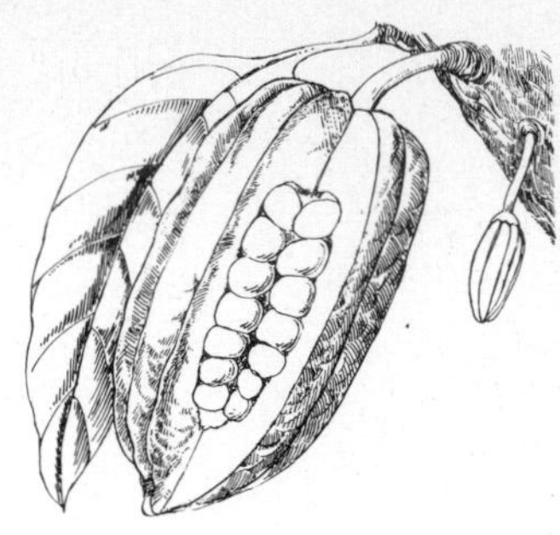

IDENTIFICATION

Dried, fermented seeds or beans of tropical cacao tree, processed to produce cocoa powder or various forms of chocolate. **Plant** Tropical evergreen growing to about 7.5m (25ft) under cultivation with long leathery leaves, small pinkish-white flowers and oval pods (russet brown when ripe), each containing about 40 pale purple beans.

Chocolate for cookies and cakes

When the Spanish general, Hernando Cortés,landed on the shores of Mexico in 1519, the Aztecs believed he was the reincarnation of one of their lost gods. Honouring him with a sumptuous banquet, the Emperor Montezuma served an unusual drink, presented in cups of pure gold, as an accompaniment. This the Aztecs called 'chocolatl' – roasted fermented cocoa beans which were mixed, some say, with powdered chillies to form a restorative (if perhaps unpalatable) drink. When Cortés returned to Spain he took the cocoa bean with him, and there it was mixed with two brand-new spices, sugar and vanilla. This sweet drink became fashionable and soon there were chocolate houses in all the capitals of Europe. Since then, chocolate's popularity has hardly waned, but in the 17th and 18th centuries, it was a very expensive drink, affordable only by the rich or privileged. Not until the 19th century, when the duty on it was lifted and various processing improvements had been introduced, did chocolate become available to ordinary people.

In its early days, drinking chocolate was thick and oily with fat rising to the surface which had to be spooned off before drinking. This problem was solved in 1828 by a Dutchman, Coenraad van Houten, who invented a press which could remove two-thirds of the cocoa 'butter', leaving a cake-like mass which could then be mixed with sugar and spices to make a more digestible drink. (The cocoa used today for drinking and cooking still has more than 80 per cent of its butter removed and the finest quality powder comes from Holland.) Soon after, the English Quaker, Joseph Fry combined the cocoa mass with sugar, gradually adding sufficient cocoa butter to achieve a solid, high-quality chocolate bar. Milk chocolate, invented in 1876 by a Swiss *chocolatier*, Daniel Pieter, included a new product, condensed milk, developed by a chemist, Henri Nestlé. Today, the finest chocolate is still made in Switzerland and the consumption of milk chocolate far outweighs that of plain chocolate.

The difference between drinking chocolate and cocoa is that drinking chocolate is lighter in colour, has more fat, and sugar and a better flavour, while cocoa is darker, has less fat and sugar but can be bitter in flavour. Block chocolates contain a high proportion of fat, some sugar, and a good flavour but can be hard to mix.

Chocolate has been variously extolled as an aphrodisiac, a hangover cure, an energy booster (it contains caffeine) and a promoter of longevity. Its use in the kitchen is extensive; cakes, biscuits, creams, mousses and ice creams, as well as home-made confectionery, all rely on it. Less well known is its use in many savoury dishes in Mexico, Spain and Italy where it adds an interesting flavour and slight sweetness to game, beef and poultry stews. In Mexico's national dish, *mole* (a turkey stew), it is combined with chillies, a traditional use as old as the Aztecs.

Cultivation A delicate tree, cacao is only grown in rain forests in the tropics, usually on large plantations, where it must be protected from wind and intense sunlight. The tree is harvested twice a year.

ESSENTIAL FACTS

Countries of origin Native to tropical America; now grown notably in West Africa (Ghana), Brazil and Mexico.
Forms of chocolate/cocoa All cocoa beans are fermented, dried, roasted, crushed into 'nibs' or pieces, then further ground into a liquid mass usually containing 50% cocoa butter.
Plain/bitter-sweet chocolate Cocoa mass partially defatted and solidified with a little sugar added; contains 30-52% cocoa solids.
Cooking chocolate Unsweetened chocolate, available in the USA, but rare in Great Britain and Europe.
Coating chocolate Contains high proportion of fat and less cocoa solids.
Milk chocolate Powdered or condensed milk added to sweetened chocolate; variously flavoured by manufacturers with vanilla, almonds etc, or filled with nuts, liqueurs; in Great Britain must contain 20% cocoa solids.
White chocolate Made from cocoa butter flavoured with sugar and vanilla.
Cocoa powder Contains only 18% cocoa butter, usually sweetened.
Drinking chocolate Made from pre-cooked cocoa powder with large quantities of sugar and added flavourings.
Preparation and storage Store powdered cocoa and all chocolates in a cool, dry place away from sunlight; plain chocolate keeps up to 1 year, milk chocolate for 6 months. Care must be taken when melting chocolate or cocoa; heat it in a bowl over hot water and never allow to boil.
Culinary uses Widely used for confectionery, cakes, pastries, sweet creams, soufflés, mousses, ice creams and sauces, often in combination with vanilla, cinnamon or coffee; in hot beverages and in liqueur *crème de cacao*; in some savoury dishes eg Mexican *mole*, beef and game stews of Spain and Italy.

Milk chocolate

Drinking chocolate

Dark chocolate

White chocolate

Truffles

Cocoa

RECIPE

Chocolate rum truffles

150g/5oz plain [dark] chocolate, in small pieces.
100g/4oz/½ cup hazelnuts, crushed
50g/2oz/4 tbsp butter, diced and softened
30ml/2 tbsp rum
2 tbsp cocoa powder

Carefully melt the chocolate over hot water. Stir in the hazelnuts. Blend in the butter and add rum. Allow to cool slightly, then refrigerate until mixture is hard enough to shape. Take heaped teaspoonfuls of mixture, roll them lightly in the hands to form walnut-sized balls, then roll them in cocoa powder and place in sweet cases.

Cinnamon (*Cinnamomum verum*, syn. *C. zeylanicum*); cassia (*Cinnamomum cassia*) LAURACEAE

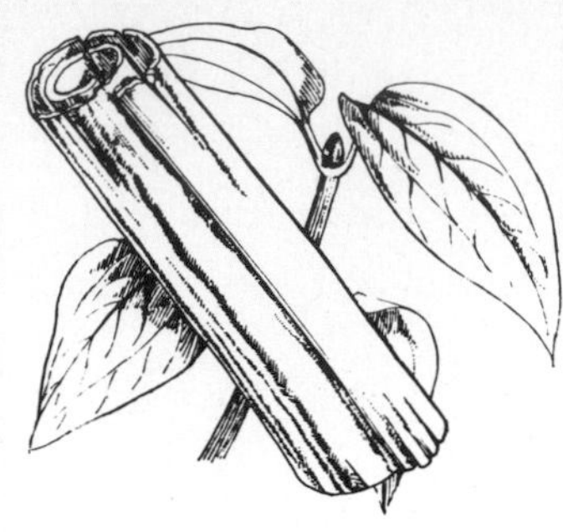

IDENTIFICATION

Cinnamon is the dried, pale-brown inner bark of a cultivated laurel-like tree which grows up to 3m (10ft); the bark is dried in thin cylindrical quills or strips, scrolled together. Cassia is the thicker, coarser bark of a small laurel-like tree; it is reddish brown in colour and dried in chips or pieces up to 7.5cm (3in) long.
Plant Tropical evergreen trees of the laurel family with long, shiny leaves, cinnamon having small, white flowers and purple-black berries, while cassia has small, pale green flowers.

Cinnamon sticks

Ground cinnamon

Cinnamon&cassia

Cinnamon is curled, paper-thin slices of dried bark rolled into sticks or quills; cassia is thicker, coarser bark dried in chips or pieces. Although they have a similar aroma and flavour and in many countries are treated as one and the same thing, in Britain they are differentiated by law. True cinnamon is, however, sweeter and milder than its cousin cassia, also known as Chinese cinnamon, which has a less refined and slightly bitter, taste.

In ancient times, cinnamon was a fabulous spice, rare and expensive, and treasured by King Solomon to whom it was given by the Queen of Sheba. It was one of the spices with which Moses anointed the Ark of the Covenant, and in Roman times Pliny deplored its wanton use by Nero, who burnt a whole year's supply at the funeral of his wife, Poppaea – thereby depleting precious treasury reserves. Although still an expensive spice in medieval Europe, it was a staple flavouring, along with ginger, in the one-pot meat and fruit dishes common at that time.

Cinnamon is no longer used so extensively in Europe but it is an essential spice for flavouring creams, custards, cakes and biscuits. Its warm, sensuous properties marry well with such fruits as apples and pears, and it has a natural affinity with chocolate – the two are sprinkled together over Italian *cappuccino* coffee.

In Middle Eastern and Arab cooking, cinnamon flavours soups and savoury dishes such as stuffed aubergines [eggplants] or lamb stew and in Indian cuisine, it is an important spice in *pilaus* and aromatic, rather than hot, curries. Cassia is also an ingredient in Chinese five-spice powder.
Cultivation Cinnamon and cassia trees grow in hot, wet tropical climates and are principally cultivated in plantations.

Cassia

ESSENTIAL FACTS

Countries of origin Cinnamon is native to Sri Lanka and now grown in hot, wet tropical regions of India, Brazil, East and West Indies and Indian Ocean islands. Cassia is native to Burma and now grown in the hot wet tropics in China, Indochina, East and West Indies and central America.
Preparation and storage Cinnamon is available whole in sticks or powdered; buy sticks for preference or the powder in small quantities to avoid loss of flavour and aroma; sticks are difficult to grind. Cassia is available in whole pieces or ground.
Culinary uses Used in sweet milk, cream and rice puddings and desserts; in cakes and biscuits; pastries, doughnuts and sweet fritters; notably in English cinnamon toast; has special affinity with apples and chocolate; also used in Middle Eastern savoury meat dishes, Indian *pilaus* and curries; for spicing wine; as an ingredient in *garam masala*, Chinese five-spice powder and some pickling mixes.

RECIPE

Cinnamon toast
This traditional and sustaining tea-time treat at Oxford and Cambridge colleges was kept warm in covered muffin dishes.
6 slices of bread
1½ tsp ground cinnamon
1½ tsp sugar
approx 75g/3oz/6 tbsp butter
Toast the bread lightly and liberally spread it with butter. Sprinkle the toast with a mixture of cinnamon and sugar then place it under a slow grill for a few minutes until lightly browned. Cut it into fingers, removing the crusts if preferred, before serving.

Clove

Cloves are the strongly aromatic, dried, unopened buds of the clove tree, which is an evergreen native to the Moluccas. Where they grow close to the sea off the coast of tropical Africa or in the East Indies, their heady scent often greets the traveller even before land is in sight. Cloves are an ancient spice known and used by the Chinese in the 3rd century BC, and later by the Romans as a culinary, medicinal and perfumery spice. In Europe, they have been popular since the Middle Ages when they were widely used, not only in the cooking pot but also as an antiseptic and in pomanders to freshen the air.

Although few kitchens in the West are without a jar of cloves, this is not a spice for everyday use, since its flavour is powerful and penetrating. It is an essential ingredient in English mince pies and Christmas puddings and is frequently added to apple dishes – but perhaps it is most useful with onions in the cooking broth for salt meats such as boiled bacon or ham, ox-tongue or silverside, where it imparts a delicate elusive flavour to the boiled joint. One of the clove's most attractive uses is in glazed ham or gammon where the fat is spread with honey or sugar, studded with cloves and glazed to a golden brown in the oven.

Cultivation Cloves are mainly cultivated in tropical plantations close to the sea. In the Moluccas, animistic beliefs and elaborate rituals are associated with the planting and cultivation of this tree – partly related, it is believed, to the decimation of the crop by 17th-century Dutch colonists.

ESSENTIAL FACTS

Countries of origin Native to the Moluccas (Indonesia); now grown in Zanzibar (Tanzania), Madagascar, West Indies, Brazil, India and Sri Lanka.

Preparation and storage Available whole dried or ground; for preference, buy whole because small heads can be easily crumbled to powder when necessary and ground cloves become musty with keeping.

Culinary uses Used in sweet and savoury dishes and sauces, notably English bread sauces; as an accompaniment to glazed ham, to flavour apple and other fruit dishes; in curries, *pilaus*, meat and game stews; in spiced wines, liqueurs and pickles.

(*Eugenia caryophyllus, Syzygium aromaticum*)
MYRTACEAE

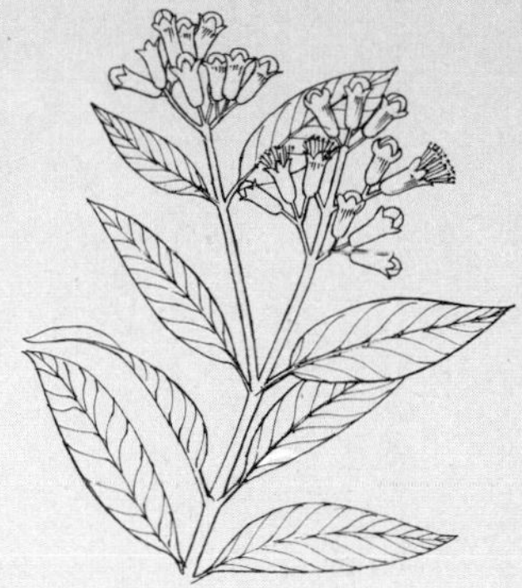

IDENTIFICATION

Pink, unopened flower buds, about 12-16mm (½-⅝in) of a tropical evergreen tree; nail-shaped buds turn red-brown when dried. **Plant** Tropical evergreen growing to about 14m (45ft), with shiny dark green leaves and small crimson flowers with yellow petals (when allowed to bloom).

Whole cloves

Ground cloves

RECIPE

Glazed gammon [ham] with apple juice

1.4kg/3lb gammon [ham] piece, boneless
1 onion stuck with 2-3 cloves
1 bay leaf
2-3 tbsp brown sugar
1 tbsp Dijon mustard
1 tbsp grated orange rind
cloves for studding
150ml/¼ pint/1 cup apple juice

If necessary, soak the gammon [ham] piece overnight to remove excess salt. Place the piece in water with an onion stuck with cloves and with the bay leaf. Bring to the boil and simmer for 1¼-1½ hours. Meanwhile, combine the sugar, mustard and orange rind. Remove the gammon [ham] from the water and carefully peel off the rind to expose the fat. Score the fat in a criss-cross diamond pattern, spread with mustard and sugar mixed together and stud the crosses with cloves. Make a foil parcel to hold the piece, leaving the glazed fat exposed. Pour half the apple juice into the parcel and place in a hot oven for about 20 minutes until the glaze is golden brown. Combine the remaining apple juice with any roasting juices, cook on top of the cooker for a minute or two and serve this separately as a sauce.

(*Coffea arabica*, *Coffea robusta* and others)
RUBIACEAE

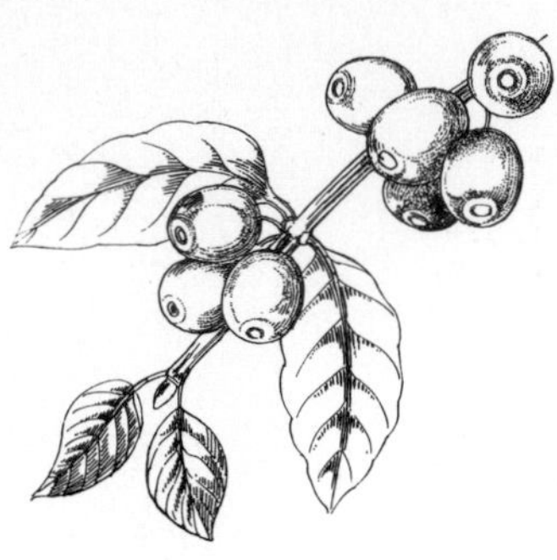

IDENTIFICATION

Green beans from berries of several species of cultivated, flowering coffee plant; extracted and cleaned by wet or dry method before marketing. **Plant** Small evergreen tree or bush bearing white jasmine-scented flowers; berries or cherries, green ripening to red, grown in clusters.

ESSENTIAL FACTS

Countries of origin Indigenous to Ethiopia, Brazil, Colombia, Mocha (South Yemen); tropical and sub-tropical lands in Central and South America, Africa, India and Indonesian archipelago.
Preparation and storage Available as green beans or beans roasted to various degrees (light, medium, full and high or continental); ground to degrees of fineness (powdered, very fine, fine and medium) depending on brewing method; as soluble granules or powder (instant coffee); as essence or syrup, sometimes combined with chicory. For best results, buy freshly roasted beans from coffee merchants, or vacuum packed beans; grind immediately before brewing according to preferred method.
Culinary uses Principally as as stimulating hot beverage (caffeine in coffee is a stimulant and should be taken in moderation), drunk black or with milk or cream, with or without sweetening agents, and in different countries with the addition of spices (eg cardomom), figs and liqueurs; often served iced; as a flavouring in sorbets, ice creams, creams, sweet sauces and cakes.

Coffee

Intrigue dominates the early history of coffee, for this plant was so zealously guarded by the Arabs of Mocha that its widespread cultivation did not begin until the 17th century – when it was smuggled into Europe by Dutch traders who then took it to their colonies in Sri Lanka and the East Indies. Coffee was, however, known in Europe in the early 1600s through travellers returning from the Levant. They acquired a taste for it and soon Venetian traders were importing coffee beans from the sole supplier – Mocha in Arabia – whose way of retaining its monopoly was to render exported beans incapable of germination. Fanciful stories abound about how tender young plants, acquired by stealth, survived misadventures and hazardous sea voyages to take root in the colonies of the New World. Mocha kept its monopoly for only 100 years; by the end of the 19th century, Brazil had become the world's leading producer, a position it holds to this day.

There are a vast number of coffee varieties, usually classified by the regional names in their countries of origin. Typical examples are Santos from Brazil, Blue Mountain from Jamaica or Mocha from present-day Yemen. They are also classified according to plant species (of which there are some 25): *arabica* plants produce the finest beans, while *robustas*, grown mainly in Africa, are of inferior quality but widely used in lower price blends and in instant coffees.

Virtually all coffee available from specialist merchants is blended; seven or eight types, for example, might be skilfully combined to develop various degrees of aroma, body, acidity and colour; this may be sold as the 'house blend' or if Mocha beans predominate, a 'Mocha blend.' Only you can know what suits your taste but, for the novice, the advice of a coffee merchant is always reliable. You can then progress to trying out your own blends.

A coffee grinder is essential if you want to produce good-quality coffee because within a mere half an hour after grinding, beans rapidly start to lose flavour and aroma. There are innumerable devices for brewing coffee but for the finest flavour coffee should *never* be boiled. The excellent filter system, widely available in automatic machines, is far and away the most popular method in the West.
Cultivation Coffee is grown mainly on plantations. Harvesting is still largely done by manual labour since the fruit ripens several times a year, the tree bearing both blossoms and berries at the same time and in varying stages of maturity. Berries must be picked when they are just ripe; if overripe the beans are spoilt, if unripe the beans will not subsequently ripen. Mechanical harvesting is carried out – principally in Africa – with inferior results. The average yield of one tree per annum is approximately 1kg (2lb) of green beans, which accounts for coffee's high cost.

Green coffee beans

Ground coffee with figs

Figs

RECIPE

Coffee granita

50g/2oz/1/4 cup finely-ground coffee
100g/4oz/1/4 cup sugar
600ml/1 pint/2 1/2 cups water
1 egg white, stiffly beaten

Bring the sugar and water to boil in a saucepan. Boil for a few minutes. Add the coffee, remove from the heat and leave to infuse for 10 minutes. Strain the coffee through a fine sieve and leave to cool. Pour it into freezer ice trays, cover and freeze for about 1 hour or until partly frozen. Remove it from the freezer and whisk in the stiffly-beaten egg white until smooth, then return it to the freezer to firm overnight. Remove the granita from the freezer half an hour before serving.

(*Coriandrum sativum*)
UMBELLIFERAE

Coriander

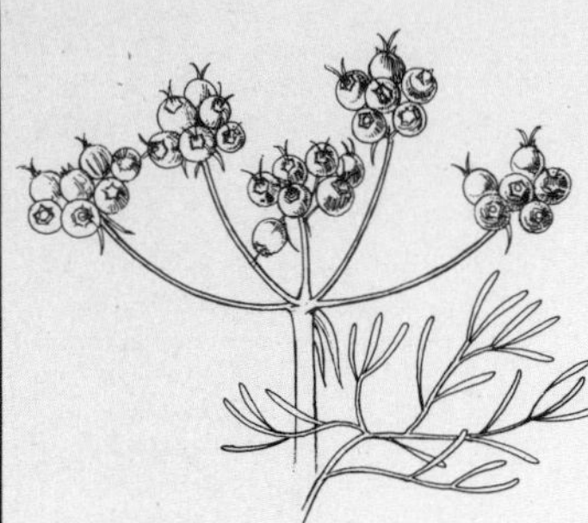

The warm, sweet and orange-like aroma of the coriander seed, makes it one of the most memorable and versatile of all the spices. Known and loved throughout the Mediterranean, the Middle East, India and China for millennia, it is also widely used in south-eastern Asia and in the Caribbean. Mild in strength, coriander can be used with a heavy hand without overwhelming the dish. It blends especially well with garlic and chilli, but is equally delightful in meat and vegetable dishes. In Greece and Cyprus, for example, large quantities of crushed coriander seed flavour olives, sausages and lamb dishes while in Britain most people will be familiar with it as a principal ingredient in *afelia* (pork stewed with red wine), a simple but delicious Greek dish. It is not much used in French cuisine except in the classic *à la grecque* vegetable dishes as one of the subtle flavours in the simmering liquid.

Coriander also has parsley-like leaves which are used fresh and have quite a different flavour. Pungent and bitter, they are perhaps an acquired, but not disagreeable, taste. When chopped and minced like parsley, coriander leaves can be added to numerous salads and cooked dishes, including stuffings, but are particularly successful in Indian recipes where they add authenticity.

Cultivation Sow seeds in early spring in light, well-drained soil in a sunny position about 20cm (8in) apart. Coriander grows quickly, flowers profusely and sets seed without difficulty. The whole plant is strongly and unpleasantly aromatic when unripe. Gather the seed heads as they colour from green to light brown (when their smell becomes pleasant) and hang to finish ripening in paper bags.

IDENTIFICATION

Dried, small cream to brown seeds of parsley-like plant growing to about 60cm (2ft); fresh green leaves (lower fan-like, upper feathery) are used as a herb. **Plant** Hardy annual with fine stem; bright green, broadly lobed lower leaves, upper thread-like and feathery; tiny white to pale lilac flowers in clusters bloom in midsummer.

Whole coriander

Fresh coriander leaves

Ground coriander

ESSENTIAL FACTS

Countries of origin Native to the Middle East and southern Europe but it is grown worldwide, notably North Africa, India, South America, Soviet Union, Hungary, Holland, south-eastern Asia.
Preparation and storage Seeds are available whole or ground; for preference, buy whole and lightly roast them before grinding (which is easy) to bring out the flavour; ground coriander quickly loses its flavour and aroma. Use fresh leaves whole or chopped.
Culinary uses An essential spice in Arab, Middle Eastern and southern European cooking where it is used to flavour meat, fish, vegetables; in sausages and vegetables *à la grecque*; in India and south-eastern Asia in curries and a wide variety of spiced dishes; it is an ingredient in *garam masala*. Coriander leaves are used like parsley in Middle Eastern, Indian and south-eastern Asian food. In Thailand, the root is pounded with garlic as paste for meat dishes.

RECIPE

Tunisian Salad (Fattoush)
2 thick slices stale bread, cubed
15ml/1 tbsp lemon juice
2 green peppers, coarsely chopped
2 large fleshy tomatoes, quartered
3 spring onions, chopped
100g/4oz Feta cheese (or similar white, crumbly cheese eg Wensleydale), cubed
100g/4oz mixed green and black olives, stoned
225g/8oz can tuna fish
salt to taste
50ml/3½ tbsp olive oil
2 cloves garlic, crushed
2 tsp crushed coriander seed
1 drop chilli sauce (harissa) or *3 drops Tabasco sauce*

Moisten the bread with half the lemon juice diluted in 30ml/2 tbsp water. Place this in a salad bowl with the peppers, tomatoes, onions, cheese, olives and tuna fish. Season to taste. Heat the oil in a pan, add the garlic, coriander and *harissa* and cook for a minute or two until the garlic is lightly coloured. Add the remaining lemon juice and pour over the salad. Let the flavours infuse for about 1 hour before serving as an appetizer.

Cumin

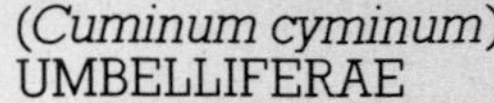

(*Cuminum cyminum*)
UMBELLIFERAE

Cumin seeds come from a delicate annual native to the eastern Mediterranean and North Africa. A venerable spice, cumin is mentioned in the Old Testament and was as widely used in ancient times as it is today. Used whole or ground, cumin's flavour, which is aromatically spicy rather than hot, is an essential ingredient in most North African, Middle Eastern and Indian cooking. It is also found in Spanish and Portuguese cuisine where it is used to flavour sausages, rice and stuffed vegetables.

In Morocco, the characteristic aroma of of this spice pervades the bazaars and food stalls where *brochettes* – kebabs – are grilled over tiny, charcoal-burning stoves by street vendors. The meat is spread with a spice mixture in which cumin predominates but which also includes turmeric, ginger, peppercorns, garlic, onions and parsley. After grilling, the *brochettes* are slipped into flat pillows of unleavened bread (like pitta) and eaten on the spot. In India, cumin is included in most curry mixes and in innumerable dishes, as well as in a refreshing drink made with tamarind water.

Remember that lightly roasting the seeds in a dry frying pan before using brings out cumin's interesting aroma and flavour.

Cultivation The cumin plant prefers a hot climate but it can be grown in northern regions if started in a heated greenhouse or under glass. As the plant takes about four months to mature, sow seed in early spring and transplant to well-drained soil in a sunny position. Harvest the seedheads as they begin to change colour and hang them in paper bags to ripen and dry in an airy place.

RECIPE

Mulligatawny soup

This is one of the many versions of this favourite Anglo-Indian soup, traditionally served with separate bowls of boiled rice.

2 chicken breasts, cut into chunks
225g/8oz dried red lentils
2 cloves garlic, crushed
1 bay leaf
2.5cm (1in) piece root ginger, finely chopped
3 dried red chillies
6 black peppercorns, ground
4 large onions, sliced
2 tsp cumin seed, roasted and ground
1 tsp ground turmeric
150ml/¼ pint/⅔ cup coconut milk
salt to taste
50g/2oz/4 tbsp butter or *ghee*
4 thin slices of lemon
Serves 4-6.

Place the chicken and lentils in 1.7 litres/3 pints/7½ cups water. Add the garlic, bay leaf, ginger, chillies, ground spices and half of the onions. Bring slowly to the boil and simmer gently for about 45 minutes or until the lentils are soft. Remove the bay leaf and whole chillies and stir in the coconut milk and salt to taste. Simmer for a further 10-15 minutes. Meanwhile, heat the butter and fry the remaining onions until deep brown. Add these to the soup along with the lemon slices just before serving.

IDENTIFICATION

Small, dried seeds (similar to caraway seeds but lighter in colour) of small, parsley-type plant growing to about 25cm (10in). **Plant** Slender annual with thread-like leaves; white or pink flowers in small clusters appear in early summer.

ESSENTIAL FACTS

Countries of origin Native to the eastern Mediterranean and Upper Egypt; now grown principally in hot countries of North Africa, Middle East, India and the Americas.
Preparation and storage Seeds available whole or ground; for preference, buy whole and lightly roast before using or grinding; ground seeds lose flavour and aroma within 1-2 months.
Culinary uses In wide variety of North African dishes (notably *couscous*); to flavour fish, lamb, chicken and vegetables especially aubergines [eggplants] in Middle East; in India (where it is known as *jeera*), in curry mixes and spiced dishes including yogurt relishes, snacks and cooked vegetables; in Mexican cooking often combined with chilli (as in *chilli con carne*) and added to commercial chilli powders and pepper sauces.

Ground cumin

Whole cumin seeds

(*Murraya koenigii*, syn. *Chalcas koenigii*)
RUTACEAE

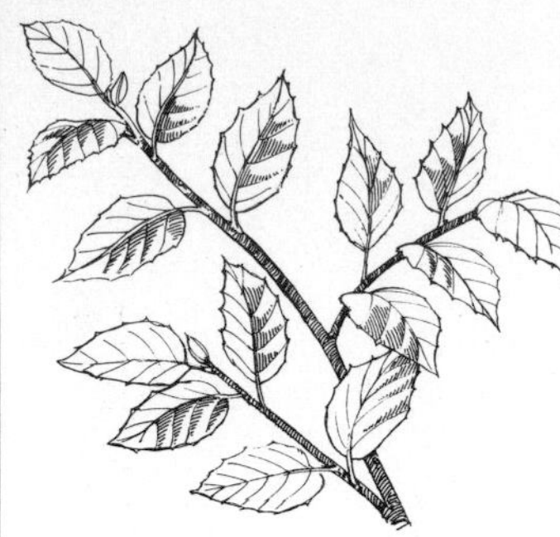

Curry leaf

Curry leaves come from a small tree of the citrus family which is a native of South-western Asia. Called *kari phulia* or *nim* leaves in India, it is used principally in southern Indian cookery, often in association with coconut, either whole or ground, as an ingredient in many spice mixtures and in commercially produced Madras curry powders and pastes. Curry leaves have a warm, appetizing aroma and impart a subtle, spicy flavour to the dishes in which they are used. Sometimes they are fried whole in butter or oil, then removed before food is cooked in this aromatic fat.

On the Kerala coast of western India, curry leaves are invariably added to fish and seafood along with onions, ginger, green chillies and coconuts. Prawns [shrimp] cooked in this mixture are quite delicious. The inhabitants of Goa in India also add curry leaves to their searingly hot fish curries.

Curry leaf is perhaps best sampled in the traditional vegetarian cuisine of southern and central India, of which the recipe is a particularly appetizing example.

Cultivation The curry leaf tree, which grows only in tropical or sub-tropical regions, is not cultivated commercially. It is found either in the wild state or as a common garden tree in southern India or Malaysia.

IDENTIFICATION

Fresh or dried leaves of tropical plant, similar in shape to bay leaf but smaller and thinner; shiny olive green when fresh. **Plant** Small tree of the citrus family with copper-coloured wood, bearing small clusters of ripe purplish berries and fragrant white flowers.

ESSENTIAL FACTS

Countries of origin Native to India and Sri Lanka; not commercially cultivated but grown in domestic gardens in India, Sri Lanka and Malaysia.

Preparation and storage Available fresh or dried from specialist Indian stores; buy fresh leaves for preference or vacuum-packed dried; once exposed to the air, dried leaves lose flavour and aroma within 1-2 months.

Culinary uses Widely used in Asian cookery, whole or ground, to flavour curries, spiced meat and fish dishes, vegetables, chutneys, pickles and relishes; essential in many southern Indian vegetarian dishes; ingredient in Madras curry mixes.

RECIPE

Okra with yogurt (Dahni bhindi)

450g/1lb fresh okra
60ml/4 tbsp vegetable oil
1/4 tsp cumin seed, lightly roasted
1 cm/1/2 in, piece of root ginger, finely chopped
2 dried red chillies
1 tsp turmeric
salt to taste
150ml/1/4 pint/2/3 cup yogurt
8 curry leaves

Wash the okra under cold running water. Snip off the stems if wished. Pat dry with kitchen towel. Heat the oil over moderate heat in a large, heavy frying pan. Add the cumin and ginger and fry for a minute before adding the okra and chillies. Cook, stirring for about 5 minutes. Lower the heat, add the turmeric, salt and yogurt and stir well before covering the pan. Cook for 10-15 minutes, then add the curry leaves and cook for a final 5 minutes. Serve with rice or stuffed into *parathas* (Indian bread).

Madras curry powder

Curry leaves

Dill

Dill was one of the herbs used by Egyptian doctors 5000 years ago and it was known as a medicinal plant by the Greeks and Romans. In Northern Europe, its use was widespread from the Middle Ages on, with dill-water renowned as a cure for hiccups, while its seeds and feathery leaves were added to sauces and pickles.

Now dill seeds are best known as the flavouring in the pickled cucumbers called dill pickles, eaten all over the world, mostly with smoked or salt fish, cold meats, hamburgers and salt beef. Although not much used in British cookery, dill seeds – which are rather bitter and taste like caraway seeds – are found a great deal in northern and central European cooking where they are used to flavour fish, grilled lamb and pork, stews, sauerkraut, cabbage, cauliflower and pickles. In France, the seeds are occasionally sprinkled on cakes and breads, and they make an excellent substitute for caraway in rye bread, especially the dark, pumpernickel type. When used in moderation dill seed can add an interesting and very agreeable flavour to conventional dishes of cauliflower and cabbage.

Aromatic dill leaves, with their subtle, delicate hint of anise, are much more popular and versatile. They are an essential flavouring in the traditional Scandinavian dish of pickled salmon known as *gravad lax* and wonderfully enhance fish and cucumber sauces, as well as yogurt and sour cream dishes. Dill leaves do not dry well, losing much of their flavour in the process but, happily, fresh leaves are fairly widely available.

Cultivation Sow in spring in well-drained soil with a sunny aspect in drills about 25cm (10in) apart. Thin to 23cm (9in). Keep well watered and free from weeds. Do not grow close to fennel as the two may cross-pollinate. Harvest the seeds on their stems just before they are ripe enough to drop and hang them in paper bags to dry in a warm airy place.

ESSENTIAL FACTS

Countries of origin Mainly northern hemisphere, especially the USA, Scandinavia, Soviet Union, Balkans and southern Europe.

Preparation and storage Seeds available whole; easily crushed if desired; will keep indefinitely in an airtight container out of sunlight; leaves available fresh or dried (dried quickly lose flavour and aroma).

Culinary uses Seeds principally used in pickling eg dill pickles (pickled cucumbers), to flavour vinegar, soups and stocks, cakes and pastry; fresh leaves used in sauces, stuffings, to flavour fish, chicken, meat and vegetables (especially cucumber); in yogurt and sour cream dishes.

RECIPE

Dill vinegar

Add a teaspoonful or two of this to a fresh red cabbage dish to give it an agreeable piquancy.

600ml/1 pint/2½ cups white wine vinegar

1-2 dill seedheads with leaves

Steep the seedheads and leaves in the vinegar in a cork-stoppered jar or bottle for 1-2 weeks, shaking occasionally. Strain the liquid into a sterilized jar or bottle and use in dressings, mayonnaise etc.

(*Anethum graveolens, syn. Peucedanum graveolens*)
UMBELLIFERAE

IDENTIFICATION

Tiny, ripe dried seeds, light brown in colour, of dill plant growing to about 1m (3ft); feathery leaves are widely used as a herb. **Plant** Hardy annual with single erect stem; leaves thin and thread-like; tiny yellow flowers in flattened clusters appear in summer.

Dill vinegar

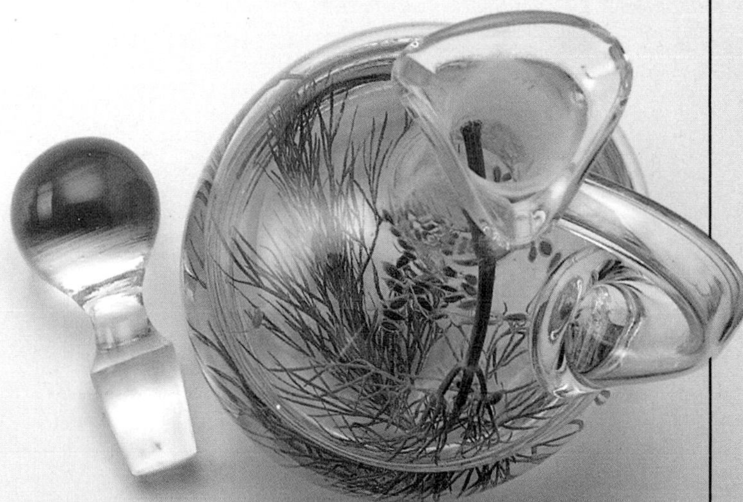

Fresh dill

Dill seeds

(*Foeniculum vulgare*)
UMBELLIFERAE

Fennel

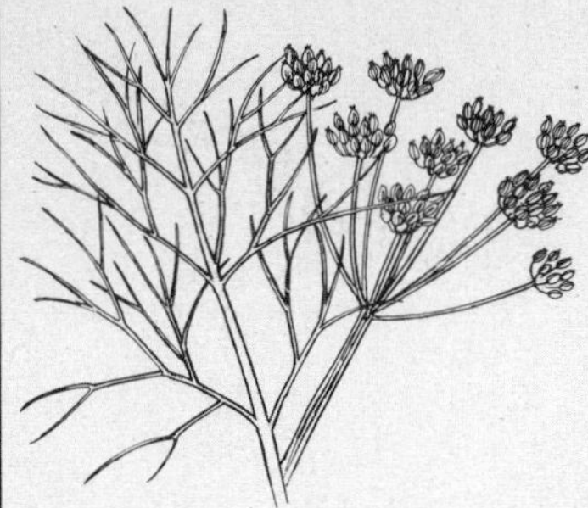

IDENTIFICATION

Small, dried light-green to brown seeds of common fennel plant grows to 2.5cm (8ft); a hardy perennial often grown as an annual; feathery leaves used as a herb; dried stalks as a flavouring. Florentine fennel (*F. vulgare azoricum*), an annual, needs a long, warm summer to swell the 'bulb'. **Plant** Short solid stem with thread-like feathery leaves; tiny, bright yellow flowers in large clusters appear in mid to late summer.

A common plant throughout the Mediterranean since ancient times, fennel is now grown worldwide, mainly for its fragrant feathery leaves which are used as a herb and also for its seeds. One variety, Florence fennel (*finnochia*), is increasingly cultivated because its bulbous stem also provides a delicious vegetable.

Like many herbs and spices, fennel was once used medicinally and a fennel decoction (obtained by boiling the leaves in water for about 15 minutes) is still an effective treatment for inflamed or tired eyes.

The seeds are invaluable in the kitchen for the subtle and agreeable anise-like flavour they can impart when fresh leaves are unavailable. The plant has a natural affinity with fish and, in Italy and the Mediterranean, fennel leaves, stalks and seeds are frequently used to enhance mullet and sardines, (especially good when grilled outdoors over an open fire). The leaves are also used to temper the richness of fatty meats such as pork, while the Florentines add the seeds to a salami called *finocchiona*, a most felicitous marriage and well worth tasting. The use of fennel seeds in the East is limited to some curry and spice mixes (for example, Chinese five-spice powder) and in India it is best known as an ingredient of *pa'an* which is an aid to digestion and sweetens the breath. Common fennel is an easy and attractive plant to grow in the garden; it is more versatile than dill and its flavour more subtle than aniseed.

Cultivation Common fennel is hardy in northern climates but needs a well-drained soil and a sunny sheltered spot. Sow seeds in the spring and thin to 45cm (18in). Harvest the seedheads in late summer to early autumn and hang to dry in a paper bag in an airy place.

ESSENTIAL FACTS

Countries of origin Native to Mediterranean regions; now grown worldwide, including India and the Far East.
Preparation and storage Seeds available whole and are easily ground if desired; store seeds in airtight containers away from light; use leaves fresh as they are unsuitable for drying, or dry the stalks at home.
Culinary uses Seeds are used to flavour fish stocks, soups and sauces, grilled fish and pork; as an ingredient in *finocchiona* salami; to flavour breads and cakes; as an ingredient in Chinese five-spice powder, in sweet pickling spices and in some curries in India, Sri Lanka and Malaysia.

RECIPE

Red mullet à la Niçoise
15ml/1 tbsp olive oil
4 red mullet, scaled and cleaned
4 shallots or 2 small onions, finely chopped
1 tsp fennel seeds, lightly crushed
1 bay leaf
150ml/¼ pint/¾ cup fish stock
150ml/¼ pint/¾ cup dry white wine
300ml/½ pint/1½ cups Italian-style tomato sauce, bottled (or if freshly made, use canned or fresh tomatoes, carrots, garlic and seasoning)
250g/4oz black olives, stoned
salt and pepper to taste
lemon and parsley to garnish

Grease a baking dish with the oil. Add the fish, shallots, half the fennel seed and the bay leaf. Pour over the wine and fish stock and bake in a hot oven (220°C/425°F/gas mark 7) for about 20 minutes or until the fish is cooked. Meanwhile heat through, or make, the tomato sauce (using tomatoes reduced with carrot, garlic, salt and pepper), adding to it the remaining fennel seeds and black olives. Pour the sauce into a warmed serving dish, place the cooked fish on top and garnish with lemon slices and parsley.

Bulb fennel with leaves

Dried fennel leaves

Fennel seeds

Fenugreek

(*Trigonella foenum-graecum*) LEGUMINOSAE

Although as a spice fenugreek is principally associated with Indian cookery, the plant has been used in the West for centuries in medicine and for animal fodder – its name is derived from the Latin for 'Greek hay'. As long ago as the 11th century, the Arab physician Avicenna prescribed fenugreek for diabetes, a use it retains to this day, and it is now also used to lower blood pressure, in the oral contraceptive pill and in veterinary medicine.

As a culinary spice, fenugreek's pungent seeds are an essential ingredient in commercially-produced curry powders and are responsible for their distinctive aroma, which is quite unlike freshly-ground mixes. The great English food writer, Elizabeth David has said, 'Fenugreek is to curry much as malt vinegar is to English salads.' But fenugreek does not really deserve such condemnation. Used in small quantities as, indeed, it is in India, it imparts a special flavour to many vegetables, especially potatoes and aubergines [eggplants]. The secret is to *lightly* roast the seeds until they barely change colour before grinding or using them; it is only when overroasted that they develop a bitter, disagreeable flavour and aroma.

Sprouted fenugreek seeds are increasingly popular in the West, particularly in health-food restautrants and, when used in salads, are refreshing and nutritious.

Cultivation This is a tender plant in temperate climates which needs to be sown outdoors in late spring with protection. Space plants at about 23cm(9in) apart in well-drained but fertile soil, making sure they get plenty of sun. The plant matures in about four months.

RECIPE

Spiced aubergines [eggplants]

2 medium aubergines [eggplants], sliced and quartered
105ml/7 tbsp vegetable oil
8 fenugreek seeds
½ tsp fennel seeds
¼ tsp cumin seeds
½ tsp nigella seeds (kalonji)
salt and pepper to taste
¼ tsp chilli powder
15ml/1 tbsp lemon juice
coriander leaves to garnish (optional)

Place the aubergines [eggplants] in a colander and sprinkle with salt. Leave for about 30 minutes, then thoroughly rinse and pat dry. Heat the oil in a frying pan, add the seeds and cook for a few seconds until lightly coloured. Add the aubergine [eggplant] pieces, seasoning and chilli powder. Lower the heat, stir to combine, cover the pan and cook, turning pieces over occasionally, for about 10-15 minutes or until they are soft and the oil is absorbed. Stir in the lemon juice and serve garnished with fresh coriander leaves.

IDENTIFICATION

Small, yellowish-brown seeds from pod of a bean-like plant growing to about 60cm (2ft). Sprouting seeds and leaves also have culinary uses.
Plant Annual with narrow, serrated leaves, yellow to white pea flowers in summer and narrow sword-like pods, each containing 10-20 seeds.

ESSENTIAL FACTS

Countries of origin Native to India and southern Europe; grown commercially in Morocco, India, Egypt and elsewhere in Africa.
Preparation and storage Dried seeds available whole or ground, lightly roast whole seeds before adding to curry mixes; commercially produced powder often bitter and pungent; use sprouting seeds in salads when at the two-leaf stage.
Culinary uses Seeds principally used in curry powders, especially in India and Sri Lanka; in pickles and chutneys, added to vegetable dishes and *dhals* (lentil purées); in some spiced dishes in Middle East and North Africa; eaten soaked and cooked like beans in parts of Africa; sprouting seeds used in salads.

Sprouting fenugreek seeds

Fenugreek seeds

Ground fenugreek

Garlic

IDENTIFICATION

Bulb of lily-like plant, leaves of which grow to between 30-60 cm (12-24 in); bulb consists of several segments or cloves, each covered with papery white skin. **Plant** Bulb case has cluster of fibrous roots; green smooth stem bears flat, long leaves; pink or whitish flowers appear in late summer.

ESSENTIAL FACTS

Countries of origin Probably indigenous to Asia; now grown worldwide in warm and in temperate climates; however, the flavour is less good in cooler latitudes.
Preparation and storage Available as whole bulbs; dried as granules or powder; dried powder with salt (garlic salt); preserved as whole peeled cloves or as purée in jars or tubes. Buy bulbs, using whole peeled cloves, or minced, crushed or mashed with mortar and pestle, garlic press or simply sharp knife or fork; keep bulbs in cool dry place. *Dried and preserved garlic* Can be used for convenience to add zest to soups, stews and some cooked sauces but are poor substitutes for real thing; garlic powder quickly loses flavour and aroma; note that preserved cloves and purée add an unpleasant, bitter flavour when added, uncooked, to salads, dressings, mayonnaise etc.
Culinary uses Innumerable uses in almost every cuisine but traditionally in robust Mediterranean cooking; also in Mexican, Central and South American cookery; essential in India, China and south-eastern Asia. Notable uses in French cuisine include *aïoli* (garlic mayonnaise), the restorative garlic soup and garlic butter served with snails; roast lamb studded with garlic and rosemary is a common and deservedly popular Western dish.

The cultivation of garlic is as old as civilization itself and since prehistoric times its powerful onion-like flavour has reputedly wrought culinary and medicinal miracles, as astonishing today as they were to the ancients. The slave builders of the Pyramids ate garlic in large quantities allegedly to build up their strength and bulbs were found in Tutankhamen's tomb, probably to keep away evil spirits. The Israelites yearned for it in the wilderness, and in Homer's epic, Odysseus escapes death at the hand of the sorceress Circe by using garlic as a charm to make her fall in love with him.

In its long and well-documented history as a remedy, Culpeper declared that it cured *all* diseases. More specifically, it was recommended for clearing the voice (by the Greeks), and for colds, coughs, bronchitis and asthma. In country lore, it cured nosebleeds and was used as a lotion for skin problems and boils. Its ability to destroy disease and infection is perhaps its most remarkable attribute. In 1722 in Marseilles, for example, four thieves, tried and convicted of robbing the graves of plague victims, maintained that they resisted contagious infection by eating huge quantities of garlic, a story reinforced in the early 19th century when French (garlic-eating) priests, treating an outbreak of infectious fever in the London slums, suffered no health hazards, unlike their Anglican brothers.

Even more renowned is its effectiveness as an external antiseptic; in World War I it was widely used on wounds when conventional antiseptics were unavailable. Known to dilate blood vessels and reduce high blood pressure, garlic could be important in the prevention of coronary heart disease, although important research findings have yet to be fully analyzed. There is some evidence that it could be a useful agent against today's industrial pollution, and in Japan there is even a clinic devoted to garlic remedies, in which one treatment is a garlic spray which is said to cure everything from hepatitis to frost-bite.

Garlic's legendary reputation against vampires is well-known but its folklore associations are numerous. In Mediterranean countries, it is used in rituals against the evil eye; it was traditionally hung on babies' cradles to ward off evil spirits and as a protection against witchcraft. It is still ceremoniously used not only in an Egyptian festival as old as the Pharoahs but also in an annual festival at Gilroy, California, the centre of garlic production in the USA.

The culinary uses of garlic are endless. Contrary to popular belief, it need not be overpowering or pungent. With ginger, it is probably the most important flavouring in Chinese cuisine, which is noted for its refinement and subtlety. It is universally used in Indian cookery and in Western cuisines it adds zest to all kinds of meat, fish and vegetables as well as salad dressings. Its lavish inclusion in Mediterranean dishes is not to everyone's taste but most people enjoy it in the garlic butter served with snails, in the Provençal mayonnaise, *aïoli*, in garlic soup and in the Greek mayonnaise, *skordaliá*. In a famous Provençal recipe, *Poulet aux Quarante Gousses d'Ail*, chicken is cooked with 40 cloves of garlic, a deliciously aromatic dish with the garlic acquiring a delicate, nutty flavour after prolonged cooking.
Cultivation An easily-grown kitchen-garden plant, garlic is propagated by planting the cloves. Plant in light, well-manured soil in a sunny position in early spring or autumn. Space to 15cm (6in). Harvest 5-6 months later. Throughly dry the bulbs and store in a cool, dry place.

RECIPE

Escargots à la bourguignonne (snails in garlic butter)

175g/6oz/1¾ cups unsalted butter, softened
3 cloves garlic, mashed
3 tbsp parsley, finely chopped
1 tbsp shallots, minced
salt and freshly ground pepper to taste
48 snails with shells

Combine the softened butter with the garlic, parsley, shallot and seasoning. In each snail shell place a knob of butter, top with snail and more butter to fill shell. Bake the snails on a bed of salt or in special snail dishes, covered with foil, in a hot oven (375°F/190°C/gas mark 5) for 10-12 minutes. Serve immediately.

Garlic flakes

Dried ground garlic

Garlic salt

Garlic purée

(*Zingiber officinale*)
ZINGIBERACEAE

Ginger

One of the earliest oriental spices known in the West, ginger was particularly popular in medieval and Tudor times in England when it was valued equally as a medicinal and culinary spice. Gingerbread was a favourite treat, stamped with a pattern and often decorated with gold leaf, and sold at fairs up and down the country by special gingerbread vendors. A medicinal cure-all and a jack-of-all-trades, it was a remedy against the plague, included in pomanders and potpourris to dispel odours and taken as a reputed aphrodisiac.

All forms of ginger derive from the root (rhizome) of the ginger plant. The dried root and powdered ginger have been traditionally used in European cookery for centuries, mainly in a wide variety of sweet dishes and it is only in very recent times that green, or fresh, ginger has become common in markets and general food stores, principally because of the West's fascination with Eastern and oriental cuisines. Jamaican dried ginger is considered of superior quality because of its delicate aroma and flavour.

Ginger has a hot, spicy flavour familiar to most people from ginger biscuits. In green ginger this flavour is stronger and hotter but oddly refreshing and pleasant. In Indian and oriental cuisines, it combines particularly well with fish to which it adds a lingering but delicate piquancy. However, like garlic, it can be put to good use in an endless variety of dishes. Dried ground ginger bears little resemblance to the fresh root because it is often blended with coarsely flavoured varieties to produce a sharp and often musty taste which many people dislike. Apart from using the spicy fresh root, serious cooks can make their own fragrant powder by grinding dried whole ginger root in a spice mill, then sieving out the fibrous matter.

Cultivation The ginger plant is a perennial usually grown as an annual only in tropical regions with pronounced wet and dry seasons. It is propagated by dividing the roots, after which plant shoots appear 10 days later. It is harvested about 7-10 months after planting.

IDENTIFICATION

Bulbous knobbed root (rhizome), dark brown to buff in colour, of tropical plant growing to about 1m (3ft). **Plant** Reed-like perennial with bright green leaf blades and yellow, purple-lipped flowers.

ESSENTIAL FACTS

Countries of origin Probably native to south-eastern Asia; now grown commercially in all tropical countries including India, China, West Africa, Caribbean and Australia.

Forms of ginger
Green (fresh) ginger Widely available in supermarkets, Indian and oriental shops and town and city markets; knobbly ginger roots vary in shapes and size. Buff or pale-skinned varieties are superior to most darker-skinned types.
Dried ginger Available as dark-skined whole root or parboiled, skinned, bleached and limed; dried whole ginger is tough and fibrous.
Ground ginger Beige-coloured powder of dried ginger, widely available in proprietary spice brands.
Preserved or stem ginger Young tender roots preserved in yellow-brown or red syrup, with concentrated spicy flavour; traditionally bottled in attractive blue-and-white Chinese jars.
Crystallized or candied ginger Young ginger steeped in sugar syrup, dried and crystallized; used as a sweet.

Preparation and storage *Green ginger* Cut off and peel piece of required size; mince, crush or slice as desired; unpeeled fresh root, wrapped in plastic film, keeps for up to 6 weeks in cool compartment of refrigerator; alternatively, preserve in dry sherry or vodka. *Dried ginger* Store in airtight container away from sunlight. Before use, beat with rolling pin to loosen fibres; add whole to cooking, especially ginger beer; remove when flavour has permeated other ingredients. *Ground ginger* Buy in small quantities and use quickly to avoid loss of flavour and aroma; or make your own (see opposite). *Preserved and crystallized ginger* Preserved ginger keeps indefinitely if airtight; keep crystallized in a dry, airtight container.

Culinary uses Green ginger is an essential ingredient in oriental and Eastern cookery where it is added to fish, meat and vegetable dishes; in spice and curry mixes. Whole dried root ginger is used to flavour pickles, chutneys, ginger beer or wine. Ground ginger used in gingerbreads, cakes, biscuits, pickles, chutneys, sauces, sweets, puddings, jams; as flavouring with fruit and melon. Preserved ginger is used in cakes, puddings and ice cream. Ginger is a common flavouring in traditional English sweet dishes; rarely used in classic French cuisine.

Fresh ginger root

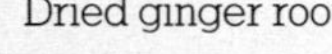

Dried ginger root

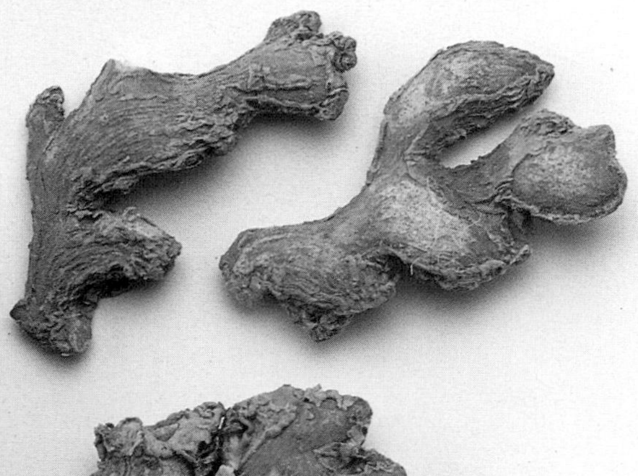

Crystallized ginger

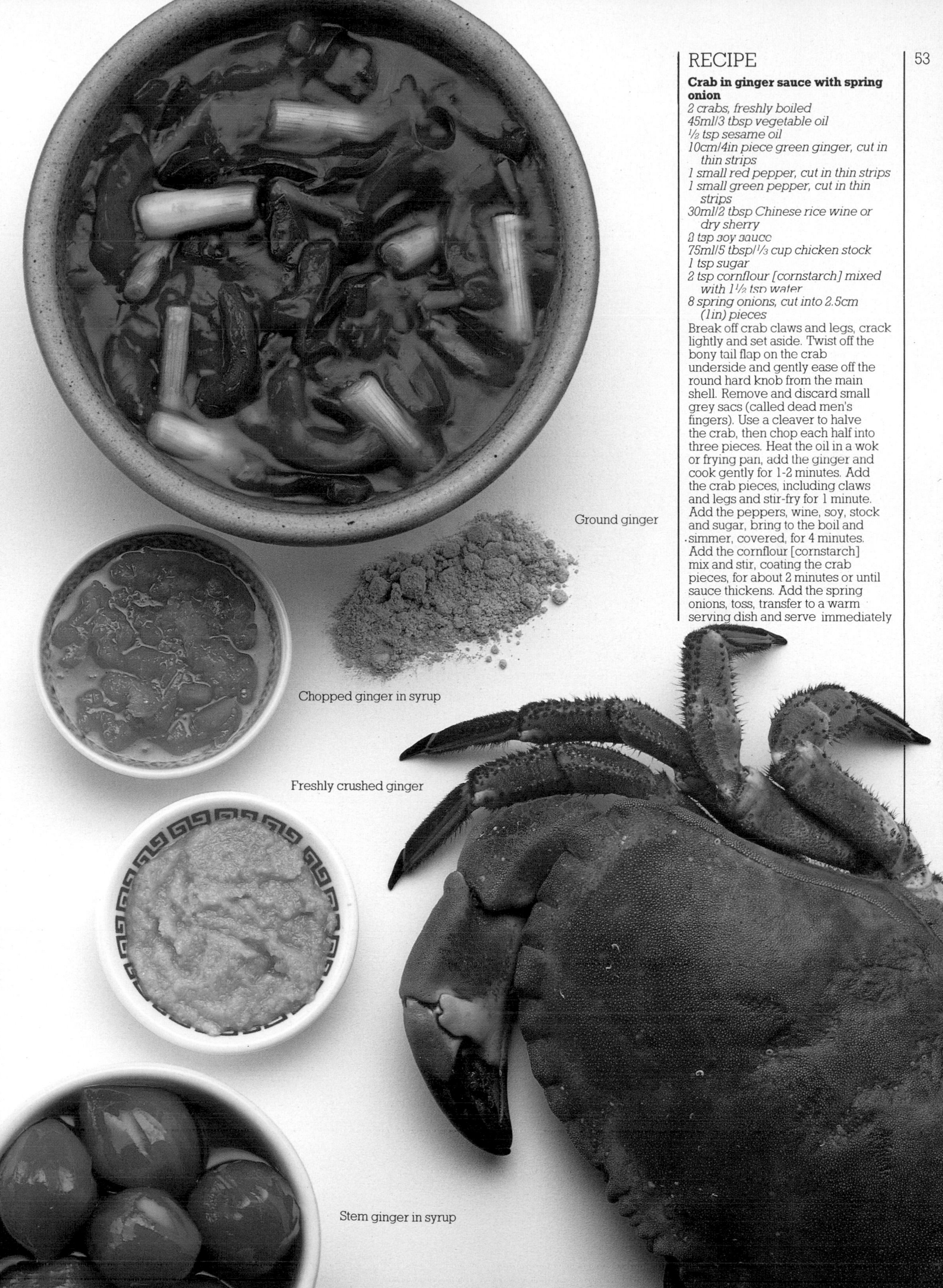

RECIPE

Crab in ginger sauce with spring onion

2 crabs, freshly boiled
45ml/3 tbsp vegetable oil
½ tsp sesame oil
10cm/4in piece green ginger, cut in thin strips
1 small red pepper, cut in thin strips
1 small green pepper, cut in thin strips
30ml/2 tbsp Chinese rice wine or dry sherry
2 tsp soy sauce
75ml/5 tbsp/⅓ cup chicken stock
1 tsp sugar
2 tsp cornflour [cornstarch] mixed with 1½ tsp water
8 spring onions, cut into 2.5cm (1in) pieces

Break off crab claws and legs, crack lightly and set aside. Twist off the bony tail flap on the crab underside and gently ease off the round hard knob from the main shell. Remove and discard small grey sacs (called dead men's fingers). Use a cleaver to halve the crab, then chop each half into three pieces. Heat the oil in a wok or frying pan, add the ginger and cook gently for 1-2 minutes. Add the crab pieces, including claws and legs and stir-fry for 1 minute. Add the peppers, wine, soy, stock and sugar, bring to the boil and simmer, covered, for 4 minutes. Add the cornflour [cornstarch] mix and stir, coating the crab pieces, for about 2 minutes or until sauce thickens. Add the spring onions, toss, transfer to a warm serving dish and serve immediately

Ground ginger

Chopped ginger in syrup

Freshly crushed ginger

Stem ginger in syrup

(*Armoracia rusticana*)
CRUCIFERAE

Horseradish

The hot-tasting root of horseradish has been in use since antiquity both for its medicinal and culinary properties. A native of eastern Europe, by the late Middle Ages it was growing wild in northern Europe and Britain where it had important medicinal applications in the treatment of gout, swellings and rheumatic complaints. By the 16th century, it had become a popular flavouring in Scandinavia and Germany and was widely used, as the English herbalist Gerard observed, as a sauce for fish and meat rather like mustard (the pungency of which it resembles). Only after the 17th century did it become commonplace in England when it was used with oily fish such as mackerel and herrings and later to add piquancy to a variety of pickles and ketchups. Its role as the traditional accompaniment of English roast beef was therefore acquired relatively recently, largely because it was difficult to oust mustard from its privileged position as the favourite British condiment.

Only when the root is scraped or cracked does it release its penetrating aroma, which makes the eyes smart and gives the grated root its sharp flavour. Subjected to heat, however, horseradish loses much of its pungency. Northern European dishes exploit this versatility; a traditional German recipe for Christmas carp, for example, includes cream, ground almonds, sugar and horseradish; in Denmark poached turbot is served in a sauce of melted butter and horseradish. In North America, it is a favourite flavouring in dips and barbecue sauces. Japanese horseradish, (an entirely different species), produces a pungent green powder, *wasabi*, which is popular as a garnish and as an ingredient in dipping sauces.

Cultivation Propagate from root cuttings and plant in late winter. Remove all side shoots before planting cuttings in holes 30cm (1ft) deep and 45cm (18in) apart. For good roots, horseradish needs moist soil and prefers sun. Keep the plant isolated and when digging it up, remove all traces of the root, otherwise it will take over the garden.

IDENTIFICATION

Fleshy roots of horseradish plant growing to 60cm (2ft). **Plant** Herbaceous perennial with long, dock-like leaves and tiny, white, scented flowers appearing occasionally in summer.

ESSENTIAL FACTS

Countries of origin Native to eastern Europe; now grown mainly in northern Europe, Britain and the USA.

Preparation and storage Available fresh whole or grated; in dried, flaked or powdered forms; and in commercially-produced sauces and creams. Thoroughly scrub the fresh root before finely grating or scraping, discarding tough inner core; home-made grated root freezes well or can be preserved in vinegar. Powdered root is reconstituted like mustard.

Culinary uses Principally added to uncooked sauces mixed with vinegar, sugar, mayonnaise, cream, yogurt or sour cream; sometimes mixed with lemon or orange juice, garlic or pepper; also used in cooked sauces where its flavour is less pungent; accompanies fish, meat (especially beef) and vegetables eg cucumber, beetroot. Grated or powdered, it can be added to vegetables, sausages, stews, soups etc.

RECIPE

Barbecue horseradish sauce

This chilled sauce is a splendid accompaniment to charcoal-grilled hamburgers, sausages and kebabs.

150ml/¼ pint/⅔ cup double [heavy] cream
1½ tsp lemon juice
2 tbsp mayonnaise
a large pinch dry mustard
1 tbsp grated horseradish

Mix the cream and lemon juice together. Beat in the remaining ingredients. Chill the sauce for about 2-3 hours before serving.

Horseradish roots

Horseradish flakes

Grated horseradish

Ground horseradish

Creamed horseradish

Horseradish relish

Juniper

Juniper berries have a sweet and aromatic woody taste and although juniper is a common culinary spice in northern Europe, it is probably most familiar as the distinctive flavouring in gin. Known since biblical times, the berries and leaves were used by the Greeks and Romans and in Europe until the 16th century as a medicinal aid against plague and pestilence as well as snake bite. Juniper is an interesting flavouring which is rather neglected in British cookery but used often in Sweden, Germany, Italy and southern Europe where, in fact, the most flavourful berries come from.

Juniper is principally used to flavour rich, dark-fleshed game such as venison, wood pigeon and wild boar but it marries equally well with pork (especially with apples and cider) and many winter dishes such as oxtail and other beef stews. An ingredient in game and coarse country patés, juniper also combines happily with chestnut and fruit stuffings and with vegetables of the cabbage family. An apple and juniper jelly can also make an agreeable change from the redcurrant jelly frequently served with game and lamb.

The blue-black berries are usually crushed before adding to dishes but can be used whole in a pickling spice mixture or in boiling broths. Juniper's flavour is quite powerful so use only about 6-8 berries at a time. However, their flavour does vary according to the area of production; northern European juniper is weak by comparison with the finer, more aromatic Italian plant.

Cultivation Juniper grows easily in north temperate climates but needs a sunny spot, preferably in soil that has chalk or lime. The berries are produced only on the female bush and ripen in the autumn after three years. Thereafter, berries are found at all stages of ripening on the bush together. Berries can also be picked wild on Mediterranean hillsides in early autumn.

ESSENTIAL FACTS

Countries of origin Cultivated widely in the northern hemisphere; found wild in Britain and the USA; main producers are Hungary and southern Europe, particularly Italy.
Preparation and storage Available as whole berries but easily broken or crushed for use in marinades, stews etc. Kept in airtight containers, berries will keep almost indefinitely.
Culinary uses Used throughout Europe to flavour strong meat, particularly game; in patés, marinades; to flavour sauerkraut and red cabbage; in preserves eg pickled mushrooms, with apple for savoury jelly. It is the principal flavouring in gin and some bitters and liqueurs.

RECIPE

Chestnut and red cabbage salad with juniper
1 small red cabbage, finely shredded
100g/4oz cooked chestnuts, finely sliced
140ml/¼ pint/¾ cup sour cream
6 juniper berries, crushed
¼ tsp paprika
salt and freshly ground pepper to taste
chopped parsley to garnish
Combine the cabbage and chestnuts in a salad bowl. Beat together the remaining ingredients except the parsley and leave for 15-30 minutes for the flavours to develop. Toss the salad in the dressing and sprinkle over the chopped parsley.

(*Juniperus communis*)
CUPRESSACEAE

IDENTIFICATION

Dried, blue-black berries, about 7-10mm (¼-⅓in) in diameter, of the juniper bush which grows, usually, to about 2m (6ft) in Britain, or on larger trees elsewhere. **Plant** Evergreen coniferous bushes or trees growing to 10m (33ft) with green, very prickly leaves; berries take 3 years to mature and are found in all stages on bush; only when ripe and blue-black are berries picked.

Juniper berries

Crushed juniper berries

(*Cymbopogone citratus*)
GRAMINEAE

Lemon grass

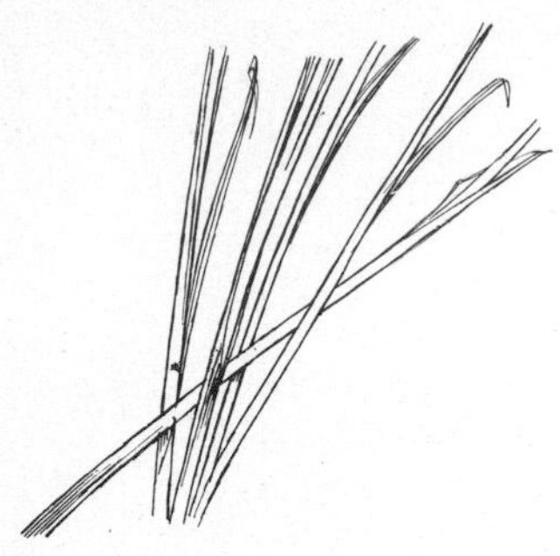

IDENTIFICATION

Bulb, white, fleshy leaf stalks and green leaves of a tropical grass, similar in appearance to a large spring onion. **Plant** Tropical and sub-tropical perennial with tall sharp-edged blades growing from 50-100cm (1¾-3ft).

Lemon grass is a tropical grass resembling a spring onion but having an attractive sweet-scented lemon flavour similar to lemon balm. It is one of the half dozen or so flavourings that give Thai and Vietnamese food their unique characteristic. Although it is used throughout all of south-eastern Asia as a culinary herb, its gentle citrus flavour is put to best advantage in these subtly spiced and scented cuisines which have more delicacy than those of their Indonesian and Malaysian neighbours.

Lemon grass goes particularly well with fish and chicken. Combined with other spices and coconut, with which it has an affinity, it is often found in the leaf-wrapped fish dishes of Malaysia or added to curried prawns [shrimp] and shellfish. It can be an ingredient in the sauces and marinades for Indonesian *saté* and it is used extensively in the Indian-derived beef and lamb curries of Burma and Malaysia, as well as with Thai stir-fried beef and salads.

Lemon peel may be substituted for lemon grass but the dish will not be so finely flavoured – although a useful tip is to add a little grated ginger to a lemon peel substitute, since lemon grass's fragrant aroma has a distinct hint of ginger.

Those seriously interested in south-east Asian cuisine will find lemon grass in Indian and oriental food shops and real enthusiasts can grow it in temperate climates, provided they give it tender care and attention.

Cultivation Select fresh plants which have traces of roots. Place the plants in a jar of water until the roots develop, then plant them in large pots (to allow for spread) in sandy soil. Make sure that the plant gets plenty of warmth, sunshine and adequate water.

Fresh lemon grass

Dried lemon grass

ESSENTIAL FACTS

Countries of origin Grown extensively throughout south-eastern Asia; also in Central and South America, Central Africa, West Indies, Australia and the USA.
Preparation and storage Available fresh from oriental and Indonesian food shops; use lower 10-15cm (4-6in) part, discarding fibrous upper leaves; use whole bruised or sliced; available also as dried stems (soak in water before using) or dried powder, often sold under local name (*serai* in Malaysia, *sereh* in Indonesia, *tabrai* in Thailand). Substitute grated lemon rind for similar, but not authentic, flavour.
Culinary uses Widely used in all south-east Asian cuisines to give delicate citrus flavour to soups, curry pastes and all types of savoury dishes including seafood, poultry, beef, pork, and in pickles and marinades.

RECIPE

Hot and sour prawn [shrimp] soup
(*Tom Yam Kung*)
This well-known soup of tender prawns [shrimp] in a rich spicy broth is a Thai favourite.

1kg/2lb raw prawns [shrimp] in shell
1.7 litres/3 pints/1½ quart fish or chicken stock
3 stalks lemon grass, cut into 2.5cm (1in) pieces
3 lemon, lime or other citrus leaves (optional)
2 dried chillies
15ml/1 tbsp fermented fish sauce (nam pla) [See pages 124-5]
30ml/2 tbsp lime or lemon juice
1 fresh red chilli, seeded and finely chopped
3 spring onions, coarsely chopped
2 tbsp coriander leaves, chopped
Serves 6-8.

Shell and devein the prawns [shrimp]. Set aside the meat and place shells and heads in a saucepan with stock, lemon grass, citrus leaves and dried chillies. Bring it to the boil and simmer, covered, for 20 minutes. Strain off the stock, return it to the heat and add prawns [shrimp], fish sauce and lime juice. Simmer for 2-3 minutes until the prawns [shrimp] are pink and just firm. Serve, sprinkled with the fresh chopped chilli (if liked), spring onions and coriander leaves.

Liquorice

Liquorice, with its bitter-sweet aniseed flavour, is rarely used in modern kitchens except for making sweets, yet it was a popular flavouring in ancient and medieval times. Liquorice comes from the crushed root of the liquorice plant which was known to be cultivated by the Arabs in Spain from around the 9th century. Exported north in considerable quantities, liquorice's main purpose was to add darkness and body to all manner of sweet-savoury dishes and in Britain, in particular, to the ever-popular gingerbreads. Until the 17th century it was a flavouring in barley water but was then replaced by the now familiar lemon. In Tudor times limited cultivation centred on Pontefract in Yorkshire, famous for its 'cakes', which are now manufactured from imported liquorice. These small, black, flat liquorice discs, which have changed little in appearance over the centuries, are still a favourite children's treat.

Today, liquorice is used almost solely in the manufacture of sweets and candies. However, extracts of liquorice have considerable medicinal application as ingredients in cough drops and syrups. To relieve coughs, colds, sore throats and bronchitis, try the soothing tisane below, as a healthier alternative to proprietary lozenges and cough mixtures.
Cultivation Plant root cuttings in early spring in light, rich soil. In northern temperate regions, liquorice needs long hot summers and plenty of moisture when plants are young. Harvest the root in the third or fourth year in spring or autumn.

ESSENTIAL FACTS

Countries of origin Native to south-eastern Europe and Middle East; now grown mainly in Russia, Spain, Italy and Turkey.
Preparation and storage Available as dried root pieces, black sticks and dried powdered root; slice, bruise or grind root pieces before use; keep the powder in an airtight container and use quickly to avoid loss of flavour and aroma; keep the sticks moisture-free.
Culinary uses In confectionery, commercial chewing gum, as a tisane and to flavour syrups, dried fruit salads and alcoholic drinks such as *raki* and *sambucca*.

RECIPE

Liquorice tisane
8cm/3in piece liquorice stick
300ml/½ pint/1½ cups water
Pour boiling water over the liquorice stick to dissolve. Strain the liquid into a cup and drink hot or warm.

(*Glycyrrhiza glabra*)
LEGUMINOSAE

IDENTIFICATION

Dried root or, more commonly, hard black sticks formed from boiled root juice of bean-like plant. **Plant** Small perennial growing to 1.5m (5ft) with purple-blue flower, small pods and vertical root reaching to 1m (3ft)

Tisane

Ground liquorice

Liquorice sweets

Liquorice roots

Pontefract cakes

(*Myristica fragrans*)
MYRISTICACEAE

Mace

IDENTIFICATION

Crimson aril (or lace-like network) enclosing nutmeg seed, which is sun dried to rusty brown, then roughly broken into 'blades'. **Plant** Tall, tropical evergreen tree usually growing to about 10m (33ft), taking 10-15 years to mature but producing 1,500-2,000 nutmegs per year for about 70 years; female trees bear peach-like fruits containing aril and seed.

Nutmeg and mace come from the same plant; the nutmeg is the seed and the mace is the aril, or lacy network, that encloses it within the fruit. Although they share a similar flavour, mace is the more delicate, tasting like an interesting blend of cinnamon and nutmeg, indeed, it is not a flavour people can easily identify.

Mace is best known in British cookery as an ingredient in potted shrimps, as well as other potted fish, meats and cheese. It also features in pickles, chutneys and ketchups (*see* pages 132-5). A blade of mace can be added to a *bêchamel* sauce or a bread sauce or to give finesse to a bread-and-butter or rice pudding. In Europe, it is traditionally used in patés, stuffings and sausages, particularly the French *boudins blancs*, the delicately-flavoured white sausages made with chicken and cream.

Mace is expensive and, as a result, is frequently adulterated in powdered form with poorer-quality nutmeg plants. Some of the best mace comes from Indonesia. Where possible, use mace blades which are less likely to vary in quality. They are, alas, impossible to grind at home because they are so brittle, so when buying the more convenient ground mace, check that it has a fairly strong, sweetly pungent aroma and purchase only in small quantities as even when kept airtight, powdered mace quickly loses its fine quality.

Cultivation The nutmeg tree is a plant which grows best in tropical insular maritime climates such as in the Moluccas (Indonesia) or Grenada (West Indies).

ESSENTIAL FACTS

Countries of origin Native to the Moluccas and New Guinea; now grown also in the West Indies and Sri Lanka.

Preparation and storage Available as small blades or powdered; better quality blades should exude a little oil when pressed with thumb, use blades in cooking liquid, mace blades are difficult to grind at home; buy powdered in small quantities and renew often to avoid signigicant loss of flavour and aroma.

Culinary uses Used in baking and sweet dishes such as puddings, creams, custards and fruit jellies; also in savoury dishes such as soups, casseroles, sauces and especially in patés and stuffings in France; a traditional ingredient in British potted meats and cheese; it is used in pickling and preserving; in drinks, especially chocolate and alcoholic punches, particularly in the West Indies.

RECIPE

Potted tongue

250g/8oz cooked ox tongue, chopped
250g/8oz/1 cup lightly salted butter, clarified
½ tsp ground mace
salt and freshly-ground pepper to taste

In a food processor or blender, combine 150g/5oz/⅔ cup butter, ox tongue and mace to form a smooth paste. Check the seasoning and add salt and pepper to taste. Pack the mixture tightly into one large or 2-3 small pots and refrigerate until firm. Melt the remaining clarified butter and pour when tepid over the paste to form a sealing layer. Store, covered, in a refrigerator. Once started, eat within five days. Serve it with toast or crackers.

Ground mace

Blade mace

Mushrooms and fungi

(*Agaricus bisporus* and others)
AGARICINEAE

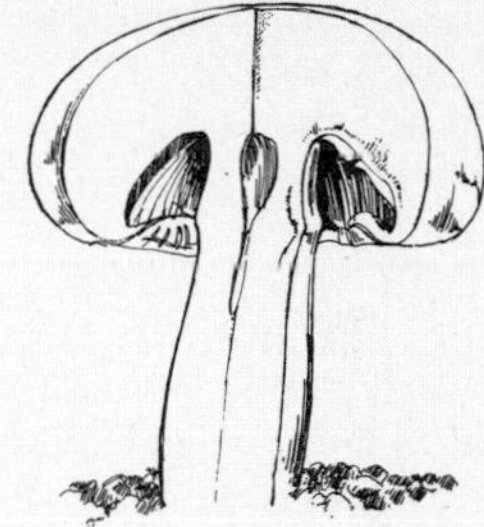

Mushrooms have fascinated mankind since prehistoric times largely because their mysterious growing habits suggested to primitive people some supernatural intervention – for mushrooms seemed suddenly to appear and disappear as if by magic. Variously described as the food of the gods, the work of the Devil and a cult object, it is not hard to understand why the mushroom is surrounded by legend. Many species are delectable to eat, others are poisonous, even deadly, and some have mind-altering properties. The Aztecs worshipped the magic mushroom *Psilocybe mexicana* and ate it in ceremonial rituals to induce visions; the ancient Egyptians thought the mushroom produced immortality; and, according to Ovid, the Romans reserved the mushroom for sumptuous banquets, eating this delicacy with the finest cutlery of silver and amber. Among the many legends about the mushroom is the story of Christ and St Peter. Walking through a forest, they were eating bread given to them by the local people, a mouthful of which St Peter spat on the ground – which instantly turned into a mushroom; close behind them walked the Devil who also spat on the ground. In an instant, up sprang a toadstool, which was brightly coloured and alluring – but poisonous.

Mushrooms are, of course, still prized and feared. Although there are countless species of finely-flavoured wild mushrooms, others are poisonous and some fatal. The most common edible mushrooms are easily identified but, if you do pick your own, check their description in a reliable field guide to make sure you have got what you think. If in doubt, do not eat them – mushroom poisoning, even when non-fatal, is an extremely unpleasant illness. Nowadays, however, wild mushrooms such as morels, ceps and chanterelles are frequently available (at high-quality greengrocers), as well as the familiar cultivated mushroom and the increasingly popular oyster mushroom. It is worth trying these delicacies in the kitchen and imaginative recipes for all kinds of wild and cultivated fungi (including the interestingly flavoured oriental species) are now commonly available. Alone or in soups, sauces and in combination with meat, fish and other

RECIPE

Mushroom ketchup
Makes approximately 1 litre/1¾ pints/4 cups. Use flat cultivated mushrooms or field mushrooms for this flavourful ketchup.

1kg/2lb large mushrooms, chopped
50g/2oz/4 tbsp sea salt
300ml/½ pint/1¼ cups red wine vinegar
1 shallot, finely chopped
1 tsp peppercorns
1 tsp ground allspice
a 2.5cm/1in piece of green ginger, roughly chopped
2 blades mace

Layer the mushrooms and salt in a large bowl. Leave covered in a cool place for 2 days, stirring twice a day. Place the mushrooms in a pan with the remaining ingredients and simmer for 1 hour. Cool. Strain, pour into sterilized jars and seal.

IDENTIFICATION

A variety of edible species of generally umbrella-shaped, soft, spongy plants (fungi), wild or cultivated and quick growing; some species are poisonous.

Large (open) mushrooms

Medium (cup) mushrooms

Mushroom ketchup

Small (button) mushrooms

Mushrooms and fungi

Continued from page 59

vegetables, mushrooms add their unique flavour, giving a dash of distinct elegance which lifts it quite out of the ordinary.

Should you be lucky enough to come across fresh truffles – especially those found in France or Italy – and rich enough to afford them, they need to be savoured. It is the perfume of the truffle which is so remarkable, permeating everything it is kept with. Some say it is faintly reminiscent of garlic; others in a more poetic vein talk of it as a precious jewel, the scent of which is heavenly but indescribable. The great French novelist, Colette, who wrote about food with almost as much enthusiasm as that other great novelist, Alexandre Dumas, lovingly described how to prepare the truffle: '. . . eat it on its own, scented and grainy-skinned, eat it like the vegetable it is, hot, and served in munificent quantities . . . its sovereign flavour disdains all complications and complexities. Bathed in a good, very dry white wine . . . salted without extravagance, peppered with discretion, they can then be cooked in a simple, cast-iron stewpan with the lid on. For twenty minutes they must dance in the constant flow of bubbles . . . No other herbs or spices! . . . Your truffles must come to the table in their own stock'. Canned truffles and the small black specks in liver paté do not inspire such eloquence, since they have lost virtually all of the truffle's magical aroma.

Cultivation Mushrooms grow on dead organic matter and when cultivating them at home, this is the reason for using composted animal manure or straw as the growing medium. This has to be thoroughly rotted down before spawn is introduced. Mushrooms need to be grown under cover in a shaded place with an even temperature and a steady supply of water. For convenient home growing, packs can be bought containing already spawned compost.

Large flat mushroom

Medium flat mushroom

Champignons de Paris

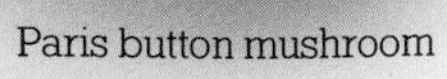

Paris button mushroom

Small (button) mushroom

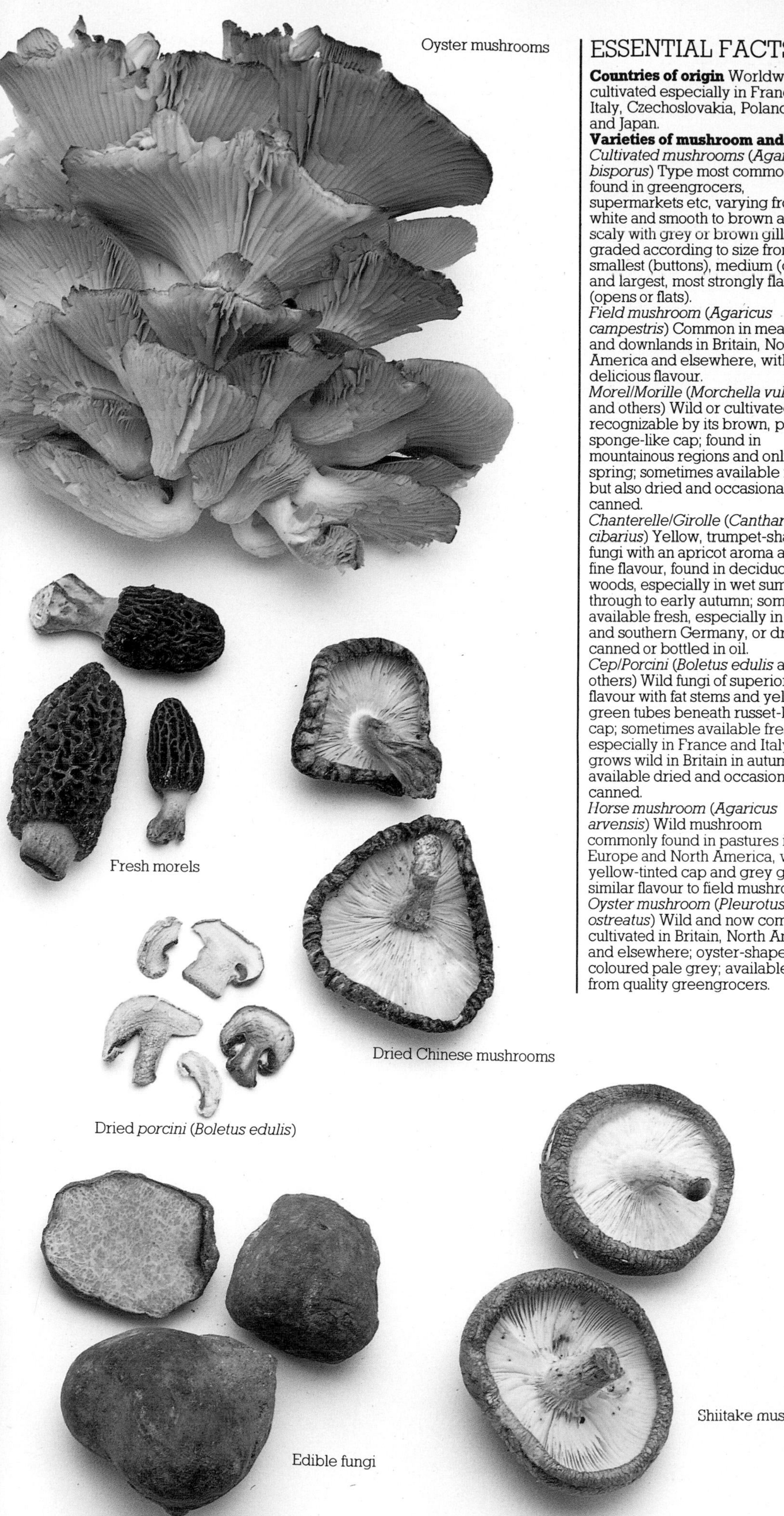
Oyster mushrooms

Fresh morels

Dried Chinese mushrooms

Dried *porcini* (*Boletus edulis*)

Edible fungi

Shiitake mushrooms

ESSENTIAL FACTS

Countries of origin Worldwide but cultivated especially in France, Italy, Czechoslovakia, Poland, China and Japan.

Varieties of mushroom and fungi

Cultivated mushrooms (*Agaricus bisporus*) Type most commonly found in greengrocers, supermarkets etc, varying from white and smooth to brown and scaly with grey or brown gills; graded according to size from smallest (buttons), medium (cups) and largest, most strongly flavoured (opens or flats).

Field mushroom (*Agaricus campestris*) Common in meadows and downlands in Britain, North America and elsewhere, with a full, delicious flavour.

Morel/Morille (*Morchella vulgaris* and others) Wild or cultivated; recognizable by its brown, pitted sponge-like cap; found in mountainous regions and only in spring; sometimes available fresh, but also dried and occasionally canned.

Chanterelle/Girolle (*Cantharellus cibarius*) Yellow, trumpet-shaped fungi with an apricot aroma and a fine flavour, found in deciduous woods, especially in wet summers through to early autumn; sometimes available fresh, especially in France and southern Germany, or dried, canned or bottled in oil.

Cep/Porcini (*Boletus edulis* and others) Wild fungi of superior flavour with fat stems and yellow-green tubes beneath russet-brown cap; sometimes available fresh, especially in France and Italy, also grows wild in Britain in autumn; available dried and occasionally canned.

Horse mushroom (*Agaricus arvensis*) Wild mushroom commonly found in pastures in Europe and North America, with yellow-tinted cap and grey gills; similar flavour to field mushroom.

Oyster mushroom (*Pleurotus ostreatus*) Wild and now commonly cultivated in Britain, North America and elsewhere; oyster-shaped and coloured pale grey; available fresh from quality greengrocers.

Shiitake (*Lentinus edodes*) Japanese and Chinese species cultivated on logs of oak and other hardwoods; available fresh in its countries of origin and in Britain and North America from quality greengrocers; more familiar in the West as the dried black 'Chinese' mushroom found in oriental food shops; also available canned and pickled.

Enokitake (Flammulina relutipes) Long thin fungi that grows in clumps on a spongy base; it has an appetizing crunchiness and delicate taste.

Matsutake (*Tricholoma matsutake*) Related to the Shiitake mushroom, growing in Japan on pine logs; available dried or canned from Japanese food shops.

Paddy straw mushroom (*Volvariella volvacea*) Cultivated in tropical regions on beds of rice straw; grey-brown in colour and toadstool-like in shape; available canned and sometimes dried from oriental food shops.

Woodear (*Auricularia polytricha*) Wild and cultivated in China; looks like the inside of a dog's ear and related to the European Jew's Ear (also edible); available dried in oriental food shops.

Truffle Perigord, Black Truffle (*Tuber melanosporum*); Italian White, Piedmont Truffle (*T. magnatum*). Prized wild and cultivated fungi which grow underground, the Black grows beneath oak trees in the Dordogne, Alsace and Provence in France; the White, in Piedmont, Italy and North Africa; hunted by truffle hounds or pigs; available fresh in its regions of origin from late autumn to winter; also available canned or bottled.

Preparation and storage

Fresh mushrooms and fungi Wipe off any grit or earth with a damp cloth, remove the stems if fibrous, do not wash or peel; slice or dice as required; store 1-2 days in cool compartment of a refrigerator.

Fresh morels Cut them in half, wash pitted caps in water to remove any grit and earth, pat dry with paper towels before using.

Fresh truffles Clean the truffle with a small brush to remove any earth from the skin. Can be stored for 2-3 days in a jar of rice in a cool, dark place (for dryness and protection), or can be cleaned, wrapped in foil and deep frozen.

Dried mushrooms and fungi
Add dried slices of *boletus* to soups, stews etc; soak dried Chinese mushrooms for 20-30 minutes in tepid water to soften, discard the stem and slice or dice as required; dried mushrooms keep indefinitely in airtight containers in a cool, dry place.

Culinary uses Used in Western and oriental cuisines in a wide variety of sauces, stuffings, soups, as a vegetable alone, stuffed, or combined with others and with fish, meat, poultry and game; shiitake mushrooms are generally used more as a seasoning, like ginger, than as a vegetable.

(*Brassica alba, B. juncea, B.nigra*)
CRUCIFERAE

Mustard

Mustard has been an important medicinal and culinary spice since classical times. In 33BC, the powerful Persian general, Darius sent a challenge to his Greek rival, Alexander the Great in the form of a sackful of sesame seeds – which represented the number of his troops. Alexander's swift reply was a small sack of mustard seeds for, although less weighty, his soldiers were much more fiery! Mustard's medicinal use can be traced back to Hippocrates, while the Romans exploited its culinary virtues, mixing it with vinegar or honey, nuts and spices to produce a variety of interesting sauces.

The words 'mustard' and '*moutarde*' come from the Latin *Mustum ardens*, meaning 'burnt must'. When introduced to France and Britain by the Romans, mustard was mixed with grape must (unfermented grape juice) to form a paste. Since then, France has been one of the world's major producers of mustard with its industry centred on the city of Dijon from medieval times and, in 1634, the town was granted the exclusive right to make mustard. Today, Dijon mustard accounts for more than half the world's mustard and, like wine, carries an *appellation controlée* – only mustard made to specific standards can carry the name 'Dijon'.

Early French mustard makers were an enterprising lot who were not afraid to experiment with different blends. In 1777, M. Grey and M. Poupon, for example, produced a strong, canary-yellow paste to a secret recipe which included white wine – a mustard which is still produced by this company in attractive stone jars or glass bottles. Maille, another familiar mustard name, cultivated aristocratic society and produced for his clients 24 different mustards of which the most fashionable were, according to author Alexandre Dumas, mustard *à la ravigote*, mustard with garlic, mustard with truffles, mustard with anchovy and mustard with

IDENTIFICATION

Small round seeds varying in colour from white or light brown to dark brown or black (depending on variety) of different species of mustard plant which grow to 1-3m (3-10ft). **Plant** Herbaceous annual bearing hairy 2.5-5cm (1-2in) pods containing about 6 white seeds (*B.alba*); long smooth 2cm (3/4in) pods with about 12 black seeds (*B.nigra*); or larger 3-5cm (1¼-2in) pods (*B.juncea*); all carry bright yellow flowers.

ESSENTIAL FACTS

Countries of origin *B.alba* is probably native to the Mediterranean; now mainly grown in North America, especially Canada, and Europe; *B.nigra* is grown mainly in southern Italy and Ethiopia; *B.juncea* is grown principally in China, India and Poland.

Types of mustard

English mustard Bright yellow, traditionally a mixture of relatively mild *B.alba* and pungent *B.nigra* seeds, with a little wheat flour and sometimes turmeric for colouring; slightly less pungent than formerly because of replacement of *nigra* seeds by slightly milder and more easily harvested *juncea* seeds; virtually synonymous with the brand name Colman, mustard powder must be mixed with water to develop characteristic pungency.

French mustards: Dijon Pale yellow in colour (owing to the removal of husks), *nigra* seeds (but now commonly *juncea* seeds), are ground wet with wine or verjuice, salt and spices; flavour sharp, varying from mild to hot; commonly used in classic French dishes, unless otherwise directed.

Bordeaux Dark in colour because of unhusked *nigra* or *juncea* seeds, blended with vinegar, sugar and tarragon; mild, sour-sweet flavour; mustard commonly sold in Britain as 'French mustard'.

Meaux or à la ancienne Yellow-brown, crunchy mustard combining partly ground and partly crushed *nigra* or *juncea* seeds, vinegar and spices, mild flavour.

American mustard Pale yellow, white (*alba*) mustard seeds mixed with sugar, wine or vinegar; pale yellow, mild, sweeter and thinner than other mustards.

German mustard

French mustard

Mustard salad dressing

Dijon mustard
Swedish mild mustard
Chive mustard
Mild burger mustard
Piccalilli
Whole grain mustard
American mustard

Mustard

Continued from page 63

tarragon. In the 19th century, another Dijon mustard maker, Alexandre Bornibus, astutely moved his business to Paris where he became well known for his 'ladies' mustard (mild and tarragon flavoured) sold in pots of Sèvres porcelain and touted with the slogan 'The contents are worthy of the container'. (Dumas, a great gourmet, agreed with him and declared that this was his favourite mustard).

English mustard developed along slightly different lines. By the 17th century, Tewkesbury was recognized as the centre of mustard production and powdered mustard balls were available which were then mixed with apple juice, cider or vinegar to form a paste. The familiar fine yellow powder we know today was developed early in the 18th century by a Mrs Clements of Durham who travelled from town to town hawking her mustard (called Durham mustard), which eventually found favour at court. So popular was her powder that it was imitated first by Messrs Keen and then at the beginning of the 19th century by a young Norfolk miller, Jeremiah Colman, names now synonymous with English mustard.

The astonishing range of mustards for the kitchen or table now cover all kinds of national styles (*see* Types of mustard). Blended mustards are coarse or fine and vary in pungency from mild to very strong; some are flavoured with chillies, sweet peppers, capers, anchovies, green peppercorns and various herbs, while others are blended with champagne, sherry or cider vinegar. New, fanciful mustards appear all the time and the dedicated cook will want to try these, or experiment with personal blends of mustard powder or paste using herbs, spices and flavoured vinegars.

An unusual and remarkably fine mustard product, *mostarda di frutta* can be found in Italian delicatessens. This mixture of preserved fruits in honey, mustard and white wine is delicious with boiled and cold meats.

Cultivation Mustard is grown from seed sown outdoors in spring. It is best grown in a sunny place and in fertile moist soil. Thin seedlings to 30-45cm (12-18in). Harvest seeds in their pods in late summer when they are almost fully developed but not ripe and allow to dry in the pods.

Salad mustard Seedlings of *alba* seeds grown on damp cloth or cotton wool and cultivated for salad greens usually with cress. Has a hot flavour.

Culinary uses Whole seeds used in pickling mixes; in India and south-eastern Asia, whole seeds sometimes fried as a garnish or freshly ground in curry mixes and pastes. *English mustard* accompanies beef, ham, gammon or bacon, pork (especially sausages); an ingredient in Welsh rarebit and spicy sauces for fish and vegetables; an ingredient in piccalilli relish. *Dijon mustard* is used in classic French cuisine with steak and other grilled or roasted meats, especially rabbit, in a wide variety of sauces and in salad dressings and mayonnaise where mustard acts as an emulsifier. *Bordeaux mustard* and *German mustard* are good with sausages, cold meats and in beer-flavoured stews. *American mustard* flavours hot dogs, ham and barbecue relishes.

Preparation and storage English mustard powder keeps well if kept in a cool dry place; mix with water and allow to stand at least 10-15 minutes to develop pungency; bottled (blended) mustards, especially Dijon can lose quality, discolour and become bitter if kept partly used for too long (in France, Dijon mustard is frequently stored in a cool part of the refrigerator).

RECIPE

Citrus mustard

25g/1oz/2 tbsp black mustard seeds
25g/1oz/2 tbsp white mustard seeds
1/4 tsp salt
1/4 tsp each dried orange and lemon peel
1 tsp green peppercorns
2 tsp honey
60ml/4 tbsp/1/4 cup cider, tarragon or sherry vinegar
a pinch of turmeric

Grind the mustard seeds, salt and peel in a spice grinder or with a mortar and pestle. Mash the peppercorns and add to the mustard. Add the remaining ingredients and mix to a thick paste. Store in a corked jar and leave for 24 hours before using.

Yellow mustard seed

White wine mustard

Mostarda di fruta

Black mustard seed

Mieux mustard

English mustard

Poupon mustard

Colman's mustard powder

(*Kalonji, Nigella sativa*)
RANUNCULACEAE

Nigella

Although nigella is largely unknown in the West, it is an essential spice in Indian cookery where its pungent, peppery flavour adds zest, colour and contrast not only to a variety of lightly-spiced meat and fish dishes but also to the delicious vegetarian cuisine of southern India. There is some confusion over the nomenclature of this spice. It is variously called black onion seed, onion seed or black cumin (although its taste is dissimilar to cumin), and you will find it called *kalonji* in the Indian stores where it is most readily available.

Nigella's tiny black seeds are really a pepper substitute and can be used as such in Western cooking, although its taste is slightly more bitter and spicy. It is an interesting flavour to experiment with, particularly in vegetarian dishes. A pinch or two of dry roasted seeds with buttered cabbage or courgettes [zucchini] looks attractive and adds an unusual exotic touch, as well as an agreeable crunchy texture to the dish.

In India, *kalonji* is an ingredient in the Bengali *panch poron* spice mixture, it is added to stews, casseroles, mild curries and to an extensive range of vegetarian dishes including *dhals*. In Egypt and the Middle East where it has a limited use, it is sprinkled, like poppy seeds, on cakes, pastries and breads.

Cultivation Sow seeds in late spring, thinning the seedlings to about 30cm (12in). Harvest the seed capsules as they ripen but before they pop open. Dry them and remove the seeds.

IDENTIFICATION

Dried, tiny, round black seeds of herbaceous annual growing to 60cm (2ft). **Plant** Has thread-like leaves, blue and white flowers in summer, seeds contained in capsules. An ornamental variety *N.damascena* (love-in-a-mist), is a common garden plant in southern Europe.

ESSENTIAL FACTS

Countries of origin Native to western Asia and southern Europe; now grown mainly in India but also Egypt and the Middle East.
Preparation and storage Available whole from Indian and Middle Eastern stores, variously called wild or black onion seed, *kalonji* or *kala jeera* (black cumin); store in airtight jars; easily crushed; gently roast the seeds to release the flavour and aroma before using.
Culinary uses Widely used in India to flavour mildly-spiced meat dishes, particularly lamb, vegetarian dishes, *dhals*, pickles and chutneys, in batters for deep-frying, as an ingredient in *panch poron*, Indian five-spice mixture. In the Middle East and Egypt it is used in cakes and breads.

RECIPE

French beans with coconut
45ml/3 tbsp vegetable oil
½ tsp nigella (kalonji) seeds
2 dried red chillies
500g/1lb French beans, cut into 2.5cm (1in) lengths
1 tbsp desiccated coconut
30ml/2 tbsp coconut milk
salt to taste
Heat the oil in a heavy-based frying pan or wok until almost smoking. Add the nigella seeds and chillies and fry for a minute until sizzling. Add the beans and stir-fry for about 7 minutes. Add the coconut, coconut milk and salt and cook, stirring, for a further 7-10 minutes or until the coconut milk has evaporated and the beans are tender.

Nigella seeds

Panch poron

Nutmeg

Nutmeg was well known in England in Chaucer's time but it was not until the Spice Islands (the Moluccas) were discovered in the early 16th century that it was in universal demand. This was one of the great spices, the monopoly of which was the subject of feuds and intrigues among the European trading nations in the 17th and 18th centuries.

An exotic spice with a sweet, nutty flavour and woody scent, nutmeg is a truly magical spice, so passionately loved in that period that people carried their own silver nutmeg graters to add the freshly-ground spice to their food, mulled wine or hot posset. This practice may be explained by one of nutmeg's remarkable constituents, myristicin, which has similar properties to the psychedelic drug, mescalin, and if taken in large quantities can induce euphoria and hallucinations. When combined with alcohol in, for example, 'spiked' punches, nutmeg can cause drowsiness, although culinary portions have no such effect.

In the kitchen, most people are familiar with its use in sweet puddings, custards and cakes, but in savoury dishes it can add a most delicate and agreeable flavour to commonplace vegetables such as puréed potatoes or boiled sprouts. In Italy, it is frequently included in the veal, cheese or spinach stuffings for *tortellini*, *ravioli* or *cannelloni* pasta. In the Middle East a hint of nutmeg enhances spicy lamb casseroles and in French cuisine, it is added to *béchamel* and bread sauces.

Cultivation The nutmeg tree is a plant which thrives in tropical insular maritime climates such as in the Moluccas (Indonesia) or Grenada (West Indies).

RECIPE

Rum cocktail

50ml/2floz/¼ cup white or dark rum
15ml/1 tbsp/1¼ tbsp lime juice
½ cup crushed ice
2-3 dashes Angostura bitters
1 tbsp castor [superfine] sugar or sugar syrup
nutmeg to grate
slice of orange

Combine all the ingredients except the ice, the orange and nutmeg in a cocktail shaker. Shake vigorously and pour over the crushed ice into a small tumbler. Grate a little fresh nutmeg on top and decorate with a slice of orange, if desired.

(*Myristica fragrans*)
MYRISTICACEAE

IDENTIFICATION

Brown kernel enclosed in shiny brown seed coat, surrounded by crimson lace-like mace of the peach-like fruit of nutmeg tree.

Plant Tall, tropical evergreen tree usually growing to about 10m (33ft), taking 10-15 years to mature but producing 1,500-2,000 nutmegs per year for about 70 years; female trees bear fruits.

ESSENTIAL FACTS

Countries of origin Native to the Moluccas and New Guinea; now also grown in the West Indies and Sri Lanka.

Preparation and storage Available as whole, dark brown or white (limed) kernels or ground; good-quality kernels should exude a little oil when pressed with thumb; buy whole nutmegs and grate as required; store in an airtight container; ground nutmeg rapidly loses flavour and aroma.

Culinary uses Mainly used in cakes and sweet dishes.; in savoury dishes especially in Middle East; also in sausages, patés, potted meats, with cheese, eggs, spinach, Brussels sprouts, broccoli; to spice alcoholic drinks eg mulled wine, egg nogs, rum and fruit punches.

Ground nutmeg

Whole nutmegs

Olives

IDENTIFICATION

Small oval fruits, green when unripe, black when ripe, of evergreen olive tree, edible only after pickling in brine. **Plant** Long-lived, often gnarled, tree with silvery-green foliage and insignificant flowers in spring, bearing fruits from late summer to winter.

According to ancient Greek legend, Athena, goddess of wisdom, created the olive tree as a symbol of peace and victory and in doing so won the patronage of the city of Athens over her formidable rival, Poseidon, god of the sea. This charming story belies the fact that the olive tree is much, much older. It was growing in prehistoric times and in ancient Egypt where leaves and branches were found in Tutankhamen's tomb, and the Scriptures relate that it was an olive leaf that Noah's dove took back to the ark. Known as the tree that will not die, it is virtually indestructible, and in Mediterranean folklore many gnarled and ancient trees, still standing, are said to be as old as Homer himself.

The olive tree has always been venerated by the peoples of the Mediterranean, whose livelihood largely depends on it, and since pre-Christian times its fruits have been associated with renewal and fertility, and its anointing oil used in baptisms and extreme unction. Ancient rituals against the evil eye include the use of olive oil. In the past (and still in remote hillside villages) it was used to fill the lamps of poor peasants, medicinally applied to sprains and bruises and considered an aphrodisiac.

The best way to savour the essential flavour of the olive is in a fine-quality oil. A simple tomato salad dressed with it or potatoes sautéed to a golden brown have a unique taste, blissfully evocative of the hot sun and fragrant scents of Mediterranean hillsides. Remember, though, that the taste of olives and their oil varies widely according to the region of production, and some have a bitter, acid quality which can be unpleasant. Persist in finding olives and oil which suit your personal taste. In market stalls in the Mediterranean, you are expected to do this by sampling the olives before you buy. Olives flavoured with herbs or garlic (available loose at many delicatessens [gourmet shops]) are wonderful as appetizers and are far superior to the 'cocktail' olives bought in glass jars which, although they look good, tend to have a somewhat bland taste. Black olives have a fuller flavour and for cooking, plump, juicy purple or black olives are essential in traditional Mediterranean dishes for an authentic taste and appearance.

With regard to the oil, it is not too fanciful to say that it should be chosen with as much care as a fine wine. Many people prefer the green, fruity varieties of olive oil and, indeed, most Greek cookery is flavoured with its powerful, earthy taste but it does tend to overwhelm many subtle salad ingredients – including the mayonnaise. It it advisable to buy the best quality olive oil you can afford and then experiment with different brands and blends to decide what suits your taste. Like wine, olive oil varies according to the vintage, some years producing finer quality oil than others.

Cultivation Olive trees are usually propagated by cuttings. They only begin to bear fruit in their fifth or sixth year and full production is not reached until trees are 15-20 years old. Olive groves are irrigated in California, resulting in high yields, but in the Mediterranean, where irrigation is rare, there is a belief that irrigated olives do not pickle well.

ESSENTIAL FACTS

Countries of origin Native to Mediterranean coasts, especially Italy, Spain, France, Greece; now grown elsewhere in Mediterranean-type climates eg North America.

Varieties of olive
Green Unripe, mild-flavoured fruits, often pickled with aromatics such as garlic, coriander and herbs; or stoned and stuffed with slivers of pimento (sweet red pepper), anchovy or almonds; also crushed and flavoured with aromatics.
Dark Violet or plum-coloured olives picked in autumn, often pickled or crushed in aromatics or packed in salt.
Black Ripe plump or shrivelled fruit picked in winter, pickled and treated as for dark olives.

Types of olive oil Oil pressed from ripe fruit varies greatly in flavour and colour depending on locality. It is graded as follows:
Extra virgin First cold pressing to produce pale yellow or greenish oil of delicate flavour with acidity of no more than 1%; finest comes from Tuscany and Provence.
Virgin Fine quality but with slightly higher acidity.
Refined Usually from pressings made under heat, subsequently refined to remove any unattractive taste or acidity.
Pure Usually a blend of refined and virgin oil.

Preparation and storage *Olives* Available in a variety of forms, including stoned and stuffed, available loose from specialist [gourmet] shops, flavoured with garlic, thyme or other herbs, or canned or bottled in brine; use loose olives within 2-3 days of purchase, olives in brine keep for a year or more in airtight containers. *Olive oil* Available bottled or canned; for preference buy from food stores with a wide variety; oil becomes rancid with long storage.

Culinary uses Universal in Mediterranean cuisines; as *hors d'oeuvres*, in salads, pastes eg *tapénade*; added to hot dishes of game, meat, poultry and robust fish dishes such as salt cod or fresh tuna; an ingredient in Italian pizza; added to vegetables eg aubergines [eggplants], tomatoes, sweet peppers; oil is used in salad dressings and mayonnaise, notably *aïoli*; to flavour Italian and Greek-Cypriot breads; as cooking or frying oil, imparting a unique flavour to food.

Black olives

Stuffed olives

Extra virgin olive oil

Dark (violet) olives

Green olives

Pure olive oil

RECIPE

Puttanesca sauce
(for spaghetti)

45ml/3 tbsp olive oil
3 cloves garlic, finely chopped, or crushed
6 anchovy fillets, chopped
100g/4oz black olives, stoned and halved
1 tbsp capers
1 dried red chilli
500g/1lb tomatoes, peeled and chopped (or Italian canned tomatoes)
salt and freshly ground pepper to taste.

Heat the oil in a pan, add the garlic and anchovies and cook gently until the garlic is lightly coloured. Add the olives, capers and chilli and cook, stirring, for 1-2 minutes. Add the tomatoes, cover and simmer, stirring occasionally, for 15-20 minutes. Check the seasoning (removing the chilli), adding salt and pepper, if necessary, before adding the sauce to boiled pasta.

Onion

The onion is one of the oldest vegetables known to man with a recorded history going back 3,500 years. Its origins are obscure but it is probably native to Asia Minor and the Mediterranean. It was certainly a favourite food of the ancient Egyptians, with at least one variety evoked as a deity and worshipped. Along with garlic, onions were one of the staple foods of the slaves who built the Giant Pyramid, and later the Isralites mourned the loss of Egyptian onions on their way to the Promised Land.

The Romans, who introduced the onion to Britain, also gave it the name *unionem* or *unio*, referring to its single bulb, and from which its English name is derived. Both a medicinal and culinary vegetable for the Greeks and Romans, it was taken for coughs, colds and sore throats, notably by the Emperor Nero, and as a breakfast food it was eaten raw with a little salt, as well as added to countless prepared dishes. Like garlic, which belongs to the same family, it was regarded as an aphrodisiac and a symbol of fertility.

There are many varieties of onion which differ in shape, size and flavour, although all share a pungency and bitter-sweet taste which can be mild or powerfully sharp. The aroma of many types of onion is so strong that it makes the eyes water, a quality which is lost in the cooking process when onions acquire a mild, sweet flavour that enhances the taste of other ingredients.

Among the many types of onion, the large, brown-skinned Spanish onions are relatively mild but full-flavoured. White and red-skinned onions also have a gentle taste and are frequently eaten raw in salads and *hors d'oeuvres*. Shallots, with their concentrated onion flavour without the bitterness, derive their name from Ascalon in Palestine where they were growing in classical times. Highly prized in France, they are essential in at least two traditional French sauces, *sauce à la bordelaise* and *sauce marchand de vin*, both of which are red wine and onion sauces served with grilled steak. The slender spring onion so widely cultivated in China and the Far East, is, of course, a must in Chinese and Japanese food and is easily available and grown in the West.

Onions are an important flavouring in almost every country in the world and are as widely used in the East as the West. So basic are they that food would be insipid and unappetizing without them, although when combined with other ingredients their flavour is rarely overwhelming or assertive. In Western cooking, they are used in all kinds of meat dishes and in robust stews, and in a wide variety of sauces and soups, including the famous French onion soup, the traditional breakfast dish of the porters of Les Halles in Paris, which is renowned as a restorative and hangover cure. Another acclaimed onion dish is the Indian *doh peeazah* (*do* meaning twice, *peeazah* onion), a spiced korma-like dish where roughly double the quantity of onions is used for every pound of meat, with some of the onion used as a paste and the remainder added as sautéed slices.

In their own right as a vegetable, onions can be boiled or baked, served with white or cheese sauces or glazed. Stuffed and baked, they can make an excellent first course and can be the main ingredient in pies and quiches.

Cultivation Many varieties of onion can be grown in temperate climates and since sowing dates and methods of cultivation differ, follow the information on individual cultivar packets. Onions are propagated by seeds or sets. For the common garden plant in northern Europe, sow seeds in early spring in well-manured, light, deep loam in drills of 30cm (12in). Thin to 5-10cm (2-4in). Or plant sets in early to mid-spring. Harvest in the early autumn.

(*Allium cepa*) ALLIACEAE

Small red onions

Onion salt

Onion flakes

Pickling onions

Spring onions (scallions)

Spanish onions

ESSENTIAL FACTS

Countries of origin Worldwide.
Varieties of onion
Common onion Medium-sized bulb, usually brown-skinned, grown in kitchen gardens and universally available; fairly pungent, used in endless variety of cooked dishes.
Spanish onions Large globe-shaped, brown-skinned onions (not necessarily from Spain) with mild, sweetish flavour; used in cooking and salads.
Pickling [pearl] onions Small bulbs with brown or silver skins used whole for pickles and in French cuisine in *boeuf à la bourguignonne* or *coq au vin* etc.
Salad onions Usually white or red-skinned varieties, mild in flavour.
Shallots Grown from bulbs and available in variety of shapes and sizes from small orange-brown to large, clove-shaped wine-coloured types; mild, subtle flavour, essential ingredient in many French sauces eg *sauce à la bordelaise*.
Spring onions. Immature plants where bulb has not completely formed with long green stem; mild, used in salads and extensively in Chinese and Far Eastern cookery.
Welsh onion Bunching onion with pencil-thick shoots, similar in appearance and use to spring onions.
Preparation and storage Available fresh, as dried flakes, powder, combined with salt or as purée. Peel fresh, slice or finely chop as required; peel under cold running water to prevent eyes watering; immerse small pickling onions in boiling water for 10-15 seconds to facilitate peeling; onions and shallots keep several weeks in cool, dry place; string home-grown onions only when completely dry; store spring onions in cool compartment of refrigerator, use within 7-10 days; store dried onion and powder in airtight containers.
Culinary uses Universally used in stocks, soups, casseroles and sauces; browned or deep-fried for garnishes. Mild varieties sliced or diced and added to salads eg tomato and green salads; pickling and small varieties used whole in pickles and many casseroles eg *coq au vin*; when stuffed can be served as *hors d'oeuvres*; main ingredient in many Venetian-style dishes eg liver, pizza, in many quiches and pies; when boiled or glazed can be served as accompanying vegetable. Shallots especially used in French cuisine, notably in dishes such as *Entrecôte à la bordelaise* (steak with red wine and butter); spring and Welsh onions widely used as garnish and in stir-fried dishes of China and Japan, and in Western salads.

IDENTIFICATION

Edible bulb in various forms such as single bulb, clusters of bulbs or small bulbs, differing in shape and size, and in colour (from white to red, brown and purple), with papery skin; spring onions are immature plants with green stems and white bulbets. (For wild or black onion seed *see* Nigella page 66). **Plant** Member of Alliaceae family which includes garlic, chives and leeks; usually cultivated as an annual.

RECIPE

Onions agrodolce (Sweet-Sour Onions)
1kg/2lb small onions
50g/2oz/4 tbsp butter
30ml/2 tbsp red wine vinegar
2tsp sugar
salt and freshly ground pepper
Plunge the onions in boiling water for 10-15 seconds to make peeling easier. Peel off the outer skin, leaving the root base intact. Gently heat the butter in a heavy-based frying pan large enough to hold onions in single layer. Add the onions and water to a depth of 2.5cm (1in). Cook over a medium heat for about 15 minutes, turning the onions frequently. Add the vinegar, sugar, salt and pepper (and a little water if necessary), cover and cook very gently for about 1 hour, turning the onions from time to time, and adding liquid as the water evaporates. Serve when the onions are soft and glazed golden brown.

(*Origanum vulgare*)
LABIATAE

Oregano

IDENTIFICATION

Leaves and top of hardy, flowering wild marjoram plant, a perennial growing to about 60cm (2ft). *O. marjorana* is grown as an annual in temperate climates. **Plant** Spreading plant bearing white and pink flowers in midsummer.

ESSENTIAL FACTS

Countries of origin Southern Britain, Mediterranean countries, Asia and North America.
Preparation and storage Available fresh in countries of origin, dried on stalks or dried crushed leaves; store dried in airtight containers away from light; use within 6 months.
Culinary uses Essential flavouring in Italian pizza; widely used in simple, earthy Mediterranean cooking; in Mexico added to chilli powders, beans, spicy soups and stews.

Few single flavours are more evocative of the sunny, spirited cooking of the south than oregano, yet the flavour and strength of this wild marjoram plant vary widely according to climate and habitat. In the hot, dry regions of the Mediterranean this is a robust, full-flavoured plant with a peppery and slightly bitter tang. Its characteristic aroma pervades Italian pizza parlours all over the world, for it is one of the main ingredients of the quintessential Neapolitan pizza. When grown in the cooler regions of Europe and North America, however, it loses its rather strident quality so that is resembles its cousin, sweet marjoram (*Origanum majorana*), a pot herb with a distinctive but more delicate aroma.

Oregano is not a subtle flavour and should be used with care. Its bitter pungency goes well with the meats and fleshy, sun-ripened courgettes [zucchini], tomatoes, aubergines [eggplants] and sweet peppers of southern Europe and North Africa. It can enchance hearty *daubes* or stews when simmered with olives, garlic and red wine.

Unless you can buy it where it grows, however, oregano is rarely available fresh so, if possible, buy it dried on the stalk and, for the best flavour, make sure it comes from a hot, dry country like Italy. The more strongly scented Aegean *rigani* is worth seeking out from Greek-Cypriot stores if you wish to discover the exquisite simplicity of Greek-style charcoal-grilled lamb or pork with lemon. It is used to such good effect in this way that oregano earns its poetic meaning 'joy of the mountains'.

Cultivation Oregano is propagated by seed in spring, by cuttings or by root division in autumn. It needs hot, dry conditions and a well-drained soil. Harvest bunches of flowers and leaves in midsummer and hang in the sun to dry for about four days.

RECIPE

Courgettes [zucchini] with oregano

450g/1lb young courgettes [zucchini]
90ml/3 fl oz/$8\frac{1}{2}$ tbsp olive oil
2 cloves garlic, finely diced
$\frac{1}{4}$ tsp oregano
salt and freshly ground pepper

Cut the courgettes [zucchini] into thin slices, sprinkle salt over them in a colander and leave to sweat for about 20 minutes. Rinse the slices thoroughly and dry them. Heat the oil in a frying pan, add the garlic and cook gently until the garlic begins to colour. Add the courgettes [zucchini], oregano, salt and pepper and cook on a medium heat, stirring frequently for 10-15 minutes or until the courgettes [zucchini] are cooked but still firm. Drain away all but 15ml/1tbsp/$1\frac{1}{4}$ tbsp oil and serve with grilled or roast meat, or fish of robust flavour such as sardines, anchovies or tuna.

Fresh oregano

Dried oregano

Paprika

The Spaniards were the first to grow the tropical *Capsicum annum* in a temperate climate where, over the centuries, it evolved as the mild sweet pepper known in Spain as *pimentó* or *pimentón* and widely used throughout the Mediterranean to stuff green olives. This same plant, in its dried, ground form, is the spice, paprika. Most people know its flavour from the goulash dishes common all over eastern Europe but associated particularly with Hungary which produces the world's finest paprika in a range from mild and sweet (the most common) to hot and pungent. Although it is regarded as Hungary's national flavouring and goulash their national dish, paprika was introduced to the country by the Turks, Hungary's traditional enemies. 'Goulash', a word derived from the Hungarian for 'cowboy', was a hearty meat stew, liberally seasoned with paprika and eaten by herders. Nowadays, there are many variations and refinements on this rough and ready dish.

Although principally a culinary spice, paprika has a surprising amount of vitamin C and since it is used in quantities rather than pinches, it can make an enjoyable and nutritious addition to vegetarian and health-food diets.

In cooking, paprika is traditionally used to give colour as well as a sweet capsicum flavour to pale soups and cream sauces and, of course, to national varieties of goulash. Chicken or veal paprika are typical Western European dishes which rely on this ingredient. Its affinity with vegetables such as cabbage, potatoes, mushrooms and cucumber is less well known and it can add a soft, delicate flavour to cream and potted cheeses, shrimps and other shellfish. Paprika is, in fact, a remarkably versatile spice and one you should have no difficulty in using up quickly – a necessity since it rapidly loses flavour and aroma, developing a dark colour and stale taste if stored too long.

Cultivation *C. annum* is quite hardy in north temperate regions if protected from frost and cold, although it grows best under glass. Sow seeds under glass in early spring, plant out in late spring or early summer in well-drained rich soil in a sunny sheltered spot. Harvest in late summer.

RECIPE

Chicken paprika

4 chicken pieces (approximately 1½lb)
45ml/3 tbsp vegetable oil
2 medium onions, chopped
salt to taste
1 tbsp mild (Hungarian) paprika
150ml/¼ pint/¾ cup chicken stock
2 green peppers, sliced
250ml/½ pint/1¼ cups sour cream
1 tbsp flour
chopped parsley to garnish

Heat the oil in a pan and brown the chicken pieces until golden. Remove the chicken and keep it warm. Add the onions to the pan and fry until coloured. Pour off the fat, add paprika and salt and cook gently, stirring for 1-2 minutes. Replace the chicken pieces, add the stock and peppers, cover and simmer for about 30 minutes or until the chicken is cooked. Meanwhile mix the flour and cream to a smooth paste. Add this to the pan, stirring, and cook for about 7 minutes or until the sauce thickens and coats the chicken. Transfer to a serving dish and sprinkle with parsley before serving.

Ground paprika

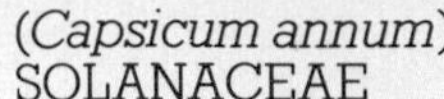

(*Capsicum annum*)
SOLANACEAE

IDENTIFICATION

Finely-ground powder, varying in colour from bright red to russet brown, of the dried fruit of certain large, mild species of capsicum peppers.

Plant Annual herbaceous plant reaching 50-150cm (1½-3ft) with white flowers and green (unripe) fruit which turn red when ripe.

ESSENTIAL FACTS

Countries of origin Native to South America; widely grown in Spain, Hungary, Turkey, Yugoslavia and the USA.

Preparation and storage In Spain and Hungary paprika is graded according to pungency from mild and sweet to hot; powder commonly available elsewhere is mild and sweet. Buy red or russet powder, preferably Hungarian, in small quantities and use quickly to avoid loss of flavour and aroma (dirty brown colour indicates staleness). Store in airtight containers away from sunlight which adversely affects it.

Culinary uses Widely used for flavour and colour in soups, sauces, vegetable and meat dishes eg Hungarian goulash and chicken paprika. It is also added to eggs, shellfish, cheese and cheese spreads, mayonnaise etc; in Spain and Portugal, it is an ingredient in many dishes including sausages eg *chorizos*.

Dried mixed peppers

Olives stuffed with peppers

Peppers

Pepper

The king of spices, pepper has dominated the European spice trade since the Middle Ages and was the single most important factor in the search for and discovery of sea routes to the East. It is not an exaggeration to say that pepper changed the course of history. Without the relentless search for this commodity, as precious as the gold for which it was so frequently exchanged, the great colonial empires of recent modern history would never have existed.

Although this commonplace condiment was known and loved by the Romans, it was the related plant, long pepper (*P. longum*) – a pungent but slightly sweeter vine pepper – that they favoured, and with which they tried to bribe the Visigoth king, Alaric in AD 408 in an attempt to prevent the sacking of Rome. He took the pepper but sacked the city anyway.

Pepper travelled the spice route from Asia for centuries; a trade principally controlled by the Islamic Arabs. After the fall of the Byzantine Empire, Venice gradually emerged as the most powerful city-state in Europe, its economic dominance maintained by wresting the Eastern spice trade from its rivals. It soon became the sole agent for the distribution of pepper and other spices in Europe and for the gold travelling East to pay for them.

Pepper's extraordinary value at this time has to be seen in the light of history. During the Dark Ages, cooking was done in one pot on the hearth with sweet and savoury flavours combined in a fairly arbitrary way. With the development of the wood- or coal-burning stove in the 18th century came a more sophisticated cuisine which isolated and elevated savoury dishes to the prominent positions they still hold today. Pepper's pleasant pungency added zest to these new dishes and its versatility was quickly recognized. In no time it had ousted cinnamon and cloves to become the most sought-after flavouring in the grand kitchens of Europe. A Pepperer's Guild was founded in London in 1180 to control its trade in England and similar organizations existed in other major European centres, all dependent for their supply on Venice.

It was the Portuguese navigator Vasco da Gama who broke the Venetian monopoly. Inspired by the visionary Prince Henry the Navigator's conviction that there was a sea route to the East, where a fabled Christian empire could be found, and in particular to the Malabar coast of western India where pepper grew, Vasco da Gama found the sea route to the East and landed on Indian soil to discover that no Christian empire existed but that there was pepper and spices a plenty. Today, India is the world's major producer of pepper and Indonesia, Malaysia and Brazil are lesser producers.

Pepper has remained an invaluable spice in the West, so fundamental to cookery of all kinds that food would seem tasteless without it. Good quality peppercorns are the only form which give the true flavour and aroma of this

Ground black pepper

Black peppercorns

Dried green peppercorns

ESSENTIAL FACTS

Countries of origin Native to southern India and Cambodia; now also grown in the whole of south-eastern Asia, West Indies, Madagascar and Brazil.

Types of pepper

Black pepper Green or unripe berries dried to black in the sun for 7-10 days; available whole (berries should be of even size and colour) or ground.

White pepper Reddish almost ripe berries, soaked in water to remove the outer skin before drying; slightly smaller than black and milder in flavour; available whole or ground.

Long pepper Minute black fruits in the form of a conical spike about 1.5cm (½in) long; pungent but slightly sweet flavour; rarely used in the West but common in India and the Far East.

Green peppercorns Fresh unripe berries preserved in brine or vinegar; also freeze-dried; easily mashed to a paste; fresh, mild yet aromatic flavour.

Pink peppercorns Usually in the West the near ripe pink berries of South American tree (*Schinus terebinthifolius*); available pickled or dried; pickled are easily mashed aromatic resinous flavour; mildly toxic in quantities.

Mignonette pepper Usually a coarse-ground mixture of black and white berries but also finely ground available; common in France as a table seasoning.

Preparation and storage Buy whole peppercorns and grind them in a peppermill as necessary; ground pepper rapidly loses its flavour and aroma and is also easily adulterated; crush whole peppercorns (for coating steaks etc) in a paper bag using a rolling pin. Whole peppercorns keep indefinitely in airtight containers; once opened, use brined green peppercorns within 4-6 weeks and store in a refrigerator.

Culinary uses Universally used as a table condiment and to flavour all kinds of cooked savoury dishes; whole peppercorns used in stocks and pickling mixtures and in some salamis and sausages; an essential spice in pastrami; in classic French *sauce au poivre* (for grilled steaks); white pepper frequently replaces black, for appearance, in pale sauces; mashed green peppercorns are added to butters, cream sauces for fish, duck or poultry or used for coating steaks etc.

RECIPE

Sauce au poivre vert (Green pepper sauce)

2tsp green peppercorns, mashed
150ml/¼ pint/⅔ cup double [heavy] cream
a squeeze of lemon juice
salt to taste

Blend the peppercorns into the cream, add the lemon juice and salt and heat gently until almost boiling. Serve as an accompaniment to grilled fish or steaks.

Fresh green peppercorns

(*Piper nigrum*)
PIPERACEAE

IDENTIFICATION

Dried unripe fruit (black), or ripened fruit with outer skin removed (white) of tropical vine pepper tree. **Plant** Climbing vine growing to about 4m (12ft) under cultivation, with dark green leaves and hanging strings of berries, green when unripe, red when mature.

Pepper

Continued from page 75

remarkable spice. The dried berries vary in size and quality but they should be of an even size and colour, hard and free from dust or powder. Coffee merchants and high-class delicatessens often sell peppercorns loose. The highest grades of pepper are Tellicherry from India and one from Sarawak, available in jars. Once ground, pepper loses a great deal of its taste and smell – so a peppermill really *is* essential in a household that cares about its food. White pepper is thought by some to be superior, and is certainly useful in white sauces or for a less pungent flavour. Green peppercorns are a relatively new and most delectable addition to the pepper repertoire. Their fresh, rather mild yet aromatic flavour can be used to great advantage in sauces and butters for fish, meat and vegetable dishes. Red peppercorns (ripened berries), do exist in their countries of origin but are not often exported. Those available in the West, mostly imported from Réunion, are not true peppercorns but the berries of a South American tree (*Schinus terebinthifolius*). Although these look attractive and have a slightly resinous flavour, they are mildly toxic in largish quantities so have fallen out of favour on the gourmet tables they once graced.

Cultivation *Piper nigrum* grows only in tropical forests. It is propagated from stem cuttings and can produce berries for up to 40 years.

White peppercorns

Green peppercorns in brine

Black pepper and Jamaican pepper mix

Dried pink peppercorns

Ground white pepper

Poppy seed

The opium poppy, from which the culinary seeds come, is among the oldest cultivated plants. The Egyptians liked the seeds as a condiment, and the ancient Greeks grew the plant specifically for its seeds which, among other uses, were mixed into cakes with honey and taken by Olympic athletes to provide an immediate burst of energy. In Roman times, poppy seed decorated mushroom-shaped breads, a practice which continues today.

Poppy seed has none of the narcotic qualities of the opium drug and its derivatives, although the plant has been lucratively cultivated for centuries in the near East and Orient for its narcotic properties (the story of the 19th century Opium Wars is an inglorious chapter in British history). Indeed, one poppy product, laudanum, an addictive tincture of opium, was a universal cure-all, widely prescribed by doctors in the 19th century – its abuse 'celebrated' by De Quincey, Coleridge and Baudelaire, among others.

The nutty sweet-spicy flavour of poppy seed is to be found in the many breads and rolls of Jewish or mid-European origin, which are common nowadays in supermarkets and bakeries and it is often used in apple strudel fillings. Poppy seed is not in much demand in British kitchens, except as a baking spice, yet it can be used in most interesting ways. It is very good in a home-made coleslaw and added to puréed potatoes and other root vegetables. Combined with noodles (a popular North American dish), it makes an excellent accompaniment to, say, a veal or chicken casserole. Indian cooks always grind the less common white seeds (available at Indian stores) to flavour and thicken curries and sauces.
Cultivation It is not possible to cultivate the opium poppy in Britain or the USA without a permit.

ESSENTIAL FACTS

Countries of origin Native to the Middle East; widely grown in China, south-eastern Asia, India; also Yugoslavia and Germany.
Preparation and storage Dark and white seeds available whole; difficult to grind without special mills (available in Austria, Germany and India); otherwise, lightly roast the seeds, then grind them in a spice blender or with a mortar and pestle; use whole or crushed in cooking and bakery.
Culinary uses Widely used in Jewish cookery and in central Europe in cakes, pastries, sprinkled on breads, buns, pretzels and biscuits; included in sweet stuffings eg Jewish *Hamantaschen*, strudels; added to salads or noodles (in the USA); in India, white seeds ground for flavouring and thickening curries.

RECIPE

Poppy seed noodles
250g/8oz noodles
50g/2oz/4 tbsp butter
1 onion, finely chopped
3 tsp poppy seeds
salt and pepper to taste
Cook the noodles in salted water. Meanwhile, lightly sauté the onion in butter until soft. Add the poppy seeds and seasoning. Drain the noodles and stir into the onion and poppy seed mixture. Serve immediately.

(*Papaver somniferum*)
PAPAVERACEAE

IDENTIFICATION

Tiny, hard, blue-grey (in Western) or cream-coloured (in Eastern) seeds, with similar flavour, of opium poppy. **Plant** Annual growing from 30-120cm (1-4ft) with large white, pink or purple flowers, pods of which contain seeds and are surrounded by a milky white juice from which the narcotic is derived.

Poppy seeds

Ground poppy seeds

White poppy seeds

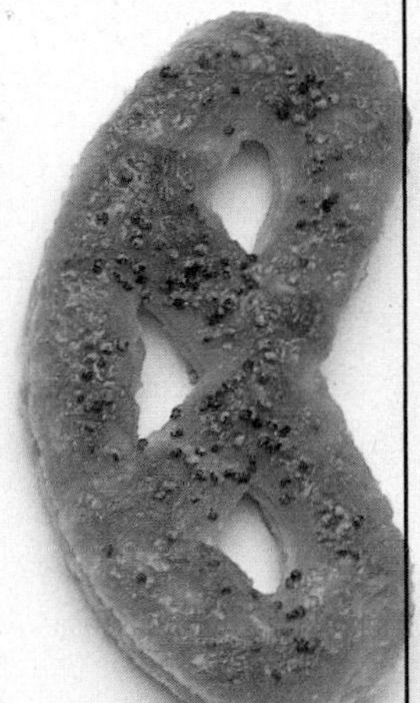

Saffron

If pepper is the king of spices, saffron is the queen. Rare and almost as precious as gold, men have risked their lives for it; even today the people whose livelihood depends on it endure great hardships to produce its fine golden strands. Known since prehistoric times, it is thought to have come from Greece and Asia Minor since it was used in ancient Greece and Rome and in biblical lands. It was almost certainly introduced to Europe by the Arabs in the 10th century – although legend has it that the Phoenicians took it to Spain, nowadays the country principally associated with its production.

The use of saffron has traditionally relied on societies with a cultured aristocracy able to appreciate its culinary advantages and a slave or peasant class, capable of carrying out its labour-intensive production – hence its widespread use under the Roman, Ottoman and Mogul empires and its relative decline in recent times. The Romans, with their typical extravagance, used it to strew paths and roads, literally creating a golden carpet for emperors and princes; and it is said that when Alexander the Great's soldiers entered the Vale of Kashmir, they found the saffron crocus growing in great profusion and were so wild with joy that they broke ranks.

According to the 16th century geographer and historian, Richard Hakluyt, saffron was smuggled into England by a pilgrim who, returning from Spain, hid a crocus head in his palmer's staff, risking death since this Spanish treasure was zealously guarded by law. Saffron Walden in Essex became the centre of its cultivation in England and the resourceful Hakluyt, with plans to solve the country's unemployment problem, attempted to extend its cultivation to other areas in the hope of exporting saffron to the Levant, but he was unsuccessful. In fact, by the end of the 18th century, its cultivation had all but died out in northern Europe, although it was introduced to Pennsylvania, USA where production continues to this day.

What makes saffron so rare and precious is its method of production. It is the orange-red stigmas of a violet-coloured crocus which blooms for only a brief two-week period in autumn. Each flower has only three stigmas which must be picked by hand at dawn before the sun becomes hot. The flowers are discarded and the stigmas are then dried, losing 80 per cent of their weight in this process, which also intensifies saffron's characteristic flavour. The result is that it takes a staggering 200,000-400,000 stigmas to make only 1kg/2lb of saffron. Because of this, some have been tempted to adulterate pure saffron – an action with dire consequences in 15th century Germany when it was recorded that two merchants were burnt to death at the stake for this offence. Adulterated saffron still abounds, especially in powdered form. Thus it is always best to buy strands which should be bright-orange (rather than yellow) without any white streaks or light patches. Pure saffron is always expensive, so be wary of anything which is cheap.

Saffron has a strong perfume and a bitter, honey-like taste which, when added to dishes in pinches, should lend a delicate but distinctive flavour. When suffusing a pinch of saffron in a cup of warm water, the stigmas should expand at once, their colour diffusing the water. Suspect impure or elderly saffron if this does not happen. As a culinary spice, saffron is mainly found in Middle Eastern, Mediterranean and north Indian cookery, although it is used to a limited extent in cakes and buns in Britain. It combines perfectly with all kinds of rice dishes from succulent Italian *risottos* to the perfumed *pilaus* and puddings of India and the Middle East. In the Mediterranean, it blends particularly well with fish and seafood. It is an essential ingredient in the Provençal fish stew, *bouillabaisse*, and is used to spectacular advantage in a (genuine) *paella*, that fragrant mix of seafood and rice.

Cultivation Saffron has ceased to exist in the wild, and is propagated from the corm. It is easy to grow in sunny, well-drained positions and can survive well in tiny, dry plots, as it does in Spain. Although, in theory, the plants can last for 15 years, they are destroyed after four years and renewed because of their susceptibility to disease.

Cornish saffron cake

Saffron powder

Saffron strands

RECIPE

Paella Valenciana

100ml/4 fl oz/½ cup olive oil
8 chicken pieces (approx 1½lb)
250g/8oz lean pork, cubed
1 large onion, chopped
3 cloves garlic, finely chopped
1 green pepper, sliced
2 red peppers, sliced
250g/8oz chorizo *sausage, sliced*
250g/8oz peeled tomatoes
16 mussels, scrubbed and bearded
salt and pepper to taste
500g/1lb long grain rico
600ml/1 pint/3 cups chicken stock
a pinch of saffron, infused in a cup of stock for 15 minutes
100g/4oz French beans, cut in 2.5cm (1in) pieces
100g/4oz peas, shelled (or frozen)
8 large [jumbo] uncooked prawns [shrimp]
8 cooked prawns [shrimp]

Serves 6-8.

Heat the oil in a large, heavy-based frying pan. Brown the chicken pieces and pork. Remove them and keep to one side. Sauté the onion, garlic and peppers and cook for about 10 minutes or until soft. Add the tomatoes and *chorizo* sausage and simmer for a few minutes before returning the chicken and pork pieces to the pan. Cook gently for about 15 minutes. Add the mussels and simmer, covered, until the mussels open. Add the rice, stirring into the mixture. Add the infused saffron and the remaining stock. Bring to the boil and simmer, covered, for 20 minutes, adding the beans and peas after 10 minutes and the uncooked prawns [shrimp] after 15 minutes. At end of the cooking time, turn off the heat, garnish with cooked prawns [shrimp] and leave, covered, for 3-4 minutes before serving.

(*Crocus sativus*)
IRIDACEAE

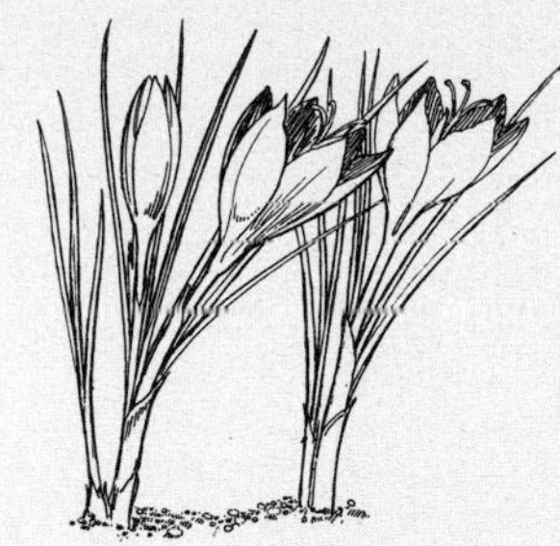

IDENTIFICATION

Dried yellow stigmas of violet flowers of small saffron crocus growing to 15cm (6in). **Plant** Autumn-flowering ornamental plant with a lily-like flower and long thin leaves.

ESSENTIAL FACTS

Countries of origin Probably native to Greece and Asia Minor; now grown throughout the Mediterranean, particularly Spain, and also in India, Turkey, Iran and China.
Preparation and storage Available powdered in small sachets or in whole strands. Buy thread-like strands for preference, soaking a pinch in tepid water to develop colour and aroma, normally adding it towards the end of the cooking process. Powdered saffron is added directly to the ingredients and may be of inferior quality or adulterated. Store saffron in airtight containers away from sunlight.
Culinary uses Used in Mediterranean regions to flavour rice and seafood dishes eg *bouillabaisse*, *paella*, Milanese *risotto* and in fish sauces and soups; in the Middle East in sweet and savoury rice puddings; in festive pilaus of Mogul (north Indian) cooking; in Britain in saffron cakes and buns (a traditional use since the Middle Ages).

Salt
(Sodium chloride)

Salt is essential to life and complete abstinence from it has not been found possible even in the most severe monastic orders. Nowadays, people are unlikely to suffer from a salt deficiency, but more of an excess, as nutritionists constantly point out. Natural foodstuffs contain about 1½ grams of salt in an ordinary diet but we may add a further 8 or 9 grams during cooking or at table simply because it is thought that without this oldest and universal flavouring, food lacks an appetizing and varied taste. Salt brings out the flavour of many foods, destroys the bitterness in some and acts as a preservative of others. In cultures where its supply is limited, substances exist which replicate its salty flavour.

Salt is not a spice but rather a fundamental flavouring. Its recognizable taste is due to sodium chloride, a mineral found in rock deposits and in sea water, and extracted from both to provide the familiar cooking and table salt. Used since early times, salt was considered a valuable commercial commodity by the Romans. The *via salaria* was the road to the port of Ostia, the source of the imperial city's main supply of salt. The word 'salary' comes from the Roman word for salt, because when Roman soldiers were serving abroad they received a salt allowance – an additional benefit in case the barbaric outposts of the empire were without it – which eventually became a cash allowance.

At this time, too, the preservation of food by salting was carried out on a very large scale in the countries of western Europe. Spain exported salt fish to the Romans for whom it was a luxury food, as was the salt pork and bacon imported from Gaul, which was a particular favourite of the Emperor Claudius. In Britain and elsewhere in Europe, fish and meat were locally cured for home use, although by Elizabethan times there was a flourishing salt-fish trade between England and Norway. The chief advance in salting was the introduction of saltpetre (potassium nitrate) which had a more penetrating and drying effect on meat tissues than just bay- or sea-salt alone. Used in tiny quantities so as not to harden the meat, it also gave the flesh an attractive rosy appearance, familiar today in bacon and salt beef.

Because we use so much salt and so regularly, many people are insensitive to the flavour of salt from different sources, and to the changes made by refinements and additives to make it free-running. Many believe that rock salt, rarely available nowadays as untreated, separated crystals but common as block or kitchen salt, has the finest and purest flavour. However, the popular sea-salt, with its attractive, crunchy crystals and faint smell of the sea, is a highly-rated, perhaps superior rival, especially when obtained by evaporation of wind and sun (and not by artificial means) as in the traditional 'bay-salt' (named from the Bay of Biscay).

Some culinary practices influence the way salt is used. In order to retain their nutrients, boiled or steamed vegetables should be salted after and not during cooking; dried beans and pulses tend to harden when boiled in salted liquid so it is best to add salt towards the end of the cooking time; meat for casseroles and stews should be browned first, then seasoned, and grills and roasts should be salted immediately before cooking so as to retain the meat juices. Many people add a pinch of salt to sweet baking to bring out the flavour. Conversely, to extract the bitter taste from vegetables such as aubergines [eggplants] and courgettes [zucchini] and the water content from cucumbers, sprinkle the sliced vegetables with salt and leave for about 20 minutes before rinsing and drying. One of the most important points to remember is that over-salting cannot be corrected except by diluting the cooking liquid, a process which can ruin a carefully prepared dish.

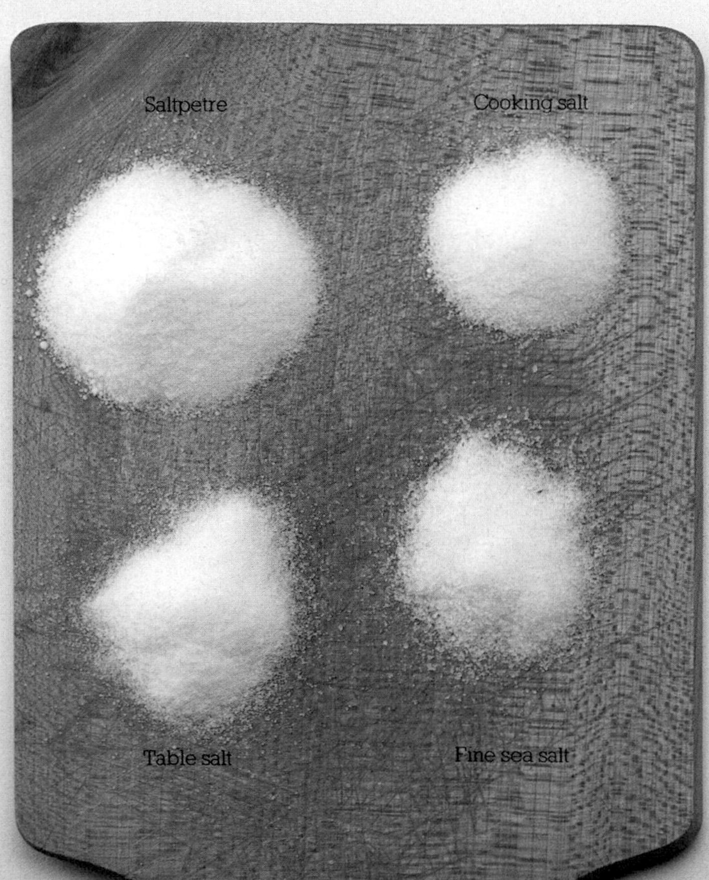

IDENTIFICATION

Free-running, block or crystallized substance, usually white in colour, extracted from rock deposits or sea water, and processed for use; salt is sodium chloride, a mineral essential for animal life.

ESSENTIAL FACTS

Countries of origin Worldwide; the Atlantic coast of Europe is a traditional region of production of 'bay-' or sea-salt from ancient times.

Types of salt

Common kitchen salt Rock salt processed to various degrees of fineness, usually free from chemical additives and available in blocks for kitchen use most readily at health-food shops.

Table salt Finely-ground rock salt with added magnesium carbonate or other substances to produce free-running table condiment; most common used of all salt types.

Sea Salt Salt derived from evaporation of sea water (either by sun and wind or artificial means); available as crystals or finely ground (often with additives to aid flow) from most supermarkets and better-quality grocery stores; Maldon salt is the finest English sea-salt, with tiny crystals which can be sprinkled directly onto food.

Bay-salt Sea-salt evaporated by natural forces of sun and wind,

traditionally used for curing fish and meat; the finest is said to come from the Bay of Biscay.
Freezing salt [Rock salt] Non-edible crystallized salt once used extensively for home freezing.
Saltpetre (Potassium nitrate) Chemically unrelated to common salt but tiny quantities are used with salt, spices etc in meat preservation; it adds a pink colour to preserved meats and is available from pharmacists.
Pickling salt Refined rock salt (same as kitchen salt above), must be free from additives for pickling.
Spiced salt Salt with spices or flavourings such as celery, garlic, onion or in French *sel-épice* with white pepper and mixed spices.
Preparation and storage Salt crystals can be crushed in a salt mill or with a mortar and pestle; fine crystals can be crushed with fingers or added directly to food eg Maldon salt; salt keeps indefinitely but needs a moisture-free atmosphere; free-flowing table salt needs no special protection but cannot be used for salting, pickling or freezing.
Culinary uses Universally employed in all types of savoury dishes; used in brines for preserved meat and fish such as bacon, beef, tongue, sardines, herrings; in dry-salt mixes for home-curing; in commercial and home-made seasoned salts eg with garlic, pepper, cayenne, celery, chilli etc; can be used to extract bitterness or water from vegetables such as aubergines [eggplants], courgettes [zucchini] and cucumbers and for pickling vegetables.

RECIPE

Chinese salt-baked chicken
Approx 2.7kg/6lb rock or sea-salt
1.4kg/3lb chicken, oven ready
30ml/2 tbsp mei kwei lu *Chinese liqueur (or dry sherry)*
30ml/2 tbsp light soy sauce
2.5cm (1in) piece green ginger, finely chopped
1 large onion, finely chopped
1/4 tsp five-spice powder (optional)
a pinch of anise pepper (optional)
Dipping sauce
45-60ml/3-4 tbsp light soy sauce
1/2 tsp ginger, chopped
a dash of sherry
1/2 a spring onion, chopped
Combine the soy sauce and the Chinese liqueur and rub into the chicken inside and out. Combine the remaining ingredients (except the salt) to make a stuffing and press into the cavity of the chicken. Leave the chicken in cool place for 2-3 hours to absorb the flavours. Put a 12mm (1/2 in) layer of salt in the bottom of a deep casserole. Place the chicken on top and cover it completely with the remaining salt. Cover it with a lid and cook for about 10 minutes over a medium heat before baking in a moderate oven (180°C/350°F/gas mark 4) for 2 1/4 hours. Remove the chicken from the casserole, brushing away any salt. Chop the chicken into pieces in the Chinese way (through the bone) and serve either hot or cold with a clear dip made by combining the soy, ginger, sherry and chopped spring onion.

Coarse sea salt
Pickling salt
Maldon sea salt
Coarse sea salt

(*Sesamum indicum*)
PEDALIACEAE

Sesame seed

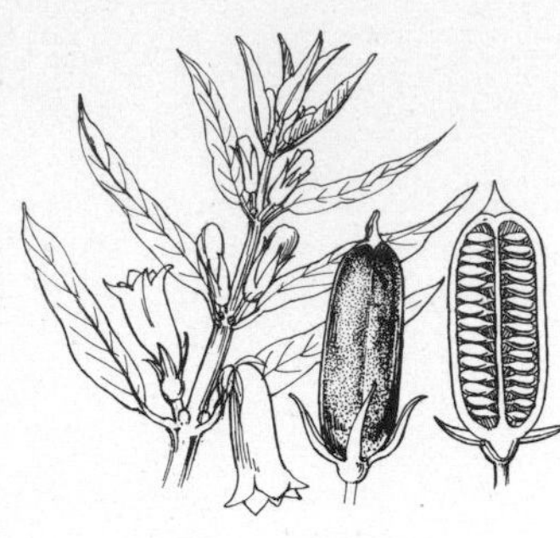

IDENTIFICATION

Tiny flat seeds, usually creamy white but also red, brown or black; available whole dried, or ground to a greyish paste, *tahina*. **Plant** Herbaceous annual growing up to 2m (6ft) with white or pink flowers.

ESSENTIAL FACTS

Countries of origin Indigenous to India; now widely grown in China and the Far East, Middle East, Africa. Central America, especially Mexico and the USA (Texas).
Preparation and storage For better flavour, lightly roast the seeds in a dry pan until they jump, or toast a batch in the oven; use whole or freshly ground (use mortar and pestle or spice grinder); ground seeds also available as *tahina* paste; store seeds in airtight containers away from sunlight.
Culinary uses Widespread use in Middle Eastern and Far Eastern cooking; sprinkled on breads and cakes especially in Middle East; *tahina* paste essential for many dishes of the Levant and Mediterranean eg *hummus*; ingredient in the sweet halva; in India often ground to add flavour and thickening to spiced dishes; seeds used in Chinese stir-fried dishes, oil for flavouring; black and white seeds used extensively in Japanese and Korean cuisines.

Probably the oldest plant known for its seed use, sesame is native to India but has been principally associated with the Middle East and China since the beginning of recorded history. The Egyptians made a flour from it and ancient Chinese civilizations made ink from the soot given off from its oil. The Greeks and Romans sprinkled the seeds on breads and pastries and also ground it to a paste, similar probably to the *tahina* still so common throughout the Middle East and Mediterranean.

In ancient Persia it was a precious commodity and no accident that in the popular story of Ali Baba from *The Arabian Nights* the enormous cave full of thieves' treasure could only be entered with the magic words, 'Open sesame'. The Greek historian Herodotus tells the curious (and perhaps apocryphal) tale of 300 boys who, ordered to be castrated by their tyrannical ruler, escaped and sought sanctuary in a temple, where they survived the long siege by eating the religious offerings of sesame seed cakes provided by the local peasants.

Early writers claimed that the seeds were an antidote to the bite of the spotted lizard and the Roman historian, Pliny (who had an opinion on everything) maintained that the powdered seeds mixed with wine 'restraineth immoderate vomits' – a medicinal use reinforced today in Africa where the seeds are taken for dysentery and a number of stomach problems.

Nowadays, the sesame plant is widely cultivated in all sub-tropical regions, but especially in India, China, Mexico and the Middle East, for its oil has extensive commercial use in the production of margarine and cooking oils, as well as in soaps, cosmetics and lubricants.

In its traditional areas of cultivation, both seeds and oil feature prominently in cookery, indeed, their sweet nutty flavour is ubiquitous in some cuisines. Most people are familiar with the taste and delightful crunchy texture of sesame seeds on Greek-Cypriot and Middle Eastern breads. Popular too is the *hummus bi tahina*, the spiced chick pea and sesame purée which appears on Greek restaurant menus all over the world. Throughout the Mediterranean and Levant, *tahina* itself which is a creamy-grey, thin paste of finely ground seeds, is often served with garlic and lemon as a *meze* or snack to be eaten with bread. Sesame seeds are an important ingredient in halva, that Middle Eastern confection available in squares or blocks, variations of which are also common in India.

In the Far East it is no less widely used. Prawn [shrimp] and sesame toasts (deep-fried bread fingers spread with mashed prawns and sesame seeds) are a favourite Chinese snack; lightly roasted sesame seeds are occasionally added to stir-fried dishes, and sesame oil is used for its subtle, nutty flavour, rather than an all-purpose cooking oil. In Japanese and Korean cuisines, sesame appears even more frequently. In Japan, it is usually roasted and then pounded, often with other ingredients, to form a sauce; in Korea, it is roasted and sprinkled whole or ground over beef or chicken dishes. It is, for example, an essential garnish on the Korean national dish, *bulgogi* – marinated and barbecued strips of beef (see below).
Cultivation Sesame is grown from seed in tropical and sub-tropical regions. It matures within 3-6 months.

Brown seeds

White seeds

Sesame snaps

RECIPE

Bulgogi

500g/1lb rump steak or beef topside, very thinly sliced in strips
3 tbsp brown sugar
125ml/4fl oz/½ cup soy sauce
3 tbsp sesame seeds, lightly toasted and ground
45ml/3 tbsp sesame oil
2 cloves garlic, minced
3 spring onions, finely chopped
2 tbsp sesame seeds, lightly roasted to garnish

Marinate the beef with the remaining ingredients (except the sesame seed garnish) for 2-4 hours, turning the beef slices from time to time. Heat a wok or frying pan, remove the beef strips from the marinade and quickly brown over a high heat until just cooked. Transfer the strips as they are done to a warmed serving dish. Lower the heat and add 45-60ml/2-3 tbsp of the marinade to the pan, allowing it to bubble and thicken without burning. Pour this over the beef and sprinkle with the reserved sesame seeds before serving.

Soy

The soy or soya bean is undoubtedly one of the world's most important crops. Cultivated in China since the third millennium BC, it is an essential foodstuff throughout the Far East where it is used in a bewildering variety of forms, including milk, bean curds, sauces and fermented pastes. In China and Japan it is known as the 'king of beans' and the 'meat of the soil' and regarded by mystics and monks as one of the five sacred grains.

Despite its long and venerable use, it was unknown in the West until the end of the 17th century and its use was barely acknowledged until the beginning of this century when it was found to be a good source of cooking oil and a base for margarine. Since World War II, however, the soy bean's value as a commodity as well as a rich source of protein has finally been recognized and the United States has increased its production sixfold to become the world's largest producer, partly for the manufacture of textured vegetable protein, a meat substitute (often added to commercially produced hamburgers and sausages) and partly for its meal which is used as a cattle feed and fertilizer.

With the increasing interest in health foods and vegetarian cookery, the soy bean has had another lease of life. Containing more protein than prime steak, soy bean products such as tofu (bean curd), miso (fermented soy bean paste) and mung bean sprouts are now commonplace in Western health-food shops and restaurants – and dedicated gardeners can now grow their own soy beans in temperate latitudes, thanks to the development in recent years of new strains of this essentially subtropical plant.

Most people are familiar with the salty, beefy taste of soy sauce, but the soy bean is astonishingly versatile. Concentrated or fermented into pastes and sauces, it becomes a spicy flavouring, yet it can be eaten as a fresh vegetable in the same way as broad beans, or dried, soaked and cooked as for haricot beans. The custard-like soy bean curd, available fresh, dried or preserved, has a delicate taste and readily absorbs other flavours; it is widely used in the East and increasingly in Western vegetarian cookery in all kinds of sweet and savoury dishes.

Soy sauce is one of the world's great flavourings, enthusiastically adopted in the West and essential in all oriental cuisines. There are many types of soy sauce, varying in colour, strength and flavour. It is usually made by fermenting a salted mixture of cooked soy beans with flour

Miso

Oyster sauce

ESSENTIAL FACTS

Countries of origin Native to China; now also grown in Japan, Korea, India, Africa, South America and the USA.

Soy bean products

Soy sauce Dark brown or light coloured salty liquid made from fermented soy beans and extensively used in all Far Eastern cuisines.

Yellow or brown soy bean paste Mashed beans mixed with spices and flavourings to form a thick paste used in, notably, Sichuan cuisine.

Fermented black beans Slightly mashed or crushed fermented beans of one soy variety, always combined with other ingredients in cooking where they add texture and a distinctive flavour; available in polythene bags or canned at oriental shops.

Sweet soy bean (or red-bean) paste Thick sweet paste used in sweet dishes or sometimes spread on pancakes for Peking duck; available canned.

Tofu or fresh bean curd Junket-like substance made from puréed soy beans available in cakes from health-food shops or oriental shops.

Dried bean curd Available in small cakes from oriental shops and added to soups, stews etc.

Bean curd cheese or red bean curd Bean curd fermented in wine and salt, strongly flavoured and used as a seasoning or condiment with rice, meat or vegetables; available in jars and cans.

Bean sprouts Sprouts of small mung (soy) beans, available fresh or canned; can be grown indoors where they will sprout in a few days.

Miso Japanese fermented soy bean paste available in varying degrees of saltiness, canned or vacuum packed.

Preparation and storage Young fresh beans can be cooked like broad beans; dried beans must be soaked overnight before boiling for about 30 minutes; tofu can be kept refrigerated in water for 2-3 days if the water is changed daily; fermented black beans must be soaked in cold water for 5-10 minutes, then drained before adding to dishes; soy sauce keeps indefinitely if airtight; bean sprouts keep 1-2 days in the cool compartment of a refrigerator.

Culinary uses Soy bean products are used extensively in oriental cookery to preserve and flavour many ingredients, principally in marinades, dips, as table condiments; added to soups and other cooked dishes and for glazing; tofu is used as a vegetable in soups and with other ingredients to enhance the flavour; in the West tofu is used in vegetarian cookery in salads, spreads, as a pizza topping and in sweet cheesecakes etc.

(Glycine max)
LEGUMINOSAE

Barbeque sauce

Dark soy sauce

Hoisin sauce

Red bean curd

Shoyu sauce

IDENTIFICATION

Small round seeds, varying in colour from yellow to black, from pods of soy plant. **Plant** A legume of which there are many varieties growing from 30cm-2m (1-6½ft) and harvested from 10-30 weeks after sowing; temperate strains have been developed.

Soy

Continued from page 85

and extracting the liquid. Light-coloured soy sauce is less strong than darker varieties and is frequently used in Cantonese cooking with fish and poultry. Soy sauce is also an ingredient in the popular *hoisin* (barbecue) and oyster sauces. Japanese soy sauce, called *shoyu*, is less salty than Chinese varieties and should, of course, be used in Japanese recipes.

Soy bean paste, usually made from mashed brown or yellow beans mixed with salt, sugar, garlic and soy sauce, is used when thicker sauces are required and is a common ingredient in Sichuan cooking. Miso, the fermented, usually dark grey soy bean paste of Japan, is used as a seasoning in a wide range of soups; it is also the mainstay of the macrobiotic diet, an alternative health regimen.

Dried, fermented black soy beans are often to be found on Chinese restaurant menus with beef, crab, mussels or pork 'in black bean sauce', adding an agreeable texture and interesting saltiness to these dishes. For desserts, there is even a sweetened soy bean paste, used as a spread or filling, which tastes and looks rather like mashed dates.

Bean curd or tofu is one of the West's recent discoveries, hailed as a wonder food because of its nutritional value, low calorie count and cheapness. It has, of course, been extensively used in the Orient for thousands of years as a 'vegetable', the blandness of which is useful in harmonizing the flavours of other ingredients. It is now available fresh, as well as canned and enthusiasts of this interesting soy product are now making their own. Bean curd 'cheese' (often labelled red bean curd) is salty and highly savoury and is used as a flavour in cooking or simply eaten with bland foods such as boiled rice.

Cultivation Although a subtropical plant, strains of soy bean have now been developed for cultivation in temperate regions. The soy bean needs warmth rather than good soil and for success it is important to create the warmest possible conditions. Sow outdoors in late spring or early summer and harvest in late summer to early autumn.

RECIPE

Bean curd with oyster sauce

30ml/2tbsp vegetable oil
250g/8oz fresh tofu, cut into cubes
1 stick of celery, sliced diagonally
6 spring onions, cut into 2.5cm (1in) pieces
1 red pepper, roughly chopped
1 green pepper, roughly chopped
100g/4oz fresh shiitake *mushrooms, sliced or 4 dried Chinese mushrooms, soaked and sliced*
3 tsp cornflour [cornstarch]
300ml/¼ pint/⅔ cup water
30ml/2 tbsp oyster sauce
15ml/1 tbsp soy sauce
15ml/1 tbsp dry sherry

Heat the oil in a wok or pan until almost smoking. Add the tofu and toss until lightly browned. Remove it to a warm plate. Add the remaining oil to the wok and add the celery, onions, peppers and mushrooms. Stir-fry for about 1 minute. Combine the remaining ingredients and add to the pan with the tofu, stirring continuously for about 1 minute or until the sauce boils and thickens. Serve immediately.

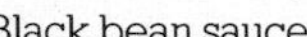

Black bean sauce

Tofu

Star anise

An unusual and attractive spice, star anise is the star-shaped fruit of a small evergreen tree, which becomes reddish-brown when dried. Of all the Eastern spices it is the most easily recognizable in grocery shops, even when it is labelled in Cantonese. Although it is almost exclusively associated with Chinese cuisine, it has been known in the West since the 17th century where it was added to fruit syrups and jams and its oil used in the production of anise-flavoured drinks such as anisette.

Its taste, unmistakeably of anise, rarely overwhelms the oriental dishes to which it is added but does tend to give them a distinctive aroma, similar to that of the Chinese five-spice powder ot which it is the dominant ingredient. Red-roasted Chinese pork, a common restaurant dish, exudes a faintly sweet anise scent because of the five-spice powder rubbed into it.

Star anise is nearly always used in very small quantities, usually in combination with other spices or soy sauce and added to a wide variety of long-simmered dishes (especially beef) and to stuffings for Chinese dumplings (dim sum). In Thai and Vietnamese cuisine, it is used to flavour pork dishes with a Chinese influence. It is said that Chinese mandarins often chewed this fruit as a breath sweetener and to revive their jaded palates. Today, in the Western kitchen, it adds authenticity to oriental dishes and aniseed is no substitute.

Cultivation This evergreen tree of the magnolia family is mainly cultivated in southern China and south-eastern Asia. It is propagated by seed and the fruits picked before they ripen; they are then sun-dried.

ESSENTIAL FACTS

Countries of origin Native to China; grown also in south-eastern Asia.

Preparation and storage Available whole or ground; buy whole for preference, grinding as necessary; store in an airtight container away from sunlight.

Culinary uses Widely used in Chinese and Chinese-influenced cuisines; a notable ingredient in Chinese five-spice powder; used to flavour pork, chicken, duck and beef often in long-simmered dishes; used in the West in commercially produced anise products eg alcoholic drinks.

RECIPE

Red-cooked beef with star anise

45ml/3 tbsp/¼ cup vegetable oil
1kg/2lb leg or shin of beef, cubed
1 star anise
1/2 beef stock cube
105ml/7 tbsp/½ cup soy sauce
2.5cm/1 in piece green ginger, finely chopped
2 tsp brown sugar
45ml/3 tbsp/¼ cup dry sherry
45ml/3 tbsp/¼ cup red wine

Heat the oil in an ovenproof casserole. Add the beef and fry until evenly browned. Pour off any excess oil. Add the stock cube, half the soy sauce and enough water to just cover beef. Bring to the boil, stirring then transfer to a slow oven (150°C/300°F/gas mark 2) and cook for 1 hour. Add the remaining ingredients and cook for a further 1-1½ hours, stirring once or twice. Serve with boiled rice.

(Illicium verum)
MAGNOLIACEAE

IDENTIFICATION

Star-shaped fruit, russet when dried, of small oriental tree growing to about 8m (26ft). **Plant** Evergreen tree of magnolia family; fruits containing seed pods picked before completely ripe.

Five spice powder

Star anise

Sugar

Although sugar is now the world's principal source of sweetness, it is a relative newcomer in the flavouring stakes, despite the fact that it was known in India over 2000 years ago. Most sugar comes from sugar cane which was probably native to south and east Asia and first cultivated in India where it was called in Sanskrit, *karkara*. Its English name derives from the Arabic *sakkara* or *sukkur* and although it was known in Britain and Europe in the Middle Ages, it was an expensive commodity, sold in small quantities by apothecaries.

Alexander the Great brought sugar to Europe in the third century BC; it was cultivated in China a few hundred years later and by AD 400 it was a common crop in southern Spain and Italy from whence the early European supplies came. It was not until the 16th century when the canes were taken to the Caribbean that its production really took off. Even so, several centuries passed before cheap sugar finally ousted honey, in the 19th century, to become the universal sweetening agent.

Today, there are various types of sugar and although most sugar used in the kitchen comes from sugar cane or the roots of sugar beet, other sugars include lactose or milk sugar, obtained from whey and skimmed milk (used in commercial confectionery and cheese-making); malt sugar, a sugar derived from the malting process (important in baking and brewing); maple sugar, derived from the sap of the North American maple tree (popular in the 19th century but now better known in Europe in the form of maple syrup) and palm sugar which comes from a variety of tropical palms (usually found in Third World countries and India where it is called *jaggery*).

The white or brown sugar most commonly used in the West, either in granules or in crystal form, is the result of various refining processes. After sugar is harvested, nowadays mostly by mechanical means, the juice is crushed out and boiled to produce the first crop of sugar crystals and molasses. The thick, dark brown unrefined cane sugar that results is known as *muscovado* sugar, an increasingly important and more easily available sugar these days because of health concerns about refined sugars. Other commercial brown sugars are not necessarily unrefined because many manufacturers colour their sugars with caramel.

During the refining process, various syrup residues are left, varying in colour from very light to dark brown; these form the golden syrup, treacle and molasses commonly available (*see* Honeys and syrups pages 114 to 117). The final, concentrated, almost black syrup left behind is black-strap molasses which contains 50 per cent sugars with minerals and organic substances.

Refined white sugar was first available as a sugar loaf, in the form of cone-shaped mountains which had then to be broken up. Sugar lumps are a reminder of this type of sugar while granulated, castor [superfine] and icing [confectioners'] sugars are merely refined sugars ground to different degrees of fineness.

Because sugar cane grows only in the tropics, alternative European sources of sugar were explored as far back as the 16th century. Carrots were tried in France but rejected and from the 19th century, the beet grown in northern countries was found to be a reliable source and is now an extensive and important crop in many Eastern European countries. The white sugar produced from the root of the sugar beet (*Beta vulgaris*) is identical to that of cane sugar. Sugar beet, however, does not produce brown sugar, although a bitter-tasting molasses which has commercial uses is obtained.

Sugar's culinary uses defy description. Probably the most popular flavouring in the world, it sweetens all kinds of beverages, puddings, cakes, pastries, fruits, desserts, jams and preserves. One of its most important uses is in commercial and home-made confectionery.

Cultivation Sugar cane is grown on plantations in humid, tropical regions and is now harvested mechanically except in peasant communities.

RECIPE

Armagnac peach conserve

750g/1½ lb ripe peaches, peeled, stoned and diced
50g/2oz/2 tbsp slivered almonds
40g/1½ oz/1 tbsp glacé cherries
½ tsp grated lemon rind
15ml/1 tbsp lemon juice
a pinch of cinnamon
625g/1¼ lb castor [superfine] or preserving sugar, warmed
45ml/3 tbsp Armagnac or brandy
120ml/4 fl oz/8 tbsp pectin
Makes 1¼kg/2½ lb

Place the peaches in a pan with the almonds, cherries, lemon rind and juice and cinnamon. Bring to the boil slowly, stirring once or twice. Add the sugar and simmer until dissolved. Remove the pan from the heat, add the Armagnac and the pectin. Stir thoroughly before pouring into sterilized jars and sealing. Label when cold. Keep for about 2 months before use. It will keep well for about 6 months unopened.

Raw cane sugar

Molasses sugar

Castor [superfine] sugar with peel

ESSENTIAL FACTS

Countries of origin Principally the West Indies but also other suitable tropical regions including Australia, southern USA, India and parts of central Africa.

Types of sugar

Muscovado Dark brown, unrefined sugar produced from the first stage of the refining process.

Barbados, demerara Brown sugars of varying degrees of colour because of molasses coatings, originally from Barbados and Guyana.

Brown or golden sugar Frequently refined sugar artifically coloured with caramel.

White granulated or lump sugar Refined, processed sugar cane or beet sugar crystals.

Castor sugar [superfine]. Finely ground white sugar.

Icing sugar [confectioners'] Powdered white sugar used in confectionary and for cake icings.

Jam or preserving sugar Commercially produced granulated sugar with added pectin for easy setting.

Flavoured sugars Vanilla, cinnamon, cloves, ginger, anise, orange and lemon peel are all used to flavour sugar.

Preparation and storage Store all sugar in moist-free conditions where it will keep indefinitely. Sugar melts at 160°C/320°F, becoming dark caramel at 190°C/374°F and black jack at 210°C/410°F. Confectioners usually have a sugar thermometer to determine the various degrees of sugar such as thread, ball and crack necessary for their craft.

Culinary uses Used as a sweetening agent in a great number of beverages such as tea, coffee, in pastries, creams etc; added to fruit; in jams or preserves; in all types of home-made and commercial confectionery; frequently used in savoury dishes to enhance the flavour of other ingredients, in glazed sauces, in sweet-sour dishes and in caramel form as a colouring agent.

Sugar cane: (*Saccharum officinarum*) Sugar beet: (*Beta Vulgaris*)

IDENTIFICATION

According to its stage of refinement, brown or white crystals, granules, powder or lumps, produced from juice of sugar cane; also white granules, lumps or powder produced from the roots of the sugar beet plant. **Plant** Sugar cane is a tall grass, growing in clumps to 3-4m (9-12ft) with solid, bamboo-like stems enclosing a fibrous, juicy centre.

Demerara sugar

Preserving sugar

Icing [confectioners'] sugar

White cane sugar

Golden granulated sugar

Castor [superfine] sugar

Small cube sugar

(*Rhus coriaria*)
ANACARDINACEAE

IDENTIFICATION

Dried brownish-red seeds of fruit of a Mediterranean plant. **Plant** Bushy shrub which grows to 3m (10ft) with white flowers and attractive red leaves in autumn.

Sumac

Sumac (Sicilian)

This interesting spice, barely known in the West, is widely used in Arab cookery and throughout the Middle East (particularly Lebanon) for its fruity, sour flavour which is used in the same way as vinegar or lemon.

A decorative plant, sumac is familiar to many gardeners in the West as different species of it grow in North America and other temperate regions, but it is the dried seeds of the *Mediterranean* species only that is used as a culinary spice. This should not be confused with North American sumac, a related species *Rhus toxicodendron*, which is a poisonous ivy causing severe skin disorders when touched. In southern Italy and Sicily where it is found wild and cultivated, it is important in the tanning industry, and its medicinal properties have been recognized for centuries. The indefatigable herbalist Gerard, for example, noted that the 'seeds . . . eaten in sauces with meat' cured stomach upsets, a use to which it is still put today in the Middle East. The Romans appreciated its culinary virtues, using it widely as a souring agent.

Sumac has a pleasant, astringent taste with a definite fruitiness which is less harsh than either vinegar or lemon. Few Middle Eastern households are without the seeds which are available whole or as a brownish-red powder. The juice extracted from the seeds is used in marinades and in salads and the powder is rubbed or sprinkled on all kinds of grilled meats, fish and kebabs, and added to spicy meat and fish stews. It is also mixed with yogurt, cream cheese and herbs to make a refreshing sauce.

This most attractive flavouring deserves to be better known, not only because it adds authenticity to Middle Eastern dishes but also because its agreeable sour flavour could give a new taste to traditional tartly-flavoured dishes.

Cultivation Sumac grows best in rocky, barren Mediterranean regions, with better-quality fruit produced in mountainous areas away from the coast. It is easily propagated from seed.

ESSENTIAL FACTS

Countries of origin Native to the Mediterranean; grown widely in southern Italy and Sicily, and in Iran, Turkey, Lebanon and other Middle Eastern countries.

Preparation and storage Available from stores specializing in Middle Eastern, Lebanese or Jewish food as whole seeds or ground powder. To make sumac juice for marinades or dressings, soak 100g/4oz/¾ cup cracked seeds in 350ml/12 fl oz/1½ cups water for 20-30 minutes. Squeeze the juice through a strainer or sieve. Store the seeds and powder in airtight containers away from light. Buy whole seeds for preference, grinding as necessary; ground powder quickly loses flavour and aroma; store juice up to 5 days in a refrigerator.

Culinary uses Widely used in Middle Eastern cookery as a souring agent in place of lemon or vinegar; powder can be rubbed or sprinkled on kebabs and grilled meats, fish and poultry; added to meat and vegetable stews; often mixed with yogurt or herbs for sauces or dips; juice used in salad dressings and marinades.

RECIPE

Samak el harrah (Hot spicy sea bass)

1 sea bass weighing about 1kg/2lb, cleaned
250g/8oz/2 cups walnuts, coarsely chopped
a small bunch of coriander leaves, finely chopped
5 cloves of garlic, minced
60ml/4 tbsp/¼ cup olive oil
2 tsp sumac juice or *a large pinch of powdered sumac*
salt to taste
¼ tsp ground cinnamon
a large pinch of cayenne pepper or *chilli powder*

Place the fish in a baking dish. Combine the remaining ingredients with sufficient water to make a sauce. Pour the sauce over the fish and bake in a medium oven (180°C/350°F/gas mark 4) for about 30 minutes or until the fish is done. Serve immediately with rice.

Tamarind

(*Tamarindus indica*)
LEGUMINOSAE

Tamarind is a handsome, decorative tree which grows all over India. The alternative name for this spice is 'Indian date' because the fruits (large bean-shaped pods) ripen to a dark brown and resemble dates. Although many Westerners may have seen the dried, sticky pulp in Indian, oriental and even West Indian shops, few are familiar with its flavour or know how it is used. Tamarind juice or paste acts as a souring agent in the same way as lemon or vinegar and, although it has a similar acid flavour, it has a refreshing, cooling property which is much valued in the areas where it is grown.

Native to tropical east Africa and possibly southern Asia, it has been used in India since ancient times. It was also popular with the Arabs who introduced it to Europe and it had become known in England in Tudor times when the herbalist Gerard remarked on its cooling qualities ('it powerfully cooles and quenches thirst'). Introduced to the West Indies by the Spaniards in the 17th century, its use there is almost as widespread as in India.

Tamarind's sour, fruity taste adds a distinctive, refreshing flavour to curries of all kinds. Tamarind fish, for example, is a well-known dish throughout India and south-eastern Asia. In chutneys and relishes, it is often combined with bananas, tomatoes and mint, and it is an ingredient in many jams and jellies. Interestingly, tamarind is one of the main ingredients in Worcestershire sauce. In both the Middle East and West Indies, tamarind combined with sugar and water provides a popular and delightfully cooling drink which tastes rather like lemonade.

Cultivation The tamarind tree, which is mainly grown in dry tropical regions where it is often found in the wild, is propagated by seed, cuttings or budding and requires little attention.

ESSENTIAL FACTS

Countries of origin India and south-eastern Asia, Africa and West Indies.

Preparation and storage Available in Indian, West Indian and oriental shops as dried, sticky masses in blocks (resembling dates); also available as concentrated tamarind, preserved in syrup or as a paste. To make tamarind juice, soak a small fistful (or 1tsp concentrated pulp) in 150ml/¼ pint/⅔ cup hot water overnight or until pulpy. Then squeeze out the juice through a fine sieve; store it in a non-metal container up to 1 week in a refrigerator; the dried mass keeps indefinitely.

Culinary uses Widely used in India and south-eastern Asia for its sour fruity flavour in curries, some *dhals*, chutneys and relishes, in some jams and jellies; an ingredient in Worcestershire sauce; used in the West Indies in Indian-influenced dishes and for lemonade-type drink (as in Middle East).

RECIPE

Tamarind and tomato chutney

500g/1lb ripe tomatoes, peeled
45ml/3 tbsp vinegar
50ml/¼ pint/⅔ cup tamarind juice (see Preparation and storage)
¼ tsp chilli powder
4 cloves garlic, minced
1 medium onion, finely chopped
a 5cm (2in) piece of green ginger, minced
½ tsp black pepper, freshly ground
2 tbsp brown sugar
1 tsp salt
¼ tsp ground cinnamon
2 tbsp raisins

Combine the tomatoes and vinegar and bring to the boil, breaking up the tomatoes with a wooden spoon. Simmer gently for 30 minutes or until reduced by a quarter. Add the remaining ingredients and simmer for a further 30 minutes or until the ingredients are soft. Cool the mixture, then pour it into sterilized jars and seal. This chutney can be used immediately.

IDENTIFICATION

Largish, bean-shaped pods, the flesh of which turns dark brown and soft when mature; usually available as sticky blocks of dried pulp. **Plant** Tropical evergreen usually growing to about 2½m (8ft) with a thick, hardwood trunk and pale green leaves.

Tamarind paste

Seedless tamarind block

Tamarind pieces

(*Curcuma domestica* or *C. longa*) ZINGIBERACEAE

Turmeric

IDENTIFICATION

Knobbly rhizome or root of a ginger-like plant with yellow-brown rind and orange interior; mature rhizomes are boiled, peeled, dried and ground to characteristic yellow powder. **Plant** Tropical perennial growing to 1m (3ft) with large, lily-like leaves and spikes of yellow-green flowers in summer.

ESSENTIAL FACTS

Countries of origin Native to south-eastern Asia; now grown in India, Sri Lanka, Java, China, Peru, West Indies, Africa and Australia.
Preparation and storage Available as dried yellow powder (occasionally whole dried); powder retains its colouring properties indefinitely but quickly loses flavour and aroma so buy small quantities at a time; store in airtight containers away from sunlight.
Culinary uses An important spice and colourant in Indian cookery, used in meat, fish and vegetable curries, as well as other spiced dishes, in pickles and chutneys, and to flavour and colour pilaus and sweet dishes; extensively used in the Middle East and North Africa in sauces, couscous and rice dishes; an ingredient in commercial curry powders and in Anglo-Indian piccalilli relish.

Turmeric is one of the great Indian spices, used since antiquity throughout the Indian subcontinent and south-eastern Asia in religious rituals, as a dye for priestly robes, for its medicinal properties and as a culinary spice to give flavour and colour to a great variety of dishes. To Westerners, it is familiar in commercial curry powders, giving them that characteristic yellow colour, it is a major ingredient in the popular piccalilli relish and it colours and flavours the pilaus commonly served in Indian restaurants.

One of the world's cheapest spices (the plant thrives in areas of production), turmeric is often known as Indian saffron, an unfortunate misnomer since its agreeable aroma and warm, spicy taste is quite different from the delicately fragrant saffron. Its Indian name is *haldi* and it is usually available as such in Indian stores.

Turmeric's medicinal importance was recognized some 3000 years ago; in the ancient Sanskrit treatise on *Ayurveda* (the Hindu science of medicine) it was recommended as a paste to be applied externally for itches, skin diseases and as a depilatory. Nowadays, it is used for cosmetic purposes in Asia to stain the skin to a light golden colour.

Turmeric comes from the rhizome or underground stem of a small plant, which has first to be boiled, dried and ground to a fine yellow powder before use. It is almost impossible to grind at home so is usually available in the West (and in India) as powder, although dried pieces of root can sometimes be obtained. Although turmeric keeps its colouring properties indefinitely, ground powder does lose flavour and aroma and can acquire a musty taste if kept too long. As with all ground spices, for the freshest, purest flavour, buy little and often, preferably from Indian stores which have a high turnover of this spice.

Tumeric's culinary uses are manifold. It has been known in the West for centuries and is used almost as much in traditional North African cookery as it is in India. It appears in a British recipe for 'pickle lila, an Indian pickle' in 1694 and in the following century was much in demand with those who wished to make 'curry the Indian way'. It flavours and colours all types of spiced dishes and is a colourant in many sweet dishes. In the Middle East and North Africa, it is an ingredient in *sofrito* sauces which flavour fish and chicken dishes, and it is often added to couscous and rice.
Cultivation Turmeric, cultivated in hot moist tropical lands, is propagated from pieces of rhizomes. In the areas where it thrives, it needs little attention.

Turmeric powder

Turmeric root

Mild mango pickle

Hot lime pickle

RECIPE

Monkfish sofrito

Both chicken and fish are commonly cooked in this sauce in Middle Eastern countries. Served cold, this dish sets in an attractive lemon-coloured jelly.

30ml/2 tbsp sunflower oil
1 clove garlic, minced
juice of 1 lemon
½ tsp turmeric
a cardamom pod, cracked
90ml/3 fl oz/6 tbsp fish stock or water
salt and pepper to taste
700g/1 ½lb monkfish, cut into four pieces
parsley or coriander leaves to garnish

Heat the oil in a pan large enough to hold the fish in a single layer. Add the garlic, lemon juice, turmeric, cardamom, stock and seasoning. Slowly bring to boil. Add the fish pieces, cover and cook gently for 10-15 minutes or until the fish is cooked, turning the pieces frequently and adding a little water if the liquid evaporates. Transfer the fish to a warmed serving dish, pour over the sauce (which should be quite thick) and sprinkle with chopped parsley or coriander.

(*Vanilla planifolia, fragrans*)
ORCHIDACEAE

IDENTIFICATION

Dried, processed bean or pod, about 20cm (8in) long, dark brown in colour, of a tropical orchid.
Plant Climbing yellow-flowered orchid which, in cultivation, is trained up trees or posts; flowers last only a day, blooming one by one over a two-month period; pods take nine months to mature.

ESSENTIAL FACTS

Countries of origin Native to Mexico, now grown in the Seychelles, Central America and other suitably humid tropical areas.
Preparation and storage Available as a long, dried bean or pod; as vanilla essence, made by extracting crushed vanilla pods with alcohol; as vanilla sugar (where the bean is used to permeate and flavour sugar); vanilla 'flavouring', an artificial substance often made from clove oil, has a harsh, bitter taste. Keep vanilla beans in an airtight container to avoid loss of aroma and flavour and contamination of other substances; use the beans to flavour creams, milk, stewed fruit etc; beans can be reused several times if washed, thoroughly dried and returned to an airtight container; vanilla essence has a concentrated flavour, use 2-3 drops at a time; for home-made vanilla sugar, store 1-2 beans in a large airtight jar of granulated sugar, allow 3-4 weeks for the flavour to permeate fully; if the jar is kept topped up with sugar, the beans will remain potent for several years. Use this in sweet dishes in place of ordinary sugar when a vanilla flavour is required.
Culinary uses Principally used as an ice cream flavouring and in combination with chocolate or coffee; also added to creams, custards, soufflés, cakes, puddings and stewed fresh or dried fruit; an ingredient in *crème caramel*, *crème brulée*, home-made confectionery, in milk drinks and alcoholic liqueurs eg *Crème de cacao*, Galliano.

Vanilla

Vanilla comes from a rare and beautiful species of pale yellow orchid which grows in clusters of a dozen or so blooms but which only flowers one by one for a day. The plant is native to Mexico but now also grows elsewhere in Central America and in Madagascar, the Seychelles, Tahiti, Réunion and other tropical areas.

The Aztecs used vanilla as a flavouring for, it has been said, their drink of chocolate but mystery surrounds the ingredients of this beverage since, according to other authorities, it was mixed with chilli powder. The Spanish adventurer, Hernando Cortés, introduced the vanilla bean to Europe (as he did the cocoa bean) and it is odd that the now commonplace association of vanilla and chocolate did not find favour in Europe until the mid-18th century. Perhaps Aztec chocolate was, in fact, variously flavoured for it seems unlikely that the *conquistadores*, having once tasted vanilla-flavoured chocolate, would have forgotten the association. It is also possible, of course, that the wily Montezuma was playing a gigantic confidence trick on the Spaniards by adding chilli to this royal drink.

Natural vanilla's flavour is sweet and fragrant but in commercial products it is often debased and frequently the result of vanilla 'flavouring', made from cloves and other substances. For a true appreciation of its flavour, vanilla pods or vanilla essence are essential, for only these produce the delicate mellow aroma that makes this spice one of the finest sweet flavourings in the world. When freshly picked, the green bean, similar in many ways to the common string or green bean, is odourless and without flavour. Only when cured in a complex process which takes six months of careful, skilful work does fragrance emerge in the dark brown, almost black bean which is frosted with a sugar-like crystal. Because of this lengthy preparation, vanilla is a relatively expensive spice, hence its numerous imitations, especially for commercial use, which tend to have a harsh, somewhat bitter taste.

For home use, however, vanilla beans are worth the expense. Once used to flavour a dish, they can subsequently be reused, if immediately washed and dried. Vanilla sugar is another convenient and economical way of using this flavour, since a vanilla bean stored in a jar of granulated sugar permeates the sugar, which can then be used alone.

In the kitchen, vanilla's exquisite flavour makes sweet foods sweeter and has a way of enhancing the flavour of chocolate, coffee and fruit. It is most common as an ice cream flavour but it is used in all kinds of puddings, creams, custards, cakes and soufflés. A vanilla bean added to stewed peaches, apricots and plums or in a dried fruit *compote* makes a particularly attractive dish. It can also be used in milk drinks and home-made confectionery.

Cultivation In tropical climates, the vanilla orchid is grown on plantations where it is trained up posts and trees. In the wild, it is pollinated by Mexican bees but when cultivated, it must be artificially fertilized. The pods are mature about nine months after fertilization and are picked when still unripe.

Vanilla pods

RECIPE

White bonnets

500g/1lb damson or purple plums, stoned
150ml/¼ pint/⅔ cup red wine
50g/2oz/¼ cup sugar
½ vanilla pod
300ml/½ pint/1½ cups double [heavy] cream, whipped

Crack six fruit kernels and place them in a pan with the sugar and vanilla. Cook slowly for about 15 minutes, add the fruit and cook for a further 15-20 minutes or until just tender. Cool. Spoon the fruit into individual dishes or glasses and top with whipped cream to serve.

Vanilla essence

Vanilla-flavoured sugar

Flavouring herbs

Among the 15 or so herbs commonly associated with cookery, there are a few which have such a dominant flavour that they qualify as flavourings in their own right. Basil, sage, thyme and rosemary are robust sun-loving herbs from the Mediterranean with aromas and tastes so unmistakable in dishes that they become a major flavouring ingredient. Among the herbs which are widely grown in temperate regions, mint with its cool but peppery taste, the onion-like chive and the distinctively flavoured tarragon each tend to make their own impact when combined with other ingredients.

The flavour of fresh herbs is incomparably superior to dried forms and since many herbs are easily grown in the kitchen garden or in containers – or are commonly available in greengrocers and markets – there is little excuse for using dried varieties which become stale and musty very quickly. When grown in cooler regions, pungent Mediterranean herbs lose their intensity of flavour. Most of these dry well, particularly on the stalk and it is worth buying imported varieties from southern France and Italy when these are available. For best results, keep all dried herbs in airtight containers away from sunlight.

Chives (*Allium schoenoprasum*)
LILIACEAE

This close relative of onion and garlic has been known since earliest times but was probably not cultivated until the Middle Ages. Chives have pretty, clove-like mauve flowers and long, straight, grass-like leaves, and now thrive in temperate regions of Europe and North America. With a delicate, onion-like flavour, they are added, snipped, to many lightly coloured and bland dishes for both flavour and colour. Their distinctive taste enhances sour cream and cream cheese and they are often used to flavour eggs, potatoes and cucumbers. They are also used in sauces such as *rémoulade* and *ravigote* and in herb butters, are sprinkled on many soups such as Vichyssoise and used to garnish tomato and potato salads in particular. Chives do not dry well, but snipped small, they can be frozen. However, they are principally used fresh and are easy to cultivate in any garden.

Fresh chives

Powdered chives

Dried chives

Mint (*Mentha spicata*) LABIATAE

Mint has been used as a flavouring since antiquity and was introduced to Britain by the Romans and taken to North America by the first settlers. There are many varieties of mint but it is principally spearmint with its long, oval, greyish-green leaves that is best for cooking. Other types include the fragrant Eau-de-Cologne mint and peppermint, the latter grown for use in sweets, candies and peppermint tea. Mint has a hot but refreshing 'peppermint' flavour which is easily recognizable and tends to dominate other ingredients. Although popular in Britain and North America in the mint sauce eaten with roast lamb, in mint jellies and with peas and potatoes, it is not much used in the cuisines of France and Italy. This is probably because mint does not combine well with other herbs nor with garlic, even though it agreeably flavours fruits such as apples and gooseberries. Mint is, however, a common flavouring in the Middle East where it is used in cucumber salads, in *tabbouleh* (parsley and mint salad with cracked wheat) and in mint teas. In India it is also quite widely used in, for example, chutneys and relishes and in yogurt-based sauces. Mint's refreshing flavour is particularly pleasant in summer drinks such as mint juleps and fruit cups such as Pimm's. Mint freezes and dries well but fresh varieties are easily grown.

Dried mint

Spearmint

Garden mint

Basil (*Ocimum basilicum*)
LABIATAE

Basil probably originated in India where, although it is rarely used in cookery, it was revered as a sacred herb. Today, it is principally associated with the Mediterranean cooking of the south of France and Italy (particularly the Ligurian coast) but its popularity is such that it is now a common pot herb in more northerly regions and is frequently available fresh in Italian delicatessens and street markets. Basil, with its strong, sweet-scented perfume and distinctive flavour is one of the most alluring herbs. Its pungent taste transforms a simple tomato salad or sauce and it is the principal ingredient in the green *pesto* sauce served in Italy with pasta. It also flavours and perfumes egg dishes of all kinds, goes particularly well with sweet peppers and aubergines [eggplants] and combines happily with fish such as red mullet. Basil does vary in quality and in northern latitudes is not as sweet and aromatic as it is in sunny climates; in cooler regions it tends to develop harshness and pungency. Dried basil bears little resemblance to the fresh herb and, although it freezes quite well, it is best preserved in the Italian manner in olive oil.

Dried basil

Basil sauce (*pesto*)

Fresh basil

Parsley (*Petroselinum crispum*)
UMBELLIFERAE

One of the oldest and longest-used herbs, parsley is so widely used in Western cookery that to describe its flavour as fresh and piquant is to state the obvious. Its use certainly dates back to ancient Greece and Rome and it was known in Britain and France in medieval times. Of the many varieties of parsley grown, the curly-leaved type is most popular in Britain and North America, while flat-leaved parsley is better known in Europe, although their flavours are not markedly different. In Western cookery, parsley is used as both a flavouring and a garnish. A sprig or two is essential in the classic *bouquet garni* and also in marinades for fish and meat, and finely chopped, it is part of the *fines herbes* mixture. Its most extensive use is perhaps as chopped leaves in sauces; in Britain, it forms the basis of parsley sauce (eaten with fish) and in France it appears in *sauce tartare* and *sauce ravigote*, among others, and is used to flavour salad dressings, mayonnaise and herb butters. Finely chopped, it is used in stuffings, soups, stocks, with eggs, fish and all types of meat and vegetable dishes. A mixture of finely-chopped garlic (or shallot) and parsley is known in France as a *persillade* and is often added to dishes at the end of cooking to enhance both the flavour and appearance of the dish. It is similarly used in Italian cuisine with grated lemon or orange peel and garlic in the simple but richly-flavoured Milanese veal dish, *osso buco*. Rich in vitamin C and a good digestive, parsley freezes relatively well but is unsuccessful dried. However, since it is easily grown and readily available there is little need to use it other than fresh.

Dried parsley

Fresh parsley

Sage (*Salvia officinalis*) LABIATAE

Since Roman times at least, sage has been cultivated for its medicinal qualities and is still considered beneficial in warding off winter ills. As a culinary herb it has been known since the 16th century. There are a number of garden varieties, differing in the colour and shape of the leaves, but the type most frequently used has furry, greyish-green leaves and purple flowers. A northern Mediterranean plant, it grows wild in parts of Spain and Yugoslavia where its musky aroma can be smelt on hillsides near the coast. Sage has a slightly bitter musty flavour and in cooking its powerful aroma penetrates a dish. It helps to make rich meat and oily fish more digestible and is widely used in Italy with pork and veal dishes and with liver, the latter a most successful combination, often found on restaurant menus. In Britain, sage and onion is a traditional stuffing for duck, pork and goose and in Germany, Belgium and other parts of Europe, it flavours eels and mackerel and is used in spicy sausages and patés. Fresh sage leaves from the Mediterranean are fuller and better flavoured than those grown in more temperate climates. Sage freezes relatively well but dried and ground varieties often have a distinctly musty taste.

Powdered sage

Dried sage

Fresh sage

Tarragon (*Artemesia dracunculus*)
COMPOSITAE

One of the great culinary herbs, tarragon is used almost exclusively in French cookery. The herb's name, which comes from the Latin means 'little dragon' and probably derives from tarragon's legendary ability to cure the bites of snakes and other venomous creatures, although in medieval times it was used for heart and liver disorders. Tarragon has a delicate flavour which is quite unlike any other, yet it is remarkably powerful and unmistakable in dishes to which it is added. It is one of the herbs in *fines herbes* (along with parsley, chives and chervil), the finely-chopped, subtle blend of mixed herbs which flavours omelettes and delicate sauces for poultry and fish. Alone, tarragon flavours the famous sauce Bearnaise (served with fish and lamb), *poulet à l'estragon* (chicken in tarragon and cream sauce) and the spectacular chicken *chaudfroid* (whole chicken in chilled aspic sauce). It is used in sauces and butters for fish and eggs, in mayonnaise and salad dressings and to flavour mustards and vinegar. It is important to use French tarragon, (a long, thinned-leaved variety) rather than the Russian type which has broader leaves and a less pleasant flavour. Tarragon freezes and dries well.

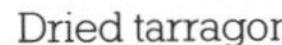

Dried tarragon

Thyme (*Thymus vulgaris*)
LABIATAE

This herb dates back to classical times when it was regarded as a symbol of courage in ancient Greece, burnt as incense in Roman times and used medicinally as an antiseptic. Garden thyme with its tiny, round, greyish-green leaves and pale pink flowers is the most common variety used in cooking but lemon thyme with its delicate citrus scent can also be used. Employed extensively in all Western cuisines, thyme's sharp, aromatic flavour adds warmth and pungency to marinades, stuffings, vegetables, fish and cheese dishes as well as all types of meat, game or poultry crockpot stews which are cooked slowly for a long time. A sprig of thyme is one of the basic herbs in the *bouquet garni* that flavours innumerable dishes and it is often combined with parsley and orange peel in Provençal beef *daubes* or stews which are cooked with wine and olives. Oils, vinegars and breads can also be flavoured with thyme. It freezes and dries well although some commercially produced dried varieties are often unpleasantly strong.

Dried thyme

Fresh tarragon

Fresh thyme

Rosemary (*Rosmarinus officinalis*)
LABIATAE

A Mediterranean plant, rosemary's name means 'dew of the sea' for it thrives on Mediterranean hillsides, especially on rocky areas near the sea. Like many other aromatic herbs from warm, dry climates, it is cultivated in cooler regions but tends to lose some of its flavour. In its wild state, rosemary has a powerful, faintly pine-like aroma with a strong, earthy taste reminiscent of camphor. Only a sprig of rosemary is needed to flavour a dish for its taste can overwhelm food if used in quantity. In Italy where it is particularly popular, it is used with pork and kid as well as roast lamb, a meat with which it has a special affinity. It can also happily add its distinctive taste to robust chicken and rabbit stews in combination with garlic and wine and be added to a *bouquet garni*. Rosemary's spiky leaves retain much of their flavour when dried, although in powdered form they can develop a bitter, acrid taste.

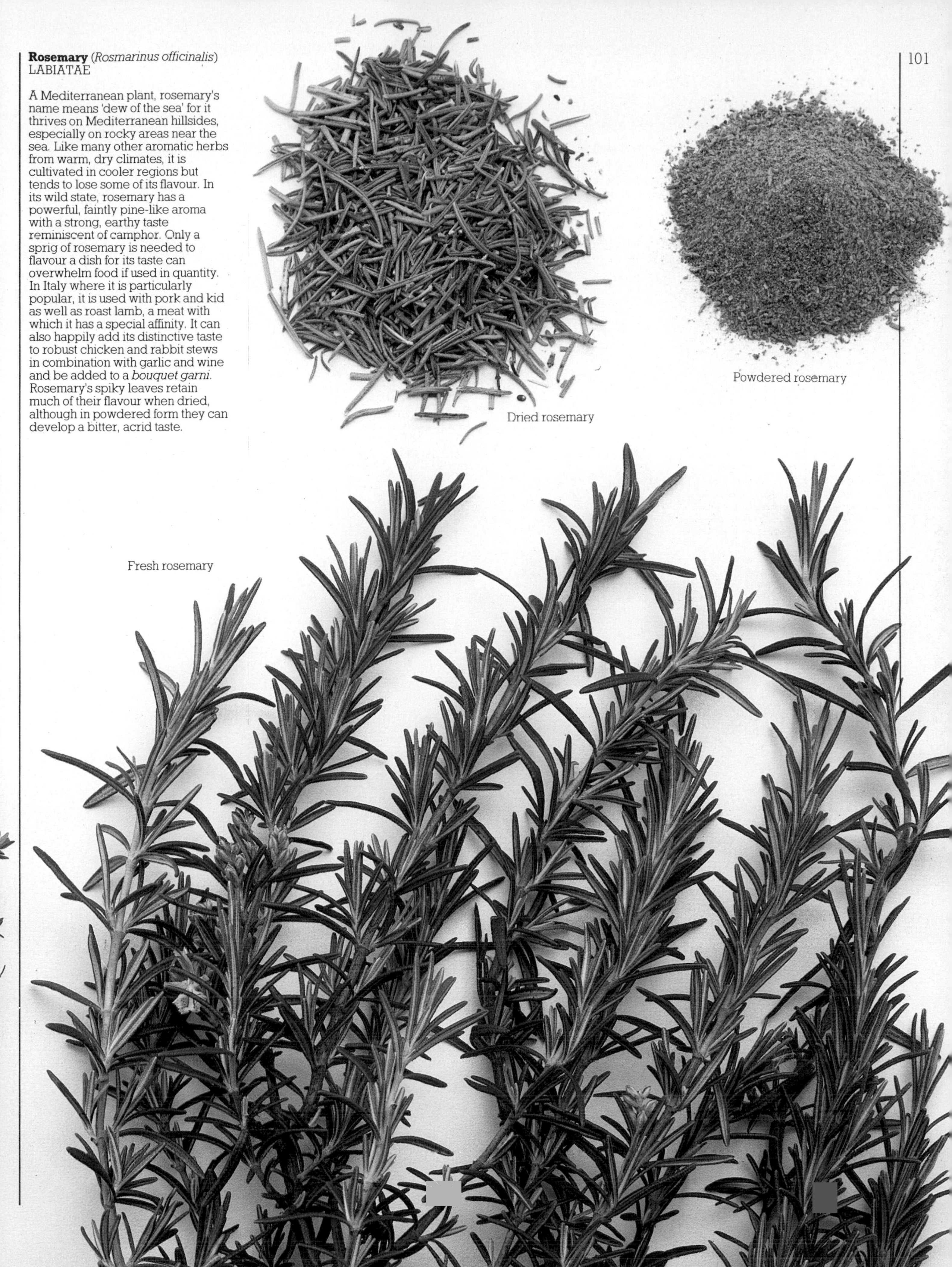

Dried rosemary

Powdered rosemary

Fresh rosemary

Citrus flavourings

All citrus fruits belong to the Rutaceae family and since earliest times, when citrons and lemons were used mainly as a souring agent and to add piquancy to food, they have provided the most important fruit flavourings in cookery. The use of sweet citrus fruits for eating and in sweet dishes is a relatively recent but significant development in culinary history. Both the juice and rind of citrus fruits have extensive culinary applications and are used worldwide in sweet and savoury sauces, added to cooked dishes and are important in preserves, baking and liqueurs.

All types of citrus fruits, including limes are widely available. Use hand or electric presses to extract the juices and a potato peeler or a special *canelle* knife (for *julienne* strips) to remove the rind, being careful to avoid the bitter white pith. Long strips can be hung to dry and used in a *bouquet garni*. To use citrus peel as a sweetener, rub a sugar lump over the peel before adding it to desserts. When using the flesh of citrus fruits in salads and desserts, remove all traces of bitter pith and ideally the white inner core and segment membranes as well as seeds. (*See also* Scented flavourings pages 126-128.)

Lime (*Citrus aurantifolia*)

Small, thin-skinned green fruit closely related to the lemon. Originally from India, the lime grows in tropical climates and in hot countries frequently replaces lemon in cooking. Lime has a stronger flavour than lemon with a sour, slightly bitter juice which is unmistakably different to lemon, as is evident in the sweetened lime juice syrups and cordials popular in Western countries. Limes are extensively used in Middle Eastern, Indian, south-east Asian, African and West Indian cookery as a souring agent and in chutneys and pickles. In Middle Eastern countries dried limes are often added to stews, while the hot lime pickles of India accompany curries and spiced dishes. Lime peel is used in sherbets and ice creams. In Thai cuisine, the rind and leaves of the knobbly Kaffir lime (*C. hystrix*) with its fragrant lemon verbena aroma, is used in curry pastes and sauces.

Limes

Lime pickle

Lemon (*Citrus limon*)

The highly scented fruit of a beautiful small tree with pretty, fragrant flowers and green leaves. Lemons grow only in subtropical regions and thrive in Mediterranean-type climates where they are cultivated in groves or orchards. The Romans knew the lemon, for it is depicted on one of the mosaics of Pompeii, and used it to sharpen sauces and spicy dishes as well as in medicinal remedies. It disappeared from Europe during the Dark Ages, was rediscovered at the time of the Crusades and was a commonplace fruit by the 16th century. Lemons have a sharp, sour taste, owing to their citric acid content and lemon juice has been used for centuries in European cookery as a souring and flavouring agent. It appears in sauces such as the Greek *avgolemono* (egg and lemon), in salads, all kinds of savoury dishes, in sweet desserts such as lemon meringue pie, as well as in jams and preserves and as a garnish. Lemon juice also prevents discolouration of sliced fruits and vegetables such as apples and artichokes and whitens and tenderizes the flesh of chicken and fish. Lemon's aromatic peel has always been important in Western cooking. Used in sauces, stuffings, marinades, salads, cakes and pastries, it adds a unique sharpness and aroma. In robust Provençal *daubes*, it is often added to the pot to enhance flavour and in the Italian *osso buco*, grated lemon rind with chopped parsley and garlic forms the *gremolata* sprinkled on the dish just before serving. Crystallized and candied lemon peel is used in traditional English baking, and the rind can, of course, be easily dried.

Lemons

Chinese dried lemon peel (Chuan-pei)

Preserved lemon peel

Preserved lemons

Ugli fruit (*Citrus* sp)

Rough-skinned fruit, native to the East Indies which is a hybrid between the grapefruit and tangerine. Its flesh is sweeter than the grapefruit's but sharper than the tangerine's. Used in the same way as grapefruit, it can be substituted for it to give an interesting sweet-sour flavour to jams and preserves, as well as sweet and savoury dishes.

Citron (*Citrus medica*)

The oldest of the sharp citrus fruits, similar in appearance to a large, rough-skinned lemon. It is said to have been cultivated in the Hanging Gardens of Babylon to make perfumed toilet waters. Nowadays, it is mainly cultivated in Mediterranean countries and in the West Indies. Unlike other citrus fruits, it is cultivated not for its flesh but for its thick, fragrant rind which is candied and used almost exclusively in cakes and confectionery. It plays an important role in the Jewish festival of Succoth.

Ugli fruit

Citron peel

Grapefruit (*Citrus paradisi*)

A large, round yellow or pink fruit from the East Indies, recognized only relatively recently (in the 1830s), as a species. Grapefruit has a sweet-sharp flavour which suggests that it may have developed as a hybrid of sweet orange and sour citron. Launched commercially in the 1880s, it has always been a popular fruit in North America (where 90 per cent is now grown) where it was probably first served as a breakfast appetizer with sugar. It features notably in slimming diets because it is thought to contain an enzyme which stimulates the metabolism. Grapefruit juice is a popular beverage in Western countries and the fruit and peel make an interesting marmalade. Recently a sweet pink variety has been produced in Texas which retains the fruit's characteristic flavour but without its traditional sharpness. Grapefruit is frequently used in both sweet and savoury salads and for a novel flavour can be substituted for lemons and oranges in many dishes.

Pink grapefruit

Grapefruit

Orange

Bitter or Seville orange (*Citrus aurantium*)

The oldest known orange brought to Europe from China and south-east Asia by Arab traders towards the end of the Roman Empire. Originally treasured for their scented flowers (used in perfumery and to flavour food) and aromatic rind, these are the oranges used by the Medicis on their coat of arms and later grown in tubs at Louis XIV's orangeries at Versailles. Nowadays, two main varieties of bitter orange are cultivated, the Bergamot orange (*C. bergamia*), used mainly for perfumery and its essential oils, and the Seville orange, which is unsuitable for eating raw but is produced for its flesh, which is used in marmalades, and its rind, which traditionally flavours classic sauces such as Cumberland and *bigarade* (for duck), and to add piquancy to fish and meat in southern France.

Sweet orange (*Citrus sinensis*)

The sweet eating orange from China introduced to Europe (Portugal) via India in the early 17th century. These were the kind of oranges which Nell Gwynne sold as a theatre refreshment only a few decades later before she was taken up by Charles II. Nowadays, sweet orange varieties are available which are usually relatively tight-skinned (eg Spanish and Jaffa) and used for juice and in salads and fruit salads. Blood oranges have a sweet juicy flesh flecked with red; and navel oranges peel easily, have few seeds and have a protrusion like a navel at one end. In French cookery, Maltese sauces use blood oranges, while sweet oranges are the ingredient in Mediterranean salads of oranges with olives, in the caramelized oranges of Italy and in the famous restaurant dish, *crêpes suzettes*, to name but a few of the uses of this most popular citrus fruit. The rind is also used in sweet baking, savoury dishes and in candied form.

Mandarin and tangerine (*Citrus reticulata*)

Small, loose-skinned oranges of Chinese origin introduced to Europe in the 19th century. These sweet oranges are usually eaten fresh but can be candied, glacéd or used to make liqueurs and marmalades. Dried tangerine peel is a common ingredient in many slow-cooked Chinese dishes. Clementines (*Citrus* sp) are a cross between the mandarin and the Seville orange developed in Algeria by a French priest. Père Clement. These have a slightly sharp, sweet flavour and although principally used as an eating fruit are ideal for orange sorbets and can be preserved in alcohol or made into syrup.

Mandarins

Preserved mandarin peel

Preserved orange peel

Kumquat (*Fortunella japonica*)

A tiny orange about the size of a large olive and known in Europe since the 17th century, kumquats have a crisp, agreeably tart flavour and can be eaten raw, rind and all. Fairly rare in the past, they are now more widely available from better greengrocers and market stalls. They are often used in fruit salads, in sauces for ham, pork and duck and make an attractive garnish.

Nuts

Nuts are seeds or fruits which consist of an edible kernel enclosed in a hard shell. Since earliest times, they have added their distinctive flavouring to both sweet and savoury dishes. Almonds are perhaps most widely used since they feature in almost every cuisine but others, such as pine nuts and pecans, have important flavouring uses in their countries of origin.

Nuts must be shelled and peeled before using. Pecans and brazils can be shelled more easily if allowed to stand in boiling water for about 20 minutes. To shell nuts such as almonds, pistachios and walnuts, pour boiling water over them and then place them in cold water. Shelled nuts can be roasted in the oven or browned in a frying pan with a little oil (but watch that they do not burn). Unshelled nuts keep well but once shelled, nuts quickly become stale and rancid. Keep them in airtight containers in a cool dark and dry place but use them up as soon as possible.

Almond (Sweet:*Prunus amygdalus 'dulcis'*;Bitter: *P. amygdalus 'amara'*) ROSACEAE

The fruit kernels of a beautiful peach-like tree which has grown in the Mediterranean basin and Asia Minor since at least classical times. In Christian ritual, the almond tree is symbolic of the Virgin Mary, denoting both fruitfulness and purity. Of the two types of nuts produced, it is the familiar sweet almond which is of major culinary importance. Bitter almonds contain prussic acid and are never eaten raw, but their essence can be distilled into a strong flavouring, similar to that produced from the kernels of peaches and other such fruits, sometimes used to flavour cakes and biscuits. Sweet almonds, on the other hand, are widely used whole, ground, roasted or slivered in an extensive range of sweet dishes and baking. Ground almonds, for example, flavour butters, pralines, fillings and nougats, while diced or whole almonds are added to cakes and confectionery. In southern Europe, the Middle East and North Africa, almonds flavour savoury dishes such as soups, fish, meat and rice dishes. In northern India and Kashmir, they are an ingredient in the delicately spiced pilaus and curries for which this area is noted. In the West, trout with almonds is just one of the many popular almond dishes, and sugared almonds are a traditional gift in Roman Catholic Spain, Italy and France at Christmas and for baptisms.

Whole almonds

Shelled almonds

Almond cakes

Chestnut (*Castanea sativa*) FAGACEAE

The nuts from the burr-like fruits of a majestic tree which grows all over southern Europe, North Africa and parts of the Middle East. A long-lived tree, venerated by the Greeks and Romans, it is a cheap source of fuel in the countries where it is abundant. Chestnuts, boiled, roasted or puréed, are used in many sweet dishes, in sauces, stuffings, as a vegetable (traditionally, in Britain, with Brussels sprouts) or as a garnish. In France, where canned sweetened or unsweetened chestnut purée is widely available, they are the basis of the delectable French pudding Mont Blanc and whole chestnuts are also preserved, once shelled, in the crystallized confection, *marrons glacés*.

Pine nut (*Pinus pinea*) PINACEAE

Seeds or kernels of several species of pine trees found in Europe (particularly the west coast of Italy), North and South America and parts of Asia. Whitish cream in colour and waxy, these tiny nuts have a distinctive, nutty flavour with the merest hint of pine. Once a delicacy in the cookery of ancient Rome, they are now traditionally associated with Italian cooking and are familiar, if expensive, items in Italian delicatessens. They are an ingredient in the famous Genoese *pesto* (fresh basil) sauce served with pasta and soups and in Italy they are also used with game, eggs and rice. In North Africa and the Middle East, they are also extensively used as a flavouring, roasted or ground, in soups, sauces, fish, meat, rice dishes and salads, and especially in stuffings for chicken and with minced lamb in *dolmades* (stuffed vine leaves), and in aubergines [eggplants], peppers and tomatoes.

Whole chestnuts

Dried chestnuts

Pine nuts

Chestnut purée

Sweetened chestnut purée

Peanut (*Arachis hypogaea*) LEGUMINOSAE

Not a true nut but the seeds from the pods of a legume native to South America and now grown in all suitable subtropical climates, including, notably, the southern states of the US. The tasteless peanut or arachide oil (also known as groundnut oil) is an important cooking and salad oil worldwide, and although whole, roasted or ground peanuts have been used in oriental and especially Indonesian cookery – most commonly in *saté* sauces – for centuries, they are best known in the West as a snack food and in peanut butter. In North America, a large portion of the peanut crop goes into the manufacture of peanut butter where it is used not merely as a spread but as an ingredient in cookies and confectionery. Unshelled peanuts for use in Indonesian dishes or home-made peanut butter can be bought from some health-food and oriental shops.

Whole peanuts

Shelled peanuts

Peanut oil

Peanut butter

Hazel, filbert or cob (*Corylus avellana*) BETULACEAE

Nuts of a hedgerow shrub or small tree of which there are many varieties, grown throughout Europe, the Middle East, Asia and North America. One of the seven sacred trees in Celtic mythology, it was also venerated as a symbol of wisdom by the ancient Greeks and early Christians, and its wood was later used for pilgrims' staffs and as divining rods. Ground hazelnuts are principally used in cakes and sweet dishes such as ice cream and in confectionery but are also added to savoury meat dishes, particularly in the Middle East, and to sauces and stuffings.

Hazelnuts

Brazil (*Bertholletia excelsa*)
LECYTHIDACEAE

The seed of a large impressive tree native to Central America and northern South America and taking its name from Brazil where it grows in abundance. These nuts, shaped like orange segments, are traditionally served as table nuts, mainly at Christmas. However, their interesting coconut flavour and creamy texture can be put to advantage in cakes and breads and as a substitute for other nuts in cooked dishes. They can also be preserved by salting, in common with many other nuts.

Brazil nuts

Shelled Brazil nuts

Walnut (*Juglans regia*)
JUGLANDACEAE

Nuts of a handsome, venerable tree, also known as the Persian nut tree, grown throughout Europe, the Middle East and in California. In ancient times, the walnut was attributed with magical healing properties, and in Roman wedding ceremonies, according to Ovid, bride and groom threw walnuts among children to symbolize their putting aside of childish pursuits. The walnut tree's wood has been prized by cabinet makers for centuries, and the versatile nut used in sweet and savoury dishes since time immemorial. A common flavouring in cakes and confectionery, walnuts are also pickled, added to salads and vegetables, made into liqueurs and used, particularly in the Middle East, in sauces and stuffings for fish, chicken and meat. Delicately-flavoured walnut oil, once used to light lamps in areas where the trees were abundant, has enjoyed a recent vogue as a cooking and salad oil.

Walnuts

Shelled walnuts

Walnut oil

Cashew (*Anacardium occidentale*)
ANACARDICEAE

The C-shaped nut of the edible fruit or cashew apple of a tree native to Brazil. Its English name derives from its Brazilian Indian names, *acaju* and *caju*, as it was known by the Portuguese. It has a refined flavour and creamy texture and although mainly used as snack food in the West, it is an important ingredient in Middle Eastern and oriental cuisines where it is used ground or roasted whole and added to soups, stews, vegetable and rice dishes. In Chinese cookery it flavours and gives texture to a variety of stir-fried dishes, of which chicken with cashew nuts is a particular favourite.

Pistachio (*Pistacia vera*)
ANACARDIACEAE

The nut of a deciduous tree cultivated throughout the Mediterranean and Middle East for thousands of years. It is said that the Queen of Sheba enjoyed the delicate mild flavour of this nut, and in the past it was used as a symbol of happiness. The flesh of pistachio is green (the greener the colour, the better the quality), and each nut is enclosed in a thin, wrinkled, red-brown skin encased in a bony tan shell which tends to split open. In Mediterranean regions, the Middle East – and increasingly elsewhere – they are eaten as a snack but are also widely used to flavour confectionery such as nougat, Turkish delight and *halva* and in the pistachio ice cream so popular in southern Europe and North America. In Middle Eastern countries, they are also used in sauces and stuffings and to flavour meat and game dishes.

Pecan (*Carya illinoensis*)
JUGLANDACEAE

The nut of a hickory tree which grows in central and southern states of North America. Pecans have elongated, mottled brown shells and are varied in size. Their flavour is similar to that of walnuts although the pecan is much oilier and contains valuable protein. (One Spanish explorer noted that American Indians were able to survive for two months by eating these nuts alone, as they did in lean winters). In North America, pecans are eaten in great quantities as dessert nuts and are also widely used chopped or whole in cakes, pies, ice cream and confectionery. Pecan pie is the best-known use of this nut. A festive stuffing for roast turkey can also include chopped pecans.

Coconut (*Cocos nucifera*)
PALMACEA

The large brown nutshell, containing white flesh and milk, of a tropical palm native to Malaysia. Its oil is important in the production of vegetable shortenings and margarines, soaps, shampoos and other commercial products, while its leaves, husk and wood are widely used in its countries of origin for timber, thatching, floor coverings and baskets. The coconut's flesh is commonly available in the West in desiccated form and used in sweet dishes and candy but in southern India and south-eastern Asia, coconut milk, extracted from the white flesh, flavours all kinds of food including soups, fish, meat and vegetable dishes such as curries and chutneys. Creamed coconut, for use in such dishes, can be bought in block-shaped packets from Indian and oriental shops.

Cashew nuts

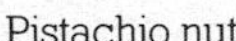

Pistachio nuts

Pecan nuts

Creamed coconut

Coconut milk
Flaked coconut
Desiccated coconut

Honeys and syrups

Honey and different kinds of sugar syrups are important sweet flavourings in the kitchen where their particular flavours – ranging from the scented honeys and the butterscotch-like golden syrup to the raw, slightly bitter taste of molasses – add individuality and interest to a wide variety of dishes. Unlike refined sugars, honeys, treacles, molasses and maple syrup contain minerals and vitamins and are increasingly used by health-conscious cooks as sweetening agents in place of sugar.

Honey is also sweeter than sugar so use less of it than you would sugar. Fine honeys should only be used for spreading or for uncooked toppings since cooking drives off some of honey's aroma and flavour and the liquid caramelizes. Because honeys and syrups are liquid sweeteners rather than solid ingredients, the liquid content of a recipe needs to be reduced when they are used as a substitute for sugar. Honeys and syrups store well, although the colour and flavour of honey tends to change if stored too long because it crystallizes and hardens with age. Maple syrup, once opened, is best kept in the refrigerator.

Honey The world's oldest sweetening substance produced from the nectar of bees. It is only in the last 200 years that honey has been superseded by the more versatile but less aromatic refined sugar. Honey was the basis of mead, the first alcoholic beverage drunk in northern Europe, and in classical times, honey from Mount Hymettus in Greece was celebrated in literature. In Spain, the Moors used it in a sweetmeat made with almonds, called *turrón*, still eaten today. Honey is gathered throughout the world wherever there are flowering plants, shrubs and trees and bees to feed upon them. It is produced in a bewildering variety of flavours, textures and colours, mostly dependent on the flowers it comes from. Essentially, honey can be divided into two types: Blended honeys and Single flower honeys. *Blended honeys* These contain the produce of many hives feeding on different flowers in different geographical regions. No single flavour or aroma dominates; colour and consistency (whether thin or thick) are uniform. This is the type widely available in supermarkets and stores and purchased for general household and culinary uses. *Single flower honeys* Honeys such as rosemary, thyme or acacia can be likened to fine wines. Flavour and aroma are the most important characteristics which, with colour and consistency, will differ from flower to flower, climate and geographical location also having a subtle but definable effect. These are honeys for the connoisseur and among the most prized are the rare *Pohutakawa*

Honeycomb

Amber eucalyptus

Hungarian acacia

Orange blossom

Buckwheat

honey from New Zealand which has an unusual salty flavour; the *Tasmanian leatherwood*, a light-coloured, delicately flavoured honey from Australia; and the almost pure white honey from Mexico, *aguinaldo*. Among the many varieties of honey are *clover*, mild, pale amber in colour and popular in Europe and North America;*heather* which is red and a British and European favourite; *hymettus*, the highly prized Greek honey with an aromatic flavour of wild thyme; the pale, delicately-flavoured *orange blossom*, popular in North America, eastern Europe and South Africa; *buckwheat*, the deep-brown, strongly flavoured honey from California used in honey cakes and wine; *eucalyptus* honey from Australia which comes in many varieties with a range of colours and flavour; *acacia*, a pale, thin and delicately flavoured honey, especially in Hungarian varieties.

Honey is widely used in European and North American cakes and puddings and in Middle Eastern and Indian sweets such as *baklava* and *halva*. It is also used in savoury dishes to flavour ham, chicken or duck, in marinades and sauces, especially sweet-sour types. One of its main uses in the West is as a spread or topping.

Tasmanian leatherwood

Greek hymettus

Honeys and syrups

Golden syrup A light, sweet syrup, gold in colour with a butterscotch flavour, produced during the sugar refining process. In Britain, golden syrup is popular as a spread for bread and biscuits and is frequently used in baking and confectionery such as toffees. It is used in English gingerbreads and is the major ingredient in treacle tart where it is combined with fresh breadcrumbs and flavoured with lemon rind and orange juice. Warmed golden syrup combined with lemon juice or butter can be used as a sauce for pancakes, sponge puddings and ice creams.

Treacle A blend of refinery syrups and extract molasses. Treacles vary from transparent, dark brown syrups to a dark, almost black syrup, which is also known as West Indian treacle. Treacles generally have a strong, sweet taste and are used in rich fruit cakes, gingerbreads and in spicy sauces for baking ham, apples and other foods. They are also used in confectionery.

Molasses Dark sugar-cane syrup of two types. Mild-flavoured molasses, often used as a table syrup, may be a blend of syrups from different varieties of cane, or a blend of refinery syrups. Blackstrap molasses, which is thicker, stronger and darker, is the concentrated syrup left over after sugar has been refined. It contains about 50 per cent sugar with minerals and organic materials. Being nutritionally rich, it is an important health food and is sometimes used in British cakes and breads where it improves their keeping qualities. It was the source of Medford rum made in New England in the early 17th century and is an ingredient in many traditional New England dishes such as Boston brown bread and Boston baked beans.

Maple syrup A brown syrup produced from the sap mainly of two species of the North American maple tree. Maple syrup has a smooth, rich taste rather like rum and is principally used as a sauce for pancakes, ice cream and waffles. It has a special affinity with nuts such as pecans and walnuts, a combination often celebrated in the sweet pastry tarts of North America. It is also used to flavour cake fillings and icings and in confectionery. Although seldom used in savoury dishes, its sweet, assertive flavour goes well with bacon and sausages and it is sometimes used in marinades for American spare ribs.

English heather honey

Pohutukawa honey (New Zealand)

Molasses

Maple syrup

Golden syrup

Fruit syrups Concentrated syrups made with sugar and the juice of fruits or flowers. The best known syrups are blackcurrant (cassis), pomegranate (grenadine) and rose hip but syrups are also made from cherries, strawberries, lemons, oranges, almonds and violets. Syrups are popular in France and Italy, and are sometimes used for dessert sauces or mixed with carbonated water to make a refreshing drink.

Grenadine

Blackcurrant (cassis) syrup

Canadian clove honey

Mexican honey

Treacle

Wines, spirits and beers

The use of alcohol in cooking dates back to early times. The Roman gourmet, Apicius, writing in the first century BC, records an astonishing variety of wine sauces, not only for meat and fish but also for cucumbers, asparagus, leeks and peas stewed in 'raisin' wine (made from muscatel grapes); wine sweetened with honey had a multitude of uses and even rose and violet wines feature in his recipes. The ancient Egyptians may have cooked with beer and certainly in medieval times, the peasant dishes of Britain and northern Europe contained it. The use of spirits and liqueurs is of relatively recent origin since these were not really developed until after the invention of distillation in the 12th century. However, early 15th century recipes tell how to pour brandy over chicken dishes (seasoned with spices and nuts) and set it alight. Since then cooks have improved on and refined these culinary traditions and created new ones so that, in many cuisines – particularly in wine-producing countries – alcohol and cooking are inseparable.

Once opened, a bottle of wine does not keep unless it is absolutely airtight. Recorking the bottle will help, as will plastic film but it is advisable to use up wine for cooking as quickly as possible. Cooking wine, however humble, should also be drinking wine, not sour or 'corked' which will add no distinction to a dish. Fortified wines such as sherry and port keep for about three weeks once opened, while spirits and liqueurs keep indefinitely.

Wine Traditionally used in the cookery of France, Spain, Italy and Greece and in other wine-producing regions of the world. It could be argued that the classic European cuisines of France and Italy owe their distinction to the wine used in both marinades and cooked dishes where its characteristic flavour adds richness and body to a wide variety of dishes. Drinking wine, with its alcoholic content and acidity, undergoes certain changes when subjected to heat. The alcohol evaporates and the essential quality of the particular wine remains to flavour and permeate the dish. When using wine in cooking, it is vital that the wine is cooked in either the long, simmering process or by boiling and reduction as in fish stocks or wine sauces. Raw acidic drinking wine does not help the flavour of any dish. Red and white wines with varying degrees of sweetness, as well as fortified wines, are extensively used in all types of food from soups to desserts. The French, in particular, have used red and white wines in cooking to such an extent that some dishes and sauces are impossible without them; frequently, they transform simple regional dishes into gastronomic feasts.

Red wine The wine used in cooking is usually dry, varying from light to full-bodied with its particular aromas and flavours varying according to the grape used in production, climatic and soil conditions and methods of viniculture. Fine, full-bodied red wines such as Chambertin (from Burgundy), Barolo (from Italy) or Cahors (from south-west France) each have a unique flavour and bouquet which is utilized in the dishes of the region. Burgundian dishes such as *coq au vin* and *boeuf à la bourguignonne* use local red wines. Bordeaux red wines flavour *sauce bordelaise* (with meat glaze, garlic and parsley) and *sauce marchand de vin*, a simple red wine flavoured with shallots. In other regions of France, red wine tenderizes and flavours casseroled pigeons and hearty Mediterranean chicken and beef stews; vegetables such as leeks and onions are braised in it and fruit such as pears and peaches are poached in it. In Greece, Italy and Spain, it is used almost as extensively but particularly with game such as hare, venison and kid. A leg of lamb, marinated for several days in red wine, will taste like venison, a discovery made by many traditional wine-producing regions. In all such regions, the addition of wine to savoury dishes is so habitual that there are few dishes that it does not enhance. Red wine vinegar is a popular culinary ingredient in France and Italy.

White wine White wines vary from light, dry wines such as Chablis and Verdicchio to the fruity wines from Alsace and Germany and the sweet rich Sauternes and Barsacs. Dry and slightly fruity wines feature in many fish and chicken dishes. *Moules marinière* (mussels), for example, are cooked in a white wine broth; sole and other delicate fish are frequently poached in a white wine and water stock; in sauces for veal, pork and chicken white wine is often boiled with the cooking juices to produce a thick, fragrant syrup; and white wine is traditionally added to the cheese fondues of Switzerland. Soft sweet wines, including not only Sauternes but also many German wines, usually flavour fruits such as pears, peaches and plums but are occasionally added in small quantities to sauces for duck or shellfish such as scallops. In the Dordogne region of France, for example, a local sweet wine called Montbazillac flavours a sauce for another speciality of the region, *magret de canard* (duck breast). White wine vinegar, often flavoured with tarragon, is popular internationally and is ideal for salad dressings and mayonnaise.

Fortified wines So called because of the addition of a little spirit (often brandy) to give a fuller, richer flavour and higher alcoholic content. *Madeira* from the Portuguese island of that name varies in sweetness and has been an important culinary ingredient for centuries. It is traditionally used to flavour consommés and aspics, while kidneys, ham, tongue and game are often served in a Madeira sauce. *Marsala*, from southern Italy and Sicily, is usually rather sweet but features heavily in Italian cookery where its best-known use is in veal marsala and in the frothy egg dessert, *zabaglione*. *Port*, which also varies in sweetness, is important in British cookery where it flavours jugged hare, Cumberland sauce and various sauces for game and lamb, often combined with redcurrant jelly. It is sometimes used to flavour melon (in France) and to refresh an aging Stilton cheese. *Sherry* is principally used in soups and in English desserts such as trifle and syllabub, to which it is added uncooked. In the West it often replaces rice wines in Chinese and Japanese cookery since the flavours are similar.

Spirits Alcoholic liquids, obtained by distillation from wine, grains, sugar and rice etc. *Brandy* is without doubt the most important spirit used in cooking. Since the time when cognac and armagnac were first distilled from wine in south-west France, it has been added to food to flavour and tenderize it. It is added to patés and a variety of fish and shellfish (lobster, prawns [shrimp] and scallops are frequently flambéed in it), as well as countless chicken and meat dishes. It appears, for example, in Chateaubriand steak, in the Gascon version of beef *en daube* and as an ingredient in many sauces for grilled meats when, at least in some restaurants, it is flamboyantly set alight to burn away the alcohol and leave a highly aromatic but delicate, faintly caramel sauce. In sweet dishes, it flavours creams, soufflés, omelettes, cakes and biscuits and is used to preserve and flavour all kinds of fruits. In Britain and North America, brandy sauce is a hard brandy-flavoured butter used mainly for mince pies and Christmas pudding. *Calvados*, the apple brandy from Normandy, has a distinctive aroma and taste which enhances dishes such as *faisan à la Normande* (pheasant with cream, apples and Calvados sauce) and a luscious dessert, the sweet Calvados omelette, where it is again combined with apples. *Rum*, distilled from fermented sugar cane, is a well-known flavouring in sweet dishes such as creams and with fruits such as pineapple and bananas and it is used in cakes and confectionery where it combines well with chocolate. In the Caribbean, it gives an interesting flavour to a number of savoury dishes such as the spicy 'calypso' sauce served with roast pork and it is often used with duck or chicken. While white rum is principally used in punches and drinks, it is the dark, strongly-flavoured rum that is mostly used in the kitchen.
Vermouth is a white wine in which various spices and roots have been infused. Sauces for fish and white meats such as chicken are often flavoured with vermouths to add an interesting herbal fragrance and a rich, smooth taste.

Anise-flavoured cordials are are popular in France and frequently used to flavour sauces for fish or seafood dishes.

Liqueurs Usually extracts from fruits blended with a spirit such as brandy and frequently sweetened with sugar syrups. Some of the better-known fruit liqueurs are Cointreau (based on oranges), kirsch (made from cherries) and *Crême de menthe* (made from peppermint). Not all liqueurs are used in cooking and cherry- and orange-based ones probably have the widest application in the kitchen. *Cherry-flavoured liqueurs* It is important to note that kirsch, made from black cherries, is dry while other cherry spirits such as maraschino and cherry brandy are sweeter (although each has a different flavour). Kirsch has an affinity with pineapples, cherries, bananas and strawberries. In France, it often flavours chestnuts, while peaches flambéed in kirsch has been a popular restaurant dish for over 100 years. Used in creams and confectionery, it also occasionally flavours meat and chicken dishes. *Orange-flavoured liqueurs* Based on bitter oranges and often including the peel, these include Cointreau, Curaçao and Grand Marnier. Widely used in sweet soufflés, as a sauce for dessert pancakes such as *crêpes suzettes* and to flavour orange sauces for fruit salads, strawberries and peaches. Less sweet varieties also enhance traditional orange sauces for duck and game. *Tia Maria* The Jamaican liqueur of rum and spices flavours creams for desserts and cakes and is particularly good in hot chocolate sauces.

Beer and cider Produced from hops and apples respectively. *Beer* This has long been employed in the cooking of Germany and northern Europe just as wine has been in southern Europe, while in Britain, where ale and stout are traditional drinks, it appears in a small repertoire of dishes. Beer's bitter hop flavouring can add interest to dishes but it lacks wine's versatility and refinement and its main use is in robust country dishes. Beer soup has long been drunk in Germany and recipes dating back to the Middle Ages include beer. In Britain, Welsh rarebit is well known but beer or stout also flavours 'hunter's' stews of beef or game, Christmas puddings and cakes once used beer for colour and flavouring and in Ireland, herrings are potted in Guinness. Perhaps the most familiar beer dish worldwide is the Flemish *carbonnade de boeuf*, a dark and richly flavoured stew. Further north, the Danes add beer to their soups and in Sweden, it is blended with molasses to make a bread. Beer's use in cooking is overlooked nowadays, but in the past, it was used in marinades to tenderize meat and for basting to give an attractive glaze and colour. *Cider* Commonly used in northern French cooking to replace wine, often in combination with apples, it particularly enhances pork but is also added to chicken and fish dishes. In Britain and North America, cider sauces traditionally flavour ham and a sweet cider sauce with sultanas and cloves sometimes flavours puddings.

Milk products

Milk has been used for as long as milk-producing animals have been domesticated, but while milk itself is an essential ingredient in a wide range of dishes, it is by-products such as creams and yogurts that are used to add a special and distinctive flavour to many sweet and savoury foods.

Fresh cream will keep for 2 or 3 days in a refrigerator but will harden unless kept covered; sour cream keeps for up to 5 or 6 days. When beating cream, be careful not to over-whip it in case the cream becomes buttery. Most bought yogurts keep for about 5 days in the refrigerator, although yogurt enthusiasts can easily make their own using special yogurt starter cultures or commercially produced natural yogurt. Home-made yogurt will keep in the refrigerator for up to 10 days. In cooked dishes, always add creams and yogurts towards the end of the cooking time and make sure the heat is low to avoid curdling.

Cream The fat that rises to the surface of milk as it cools which is skimmed off to produce butter or cream. When fresh and unadulterated with other flavourings, cream has a concentrated rich 'dairy' flavour faintly reminiscent of the natural pastures on which the cows have grazed. Despite its own special flavour, it enhances other ingredients and in savoury dishes, it thickens and enriches them while adding its own smooth taste. For cakes and desserts, it is often combined with sweet spices such as vanilla (in *crème chantilly*) or mixed with sweet fruits for puddings or toppings. The fat content of cream varies from country to country and largely determines cream's culinary use. In Britain, single cream is a thin liquid used with coffee and poured over desserts. Richer and thicker double [heavy] cream can be used in semi-liquid form or whipped for spreading or toppings, as can 'whipping' cream which has a slightly lower fat content. Clotted cream, made from cream which is scalded, skimmed and cooled quickly is invariably used as a sweet

Single cream

Milk

Double (heavy) cream

Whipping cream

topping or dessert cream. *Crème fraiche*, a thick cream much used in France and often specified in recipes, has a lively flavour which is slightly sour, making it ideal for the wide variety of savoury cream sauces used in traditional French cookery.

Sour cream Cream inoculated with a lactic acid culture to give this thick cream its agreeable, slightly acid flavour. In the days before pasteurization and refrigeration, cream which was spoiled was not thrown away but utilized by the Russians and other Eastern Europeans to flavour the famous beetroot soup, *borsch*, and beef stroganoff as well as many vegetables and paprika-flavoured dishes. Known also as *smetana*, sour cream is now commercially produced and can be used in a wide variety of dishes, including soups, stews such as goulash, with cucumbers and other vegetables and, often in combination with chives, as a salad dressing for, especially, potatoes.

Yogurt Milk inoculated with different types of lactic acid to make a semi-solid creamy curd. According to an ancient Eastern legend, the patriarch Abraham is said to have invented yogurt after an angel whispered to him the secret of souring milk. Although yogurt is now eaten all over the world, it is traditionally associated in its various forms with southern Russia, the Balkans, the Middle East, North Africa and India. Yogurt has a pleasantly acid, rather than sour, flavour and sheeps' milk is said to make the finest type although it is, of course, more commonly made with cows' milk in the West and in India with buffaloes' milk. It can be eaten plain but often has honey or fruit added to it. In the Middle East, it is a flavouring in cakes and sweets with dried fruits and nuts, and is added to savoury dishes such as lamb and chicken. In India and Pakistan, it is an ingredient in curries and *pilaus*, in Indian vegetarian food and is the basis of various *raitas*, the cooling relishes served with Indian curries. Yogurt can also be used, like sour cream, as a salad dressing. It is easily made at home with either bought yogurt or yogurt culture.

Buttermilk The sour milk residue left over from butter-making but now commonly made from pasteurized skimmed milk. It makes a refreshing drink and its slightly sour flavour gives a special taste and extremely light texture to scones, griddle cakes, breads and cakes.

Sour milk drinks Sour milk products are made into a number of cooling drinks in many parts of Asia and the Middle East. *Dough* (from Iran) and *laban* are refreshing beverages of yogurt beaten with salt, water and sometimes crushed mint, often sold by street vendors or available as bottled soft drinks. In India, *lassi* is a similar yogurt drink but cumin-flavoured. *Kefir*, a popular drink in Eastern Europe, is made from fermented cows' milk and is sour and slightly alcoholic. Fermentation is started by dried grains known as kefir grains.

Soured cream

Plain and fruit yoghurts

Laban

Buttermilk

Meat, fish and vegetable extracts

Concentrates of meats, fish and vegetables have been used for centuries to season and flavour food and although once produced in the kitchen, these food extracts are now largely made commercially. The ancient Greeks and Romans produced sauces from the juice of dried and fermented fish which were widely used in cookery, particularly in Roman times, to season seafoods and meats and as a dressing for salads. Today, in China and south-eastern Asia, preparations remarkably similar to these ancient condiments are used. Recipes for 'stock cubes' exist from the 17th and 18th centuries when they were useful for travellers and, of course, for long sea voyages. One French recipe of 1769 recommends these home-made cubes as 'easy to carry . . . and will keep for 100 years or more.' In theory, food extracts such as concentrated beef pastes and stock cubes are made from the natural juices of the particular animal or vegetable, but colourings, spices, salt and monosodium glutamate (to intensify flavour) and sometimes preservatives are now also added. According to the degree of evaporation, a moist or dry extract can be obtained.

Fish pastes and sauces keep indefinitely, as do yeast and malt extracts. Stock cubes can absorb moisture in damp conditions and should always be kept dry, preferably in airtight containers.

Chicken extract cubes

Vegetable extract cubes

Meat extracts Obtained principally from beef by various chemical processes and first developed by the German chemist, Justus von Liebig at Fray Bentos, Uruguay in 1847. He found that if raw meat is ground with water, the resulting liquid contains about 20 per cent meat. When this is further processed and concentrated, a thick, dark brown, salty paste with the smell and taste of meat remains. It takes 32lbs (14kg) of meat to produce 1lb (½kg) of extract. One of the best known brands of beef extract in Britain is Bovril, first made in Quebec in 1874 and then known as 'Johnston's Fluid Beef'. Although principally used as a beverage, small quantities can be added to soups, sauces, stews and gravies for flavouring but note that the taste is rather pronounced.

Stock cubes Dehydrated extracts from the juices of meat, fish or vegetables. These have been made in the kitchen since the 17th century at least and were an obvious bonus to travellers and seamen on long voyages, since they kept for over a year and merely needed water to rehydrate them. In old recipes, the meat or vegetable product was boiled in water for about 6 hours, put through a press and the resulting liquid allowed to dry. Today, commercially produced stock cubes are convenient aids in the kitchen, and vegetable, fish, chicken, beef and lamb cubes are commonly available. Precise ingredients differ according to the manufacturer and some are more highly seasoned and pungent than others. Many also contain flavour enhancers such as monosodium glutamate (MSG), artificial colouring and preservatives. It is important to experiment with different brands until you find ones which have the genuine flavour of what they purport to represent. Health-food shops are a good source of fish and vegetable cubes or powders which are free from additives. Although very convenient, stock cubes have a distinctive taste which will be obvious in delicate sauces or soups. Generally, only half a cube is needed in most dishes, and rarely more than one.

Malt extracts Made by soaking powdered malt in water, filtering and finally evaporating it to a syrup or paste. Malt extract, a brown, sticky substance contains malt sugar which is less sweet than cane sugar, and malt retains moisture so it is often added to breads and cakes. It also releases carbon dioxide during proving and baking which helps dough to rise. It imparts a distinctive 'malty' flavour to food, quite apart from its sweetness.

Malted milk Originally developed as a nutritious drink for invalids and infants in the mid-19th century, malted milk has long been a popular drink in the soda fountains of North America and elsewhere; in Britain powdered Horlicks (of late 19th century origin) is mainly thought of as a comforting, bedtime beverage. In North America in particular malted milk products are used in crackers, biscuits, cake mixes, creams and fillings as well as in ice cream.

Yeast extracts A paste produced when yeast cells are broken down and the resulting liquid drawn off for evaporation. Yeast extracts, with a taste similar to meat extracts, are a good source of Vitamin B and are principally used for spreading on bread or crackers, or to flavour soups and stews, particularly in vegetarian cookery. They are commonly available in health food shops and in Britain under the brand names, Marmite and Vegemite.

Fish extracts Pastes or sauces produced from fermented, dried or salted fish used principally in Chinese and south-east Asian cookery. *Balachan*, essential in Burmese and Malay cuisines is composed of prawns [shrimp] and salt allowed to ferment in the sun and then mashed into a paste. Its strong smell disappears in cooking, leaving a delicate taste and aroma which flavours meat and poultry dishes. *Shrimp paste* and *dried shrimp* flavour Chinese and south-east Asian food where they are added in small quantities to soups and stews to bring out the flavour of other ingredients. *Fish sauces* (*nam pla*), the fermented juice of salted fish, gives Thai food its characteristic flavour. Similar in colour to light soy sauce, it has a faint smell of overripe cheese but adds a delicate flavour to dishes, and is also used as a dipping sauce. *Anchovy pastes and sauces* were commonly used in Victorian times to flavour meat and fish and can still be added to good effect to sharpen or heighten the flavours of meat, fish and poultry.

Beef extract cubes

Horlicks malted milk drink
Yeast extracts
Malt extract
Fish paste
Anchovy paste
Mackerel sauce
Balachan
Anchovy sauce

Scented flavourings

Although scented food is now unfashionable, the use of perfumed waters in cooking is very old. One suspects that when sweet fragrances were first popular in the Middle Ages they were used to disguise slightly rancid, tough or old ingredients but by the 17th century in England, rose water, for one, was included in a number of sophisticated dishes such as spiced cakes and knotted biscuits, and in a wonderful egg and cream boiled pudding called 'quaking pudding', which was also served with a rose water and sugar sauce. Early recipes which often include rose water in sauces for chicken and other white meats, are a good source of imaginative ways to use scented waters.

Orange and rose are the most commonly used scents in cooking and both are essential store cupboard items in the Middle East and India. You can, of course, make your own rose and orange water by infusing the petals or blossoms in boiling water or, for convenience, they can be bought at Middle Eastern or Indian food shops. Although scented waters can be purchased from pharmacists, they are designed mainly for toiletries so check that the waters are unadulterated and suitable for consumption.

Orange blossoms and orange flower water (*Citrus* spp) RUTACEAE

These are common flavourings in Middle Eastern cuisines. Orange flower water is produced in many countries, particularly in France, but mainly as a toilet water. In the Middle East, however, it adds a delicate perfume to syrups, pastries, puddings, fruit dishes and confectionery. A drop or two is sometimes added to Turkish coffee and it adds an interesting fragrance to salad dressings and stews. In the Lebanon, a teaspoonful with boiling water in a coffee cup provides a soothing and digestive drink known as 'white coffee'. The best orange water is said to come from Cyprus and it is advisable to buy it from Middle Eastern food shops rather than chemists. Orange flowers themselves are the ingredient in a jam popular in Iran and other parts of the Levant. (*See also* Citrus flavourings pages 102-107.)

Scented-leaved geraniums (*Pelargonium* spp) GERANIACEAE

Of the variously scented geraniums mainly used in perfumery, only one variety, the rose-scented geranium, with its delicate rose-water scent has an interesting if not very common culinary use. It is the leaves, not the flowers, which provide the fragrance just as they turn yellow and before the plant flowers. In England in Victorian times, the fresh leaves flavoured milk puddings, custards, jellies and fruit punches, for which they can still be used today. When crushed, they make a sweetly scented butter for cake fillings or a spread, and they have a special affinity with blackberries when added to stewed fruit. Modern cookery writers have also combined them with lemons and apples in sorbets and jellies.

Rose petals

Orange water

Scented-leaved geraniums

Rose petals and water (*Rosa* spp)
ROSACEAE

This is the oldest culinary perfume, which has lent aroma to drinks and sweet dishes for centuries. The Persians, who made rose petal wine, were exporting rose water to China at the time of Christ, while to this day, the Chinese produce a rose-flavoured liqueur, called *Mei Kwei Lu* (rose dew) which is wonderfully scented, very potent and served as a digestive or used to flavour some pork dishes. The Romans put rose petals in their wine and in Elizabethan times in England, rose water flavoured many sweet dishes. Rose petals are now principally used in the rose petal jam renowned in Bulgaria, Turkey and the Middle East. Honey is often flavoured with roses and the Bulgarians make a very sweet liqueur from them. Rose water and rose essence are especially important in Indian sweet cookery where they appear in sherbets and many other puddings. *Gulab jamun* is a famous Indian dessert of deep-fried milk balls in a rose-flavoured syrup. In the Middle East, rose water is used to scent syrups, pastries, puddings and drinks, often in combination with orange water or as a substitute for it, and also as a glaze for chicken. In the West, crystallized rose petals make an appearance in confectionery and the great food writer, Elizabeth David, mentions laying rose petals on the fruit of a cherry pie before closing it with pastry, a use first recorded in the 16th century. Although not a common vinegar, rose-petal vinegar (made with an infusion of the petals) is agreeable in a salad of mixed green, slightly bitter leaves.

Violet (*Viola odorata*)
VIOLACEAE

Violet is a once-popular flavouring with few culinary uses nowadays. Violet water can be made by infusing the flowers and is sometimes used to flavour cream, sorbets and liqueurs. Its principal use is in crystallized form where the petals decorate cakes, puddings and confectionery and the cloyingly sweet, violet-coloured liqueur, *parfait d'amour* is made from it. Young fresh leaves and flowers can be used in salads and make an attractive garnish.

Parfait d'amour liqueur

Rose water

Crystallized violet petals

Crystallized rose petals

Rose petal vinegar

Buying, storing and preparation

Today, spices and flavourings are widely used in the kitchen and are readily available at reasonable prices in supermarkets and grocery stores. Most people buy common spices such as cloves, cinnamon and peppercorns from such outlets and also dried flavouring herbs such as oregano, rosemary and bay leaves, but are usually obliged to go to specialist [gourmet] shops for Indian and oriental spices or for more unusual kinds. (*See* Specialist suppliers, pages 140-141.)

Buying spices and dried herbs

Common spices and flavourings are usually prepackaged in attractive glass jars or in packets and purchased at large grocery stores or in supermarkets. This is a perfectly acceptable and practical way of acquiring them since large shops generally have a fairly rapid turnover of such products and you can usually be assured that the jars have not been sitting on the shelves for too many months. This is not always so when you buy herbs or spices from small corner shops, whose customers are more likely to be cooks in an emergency. Admittedly, whole seeds and berries such as peppercorns do have a long shelf life and many will keep indefinitely if kept airtight and, specifically, away from the light – this is not possible when, for obvious reasons, they are on display. Before buying herbs and spices, check that they are a good colour and not faded, that whole spices have not become powdery and that they have the distinctive aroma of the ingredient without any musty undertones.

Remember too, that because spices may come from third world countries where they are harvested in archaic conditions, there can be a risk of contamination when buying loose spices. Packaged spices are cleansed both physically and bacteriologically and are safe to use in food. This is the main reason why packaged products are of a higher price.

Buying fresh herbs and flavourings

Garlic, onions, horseradish, ginger and onions are commonly used fresh and with the exception of horseradish (which can be grown) are easily available in markets and from greengrocers and supermarkets. Herbs, such as mint, basil, thyme and tarragon, should always be used fresh for the finest flavour and these too are increasingly easy to buy, or may be grown without difficulty in kitchen gardens or in containers. When these are unavailable, use home-dried herbs or imported ones from the Mediterranean and dried on their stalks. Remember, though, that while the above herbs dry relatively well, they cannot always be substituted for fresh ingredients; a *pesto* sauce, for example, is impossible without quantities of fresh basil.

Dried herbs become stale and flavourless much quicker than spices and should really be used within a couple of months of drying, otherwise they lose much of their potency and begin to smell hay-like. Bear in mind also that dried herbs bought at the beginning of summer will already be nine months old, since they would have been harvested in early autumn. Dried herbs are therefore best used over the winter months.

Buying Eastern and oriental spices

For Middle Eastern, Indian and oriental spices, it is essential to go to shops specializing in ethnic foodstuffs. These can sometimes be purchased loose in whatever quantity you want or, more commonly, are packaged in plastic bags. The difficulty here is not so much the quality or age of the spices but their identification. Frequently, they are labelled by their name in the country of origin, and this is further complicated by the innumerable English versions of their Arabic, Hindi or Chinese names. Anise pepper, for instance, is rarely so labelled in Chinese supermarkets and appears as *'farchiew*

An excellent way to store roots like garlic, ginger and onions, which need air to prevent them from rotting, is in hanging baskets.

spice' or 'Szechwan (Sichuan) pepper' while nigella is commonly called '*kalonji*' or 'black onion seed'. Shop assistants are rarely experts in nomenclature so finding some of these spices can be a hit-or-miss affair. It helps to know what the spice or flavouring looks like (in the encyclopedia section, refer to the spice description and identification photograph) and also its alternative names (*see* Botanical and common names, pages 136-137).

Whole spices versus ground spices

Where possible, always buy whole berries and seeds, rather than powdered forms. Most are easy to grind or crush just before cooking and this way you will get the full flavour and aroma of the spice. The action of grinding dried herbs and spices releases their bouquet and fragrant oils, which are essential for their characteristic flavour. Once exposed to the air – and even if bottled in an airtight container soon after – these are dispersed, and within a short time the spices become relatively flavourless and odourless. (Perhaps some enterprising spice manufacturer could include a 'sell by' date on ground herbs and spices which would help cooks enormously.) Some spices are, of course, only sold in powdered form, such as turmeric, paprika, cayenne and chilli powder and these tend to hold their flavour fairly well. However, it is advisable with all powdered spices and flavourings to buy often and in small quantities to get the best from them.

Storing spices and herbs

Herb and spice racks containing rows of clear glass jars look good in the kitchen, are easily identifiable and convenient for the cook – but bad for the flavourings. Herbs and spices should not be exposed to direct sunlight which fades their colours and affects flavour. Nor should they be kept near a cooker where moisture and condensation can have adverse effects on them. To retain their quality, spices and herbs must be kept in airtight containers in a dark, cool and dry place. Racks are convenient for the storage of glass bottles but these are best positioned on the inside door of a kitchen cupboard or larder. If you want to keep spices on open shelves, store them in small earthenware or pottery containers, suitably airtight and labelled. If either whole or ground herbs and spices are bought in plastic or cellophane bags, do transfer them, once opened, to airtight containers since exposure to the air causes rapid deterioration. Beware, also, of storing opened plastic bags of, say, various Indian spices in one jar. For the cook, it may seem logical to store them together but, in fact, the spice flavours permeate each other.

Using spices and flavourings

As a general rule, only small quantities of spices are used at a time – ranging from a pinch in many instances to a tablespoon or more (of chilli powder in many Mexican dishes). Precisely how much is a matter of individual preference and traditional habits. Some people positively relish searingly hot dishes in which large amounts of chilli predominate, others find garlic offensive even in small quantities. Fresh leaves, bulbs and roots are nearly always used in larger quantities than their dried equivalents but there are no hard-and-fast rules for the use of spices and herbs. If you like the taste of a particular flavour, try adding a little more of it than the recipe indicates or experiment by combining it with a different food. Try these unusual flavour combinations: crush anise pepper over steaks for an unusual steak *au poivre*; cook shellfish such as scallops, prawns [shrimp] or crab in sweet white wine, rather than dry, for a different fragrance and smoothness; or poach chicken in a

sauce of 250g/8oz/2 cups crushed walnuts, 45ml/3 tbsp/ pomegranate syrup and 450ml/¾ pint/2 cups water for a sweet-sour Persian flavour.

Fresh garlic, ginger and onion are usually finely chopped or minced before being added to the cooking pot or pan; cloves, cinnamon sticks and vanilla pods are generally used whole to flavour cooking liquids or creams and then removed before serving; some berries and pods like juniper and cardamom are lightly crushed so they can release their flavour in the cooking; others such as saffron and tamarind need to be infused before use; whole seeds such as sesame are often roasted for colour and flavouring.

Grinding spices

The final dish always benefits if berries and seeds are freshly ground before being added to the pot. This really will produce superior results in the kitchen and with nearly all spices is very easily done in the old-fashioned way with a mortar and pestle, or with a coffee or spice grinder reserved only for this use. A peppermill is also useful for spices like coriander and even a liquidizer can be put to use if you add a lubricant such as a little cooking stock. The same implements can be used for the purées and pastes which feature in much Indian and south-east Asian cookery. By grinding your own spices, not only will you get the best – and freshest – flavour and aroma, but you can also be assured that your mix is unadulterated. Needless to say, measure out your spices and grind only what you need for the particular dish.

Handling chillies

Remember that chillies are hot and can burn the skin and sting the eyes. Some people wear rubber gloves when preparing chillies but this is usually only necessary if you are handling a great many of them. In most instances it is sufficient to carefully wash your hands and implements such as knives and chopping boards afterwards and to avoid touching sensitive areas such as the lips and around the eyes with 'chillied' fingers.

Those unused to cooking with chillies regularly may be uncertain about how to control the strength of chillies. As a general rule, fresh chillies are milder than dried and red chillies (whether fresh or dried) are hotter than green. To add piquancy and flavour without too much hotness, add one or two whole chillies to your pot, discarding them when the degree of pungency you want has been reached. For a relatively hot flavour, halve the chillies and remove the seeds and veins before adding them to the cooking, and for extreme heat, include the entire chilli, seeds and all, finely

Left Large glass jars are suitable for storing spices in shops but, for home, it is better to buy in smaller amounts more frequently to ensure they are fresh and aromatic.

Right Coffee grinders like these are ideal for grinding spices if kept solely for that purpose.

Left Bone pots used in Hong Kong for preserving and pickling.

chopped. The best way to counteract the heat of chillies if you are suffering is to sip milk or yogurt; water will not help.

Preparing spices for curries

Heat aromatizes whole ground spices, thereby heightening their flavour, and in almost all Indian cookery freshly ground mixes or pastes are dry roasted or sautéed before being used. The important thing is to cook dry mixtures over very gentle heat either in a dry non-stick frying pan until they release their aroma, or in a warm oven (160°C/325°F/gas mark 3) for about 10 minutes. It is vital not to let the spices burn.

One spice mixture which is usually made up and stored by Indian cooks is *garam masala*, which is sprinkled on food just before it is served or added towards the end of the cooking. Its purpose is to add piquancy to fairly bland or mildly spiced dishes and it is emphatically not used as a curry powder. You can make up small quantities of this at a time by first gently heating the whole spices in a dry pan, stirring all the time. When they are cool, grind the spices to a powder, store in an airtight container away from the light and use up within a month or so before the mixture becomes stale.

The pastes used in Indian cookery are simply ground spices mixed with a little water or cooking liquid. They are usually cooked in a little oil or *ghee* (clarified butter) over a medium heat for about two minutes, constantly stirred. Pastes are less likely to burn than dry mixtures and blend better and more evenly into the prepared dish.

Purées are usually made of onions alone or with garlic and ginger. Dry spices can be mixed with purées to make a paste or the purées can be added during cooking to give flavour and evenness of texture to the food. Use a large amount of oil and sauté the ingredients over a medium heat until soft and lightly coloured. Drain off the oil and purée the mixture in a liquidizer or food processor. You can freeze any leftover purée, measured out in freezer bags or yogurt pots, for future use.

The coconut milk used in curries in southern India and Sri Lanka can be obtained in three ways. Ideally, use freshly grated coconut meat, add an equal quantity of hot water, knead, then allow to cool and strain. The same results can be obtained with desiccated coconut which is easily available in the West. Creamed coconut blocks are available from Indian shops and many supermarkets; to make coconut milk, dissolve 25-75g/1-3oz/1-3 tbsp of creamed coconut in approximately 300ml/½ pint/1¼ cups hot water, using the smaller quantity if a thinner cream is required.

Condiments, sauces and chutneys

Above Indonesian *Saté*.

Right Chilli paste on sale in Sumatra.

Spices and flavourings can be used singly, as tarragon is in *bearnaise* sauce, or in combination with other spices to make spicy sauces and condiments, of which there are a large number traditionally used in different parts of the world. Many are based on chillies, variously called hot pepper, chilli or barbecue sauce, depending on their country of origin. Ketchups, chutneys and relishes, where pungent spices combine with fruits and vegetables, such as tomatoes, mangoes or sweetcorn, are also age-old condiments in many countries.

Chilli and pepper sauces

The most famous chilli sauce in the world is Tabasco, the pungent red pepper sauce made in Louisiana, and a notable ingredient in the Bloody Mary cocktail. However, there are many other hot pepper sauces produced commercially to West Indian, Mexican, South American and Chinese recipes. Sometimes they are combined with tomatoes and other spices to produce a piquant blend – and it can only be said that there are as many chilli sauces as there are varieties of chillies. These are favourite condiments worldwide and can, of course, be easily made at home.

Harissa, the fiery red paste which flavours and colours many North African foods including *couscous*, is available ready-made in small cans. It can, however, be easily home-made by combining the following in a liquidizer: 25g/1oz dried red chillies, ½ tsp salt, 1-2 cloves garlic, 1 tsp caraway seeds, a little olive oil and lemon juice. Blend to a paste and use sparingly.

Almost every island in the Caribbean has its own version of pepper sauce, made from local chillies such as Scotch bonnet in Jamaica and including the hot yellow ones found on all islands. Caribbean peppers have a fine, distinctive flavour but are not easily available in Britain and Europe except in specialist [gourmet] West Indian shops where they sometimes appear canned or bottled. In a recipe any hot chilli can be substituted but the flavour will not be as fine. Chilli enthusiasts will also look for the Pickapeppa Hot Pepper Sauce from Jamaica or the various bottled pepper sauces from the Caribbean, each one of which varies in

colour, texture and ingredients and all are quite different from, say, Mexican or Chinese chilli sauces.

Mexican and Central American chillies are astonishing in their variety, differing as they do in flavour and heat as well as size, colour and shape. Among the most commonly used are *ancho*, a mild, richly-flavoured dried pepper; *mulato*, similar but sweeter; and *pasilla, jalepeno* and *serrano*. Although widely available in North America, they are hard to find in Britain and Europe except from high quality grocers, usually canned or bottled. When *ancho, mulato* or *pasilla* are called for, substitute 2 tsp paprika for each teaspoon indicated plus ½ tsp cayenne for the pot.

Saté sauce is the traditional Indonesian accompaniment to the famous dish of skewered meat (*Saté*) grilled over charcoal. Particularly popular in the West, the sauce can be bought ready-made in jars. Its principal ingredients are chillies and peanuts, ground to a paste and flavoured with lemon grass, dried shrimp, coconut milk, lemons, sugar and salt, and home-made versions can be easily made.

Traditional British condiments

Few European countries have the pungent bottled condiments so loved by the British such as Worcestershire, anchovy essence or ketchup, mushroom ketchup and the ubiquitous tomato and HP sauces. Nor do they have chutneys and pickles such as piccalilli and mango chutney, known for well over a century and still popular today.

Nineteenth-century cookery books give recipes for these spicy condiments which were commonly home-made and it is fun to try these for an agreeable change from bottled varieties. Although Worcestershire sauce is now made by more than one firm, Lea and Perrins were the original makers, and the story goes that around 1836 the recipe was given to Mr Lea in his Worcester shop by the second Baron Sandys, an ex-governor of Bengal, who asked for it to be made up for him. This was done but the sauce was not to Lord Sandys' liking and he rejected it. A couple of years later, a barrel of the sauce was discovered in the cellar. It was tasted, pronounced excellent and the firm decided to sell it to local customers. It rapidly became popular, was soon

found on tables in the grandest households and Mr Lea, the founder of the firm, not unpredictably, died a millionaire. The recipe here does not include the tamarind or molasses used in Lea and Perrins sauce but is a traditional 19th-century recipe nonetheless.

Mango chutney, also of Indian origin, has been known in Britain since 1750, invariably marketed under military brand names such as 'Major Grey's Mango Chutney', presumably to add 'authenticity' to the blend. It is, without doubt, one of the most delicious condiments and, now that fresh mangoes are regular imports from the tropics, can be home-made.

Until the mid-19th century, anchovies were frequently used in Britain to season meat dishes and to this day are used in small quantities in Italy particularly to enhance rather than specifically flavour fish, meat and tomato-based sauces for pasta. Anchovy essence or ketchup, made in a similar way to mushroom ketchup, proved to be a more convenient way of accentuating flavours, although it is nowadays not much used in Britain. However, this relatively unfamiliar seasoning is well worth trying not only in pasta sauces but in beef stews or fish pies or casseroles. It really does pleasantly enliven flavours without being any more detectable than salt or pepper.

Tomato ketchups and barbecue sauces
Few home-made blends can imitate the flavour of bottled tomato ketchup – one of the great flavourings for insipid food, though scorned by gourmets, and loved by adults and children alike. Spicy tomato relishes are found wherever the tomato is eaten, for this vegetable has a special affinity with full flavoured spices and herbs. Such relishes can wonderfully enhance simple grilled meats or cold chicken and meat salads and are sometimes added to dressings, such as seafood dressing, and sauces. The recipe for English tomato ketchup (right) dates from 1857. The barbecue sauce is a mixture of commercial condiments with common herbs and spices that is easy to make.

Angostura bitters
Angostura bitters, made from the bark of a West Indian tree and flavoured with cinnamon, cloves, mace, nutmeg and other ingredients, achieved popularity throughout the British Empire as a cure for malaria and other tropical diseases. Nowadays, it principally flavours pink gin and champagne cocktails but it was once used to pep up fruit salads and ice creams and, most unusually, soups such as beef and chicken consommé.

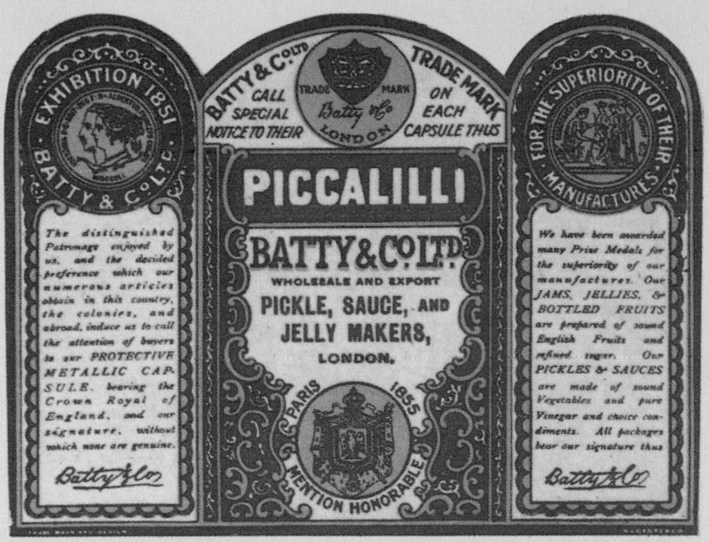

Early examples of bottled piccalilli and nabob sauce – an old Indian recipe made from fruit, vegetables and spices.

RECIPES

Mexican jalepeño sauce

4 jalepeño chillies or *100g/4oz canned jalepeños*
2 cloves garlic, chopped
1 small onion, chopped
150ml/¼ pint/½ cup water
2 tbsp/30ml vegetable oil

If using loose chillies, remove the stems and seeds, chop roughly and soak in warm water to barely cover for 30 minutes. Combine canned chillies and juice or soaked chillies and liquid with the garlic, onion and water in a liquidizer. Blend until smooth. Heat the oil in a saucepan, add the mixture and cook gently for about 10 minutes or until the garlic and onion are cooked. Cool this and use to flavour meat, beans or vegetables. This is not a long-lasting sauce but can be kept, covered, in the refrigerator for up to 5 days.

Trinidad hot pepper sauce

1 small green papaya
10 fresh red chillies, seeded and chopped
2 onions, finely chopped
3 cloves garlic, minced
3 tsp salt
½ tsp turmeric
1 tsp mild curry powder
3 tbsp mustard powder
450ml/¾ pint/2 cups malt vinegar

Simmer the unpeeled papaya in water for about 15-20 minutes or until tender. Cool, peel and roughly chop it. Combine the mustard and vinegar and place in a saucepan with the papaya and the remaining ingredients. Bring slowly to the boil and simmer gently, uncovered for about 20 minutes. Cool and bottle in sterilized jars.

English tomato ketchup

Bake quite ripe tomatoes till they are perfectly soft. Rub the pulp through a sieve. Add as much chilli vinegar as will make a fairly thick cream. Add ½ oz garlic or 1 oz shallots, sliced, to each quart [2 pints] and salt and boil all together for 15 minutes. Take the scum off. Strain through a sieve to remove the garlic or shallot. When it is cold, bottle and cork it well. NB If when the bottles are opened, it is found to have fermented, put more salt into it and boil it up again. The thickness when finished should be that of very thick cream.

Mango chutney

6 green mangoes
2 tsp salt
3 red chillies, seeded and chopped or 2 tsp chilli powder
300ml/½ pint/1 cup malt vinegar
400g/14 oz/2 cups sugar
40g/1½ oz green ginger, peeled and chopped
3 cloves garlic, crushed

Peel and chop the mangoes, sprinkle with salt and set aside for 20 minutes. Grind the chillies or powder with a little vinegar to form a paste. Place the remaining vinegar in a saucepan with the sugar and simmer gently until the sugar dissolves. Pour off all the juice from the mango flesh and add the flesh to the pan. Simmer for about 10-15 minutes. Add the ginger, garlic and chilli paste and stir well. Cook for a further 10-12 minutes. Cool and bottle in sterilized jars.

Quick barbecue sauce

450ml/¾ pint/2 cups bottled tomato ketchup
dash of Tabasco sauce
dash of Worcestershire sauce
45ml/3 tbsp red wine or tarragon vinegar
1 tsp paprika
½ tsp garlic powder

Combine all the ingredients until thoroughly blended. Store in a screwtop jar and use as required.

An old recipe for Worcestershire Sauce (1857)

1 oz capsicum [chillies]
8oz shallots
4 drams cinnamon [large pinch]
6 oz garlic
2 oz cloves
2 oz nutmegs
1 dram cardamom [one or two seeds]
1 pint soy
2 pints mushroom ketchup
1 gallon vinegar (brown) [16 fl oz to each pint using old measurement]

Bruise the shallots and garlic and boil for one half hour. Add the remainder of the ingredients and let them boil for another half hour in a closed vessel. Let the whole remain for a month, covered over. Strain through a fine sieve. And bottle the sauce. The spices when drained off may be boiled in a few pints of vinegar which they will flavour, and which will be most useful for making pickles when once more strained through a hair sieve.

Botanical, common and foreign names

The botanical classifications given here are an aid to the identification of plants from which the spices and flavourings are obtained. They are of particular use to the gardener since common names vary widely from country to country. To confuse matters, because in some instances botanists disagree about the classification of a number of plants and in other cases plants have been reclassified, scientific names may differ from older reference books.

Names have also been given for spices and flavourings in the major European languages as well as, where appropriate, some ethnic languages, mostly Asian. Anglicized versions of the latter vary widely and, while an attempt has been made to include the most common transcriptions, readers may well find others in shops and restaurants.

Key for European languages: **F** = French; **G** = German; **I** = Italian; **S** = Spanish.

Aframomum melegueta: grains of paradise, Melegueta pepper; **F** graines de paradis; **G** Malagettapfeffer; **I** grani di Meleguetta; **S** malagueta.

Agaricus bisporus: cultivated mushroom; **F** champignon de Paris; **G** Kulturpilz; **I** funghi di serra; **S** hongo plantado.

Agaricus campestris: field mushroom; **F** champignon des prés; **G** Wiesenchampignon; **I** prataiolo; **S** hongo silvestre.

Allium cepa: onion; **F** oignon; **G** Zwiebel; **I** cipolla; **S** cebolla.

Allium savitum: garlic; **F** ail; **G** Knoblauch; **I** aglio; **S** ajo.

Alpinia galanga: greater galangal; **F** grand galanga; **G** galangawurzel; **I** galanga; **S** galanga; **Indonesian** laos; **Malay** leuguas; **Thai** kha

Alpinia officinarum: lesser galangal; **F** galanga vrai; **Indonesian** kenchur.

Anethum graveolens: dill; **F** aneth; **G** dill; **I** aneto; **S** éneldo.

Apium graveolens dulce: celery; **F** céleri; **G** Sellerie; **I** sedano, apio; **S** apio.

Armoracia rusticana: horseradish; **F** raifort; **G** Meerrettich; **I** rafano; **S** rábano picante.

Bixa orellano: annatto; **F** roucou; **G** Annatto; **I** anotto; **S** achiote.

Boletus edulis: cep; **F** cèpe; **I** porcini.

Brassica alba: white mustard seed, yellow mustard (USA); **F** moutarde blanche; **G** Weisser Senf; **I** senape bianca; **S** mostaza silvestre.

Brassica juncea: Brown, Indian or black mustard seed; **F** moutarde de Chine; **G** Indischer Senf; **I** senape Indiana; **S** mostaza de Indias; **Indian** rai.

Brassica nigra: black or brown mustard seed; **F** moutarde noire; **G** Schwarzer Senf; **I** senape nera; **S** mostaza negra.

Cantharellus cibarius: chanterelle; **F** chanterelle, girolle; **G** Pfefferling; **I** capo gallo; **S** canterelo.

Capparis spinosa: 'inermis': caper; **F** câpre; **G** Kaper; **I** càppero; **S** alacaparra, tápana.

Capsicum annuum: paprika, pimento pepper; **F** piment; **G** Paprika; **I** paprica; **S** pimentón.

Capsicum frutescens: cayenne pepper; **F** poivre de Cayenne; **G** Cayennepfeffer; **I** pepe di Caienna; **S** pimentón picante.

Capsicum frutescens: chilli [chili], pepper, bell pepper, bird chilli, long pepper; **F** piment fort; **G** Roter Pfeffer; **I** peperoncini; **S** chile, pimentón; **Indian** mirich; **Mexican** chile.

Carica papaya: papaya, pawpaw; **F** papaye; **G** Papaie; **I** papaia; **S** papaya.

Carum ajowan: ajowan, lovage; **F** ajowan; **G** Ajowan; **I** ajowan; **S** ajowan; **Indian** ajvini.

Carum carvi: caraway; **F** carvi; **G** Kümmel; **I** carvi; **S** alcaravea.

Ceratonia siliqua: carob, St John's Bread, Locust bean or seed; **F** caroube; **G** Johannisbrot; **I** carruba; **S** algarroba.

Cinnamomum cassia: cassia; **F** casse; **G** Kassia; **I** cassia; **S** casia.

Cinnamomum zeylanicum: cinnamon; **F** cannelle; **G** Kaneel; **I** cannella; **S** canela.

Coffea arabica: coffee; **F** café; **G** Kaffee; **I** caffe; **S** café.

Coriandrum savitum: coriander, Chinese parsley; **F** coriandre; **G** Koriander; **I** coriandolo; **S** cilantro; **Arabic** kizbara; **Indian** dhania.

Crocus sativus: saffron, autumn crocus (USA); **F** safran; **G** Safron; **I** zafferano; **S** azafrán; **Indian** kesar.

Cuminum cyminum: cumin; **F** cumin; **G** Kreuzkümmel; **I** cumino; **S** comino; **Arabic** kammun; **Indian** jeera, zeera.

Curcuma domestica/longa: turmeric; **F** curcuma; **G** Gelbwurz; **I** curcuma; **S** curcuma; **Indian** haldi.

Cymbopogon citratus: lemon grass; **F** herbe de citron; **G** Zitronengras; **I** erba di limone; **S** hierba de limon; **Indonesian** sereh; **Malay** serai; **Thai** takrai.

Elettaria cardamomum: cardamom; **F** cardamome; **G** Kardamom; **I** cardamomo; **S** cardamomo; **Indian** elachie.

Eugenia caryophyllus: clove; **F** clou de girofle; **G** Gewürzenelke; **I** chiodo di garofano; **S** clavo de especia.

Ferula assafoetida: asafoetida, laser (Roman), **F** assa foetida; **G** Teufelsdreck; **I** assafetida; **S** asafétida; **Indian** heeng.

Foeniculum vulgare: common fennel, large fennel (USA); **F** fenouil; anet douce (Florence fennel); **G** Fenchel; **I** finocchio; **S** hinojo.

Glycine max: soy bean; **F** pois Chinois, soja; **G** Soja; **I** soia; **S** soja; **Japanese** shoyu; **Chinese** Ch'au-yau (soy sauce), tofu (soy curd).

Glycyrrhiza glabra: liquorice, licorice (USA); **F** réglisse; **G** Lakritze; **I** liquirizia; **S** regaliz.

Illicium verum: star anise, badian; **F** anis de la Chine, badiane; **G** Sternanis; **I** anice stellato; **S** badián; **Chinese** ba chio.

Juniperus communis: juniper; **F** genièvre; **G** Wacholder; **I** ginepro; **S** enebro.

Laurus nobilis: bay leaf; sweet bay; **F** feuille de laurier; **G** Lorbeerblatt; **I** foglia di alloro, lauro; **S** hoja de laurel.

Mangifera indica: mango, amchur; **F** mangue; **G** Mango; **I** mango; **S** mango; **Indian** amchur, amchoor.

Mentha spicata: mint, spearmint, garden mint; **F** menthe verte; **G** Grüne Minze; **I** menta verde; **S** menta verde.

Morchella vulgaris: morel; **F** morille; **G** Speisemorchel; **I** spugnola rotonda; **S** murgula.

Murraya koenigii: curry leaf, nim leaf; **F** feuille de cari; **G** Curryblatt; **I** foglia di curry; **S** hoja de cari; **Indian** kari phulia, neem.

Myristica fragrans: mace; **F** macis; **G** Muskatblüte; **I** macis; **S** macía.

Myristica fragrans: nutmeg; **F** noix muscade; **G** Muskatnuss; **I** noce moscata; **S** nuez moscada.

Nigella sativa: nigella, wild onion seed, kalonji; **F** cheveux de Vénus; **G** Schwarzkümmel; **I** nigella; **S** neguilla; **Indian** kala zeera; kalonji.

Olea europea: olive; **F** olive; **G** Olive; **I** olive; **S** aceituna, oliva.

Origanum vulgare: oregano; **F** origan; **G** Oregano; **I** oregano; **S** oregano.

Pandanus odoratissimus/odorus: screwpine, pandan; **F** pandan; **G** Pandanus; **I** pandano; **S** pandano; **Indian** kewra; **Indonesian** daun pandan; **Malay** daun pandan.

Papaver somniferum: poppy; **F** pavot somnifère; **G** Mohn; **I** papavero; **S** adormidera; **Indian** kus-kus.

Pimenta dioica: allspice, Jamaica pepper; **F** poivre de la Jamaïque; **G** Jamaikapfeffer; **I** pimento; **S** pimiento de Jamaica.

Pimpinella anisum: anise, aniseed; **F** anis; **G** Anis; **I** anice; **S** anís.

Piper cubeba: cubeb, Java pepper; **F** cubèbe; **G** Kubebe; **I** cubebe; **S** cubebe; **Indonesian** tjabé djawa.

Piper nigrum: pepper, black; **F** poivre; **G** Pfeffer; **I** pepe nero; **S** pimienta negra;
pepper, white; **F** poivre blanc; **G** Weisser Pfeffer; **I** pepe bianco; **S** pimienta blanca;
pepper, green: **F** poivre vert; **G** Grüner Pfeffer; **I** pepe verde; **S** pimienta verde.

Pistacia lentiscus: mastic; **F** mastic; **G** Mastix; **I** lentischio; **S** mastique; **Greek** mastikha; **Arabic** aza.

Pleurotos ostreatus: oyster mushroom; **F** pleurotte.

Punica granatum: pomegranate; **F** grenade; **G** Granatapfel; **I** melagrana; **S** granada; **Indian** anar.

Rhus coriaria: Sicilian sumac; **F** sumac; **G** Sumach; **I** sommacco; **S** zumaque; **Arabic** sammak.

Saccharum officinarum: sugar; **F** sucre (de canne); **G** Rohrzucker; **I** zucchero; **S** azúcar (de caña).

Santalum album: sandalwood; **F** bois de santal; **G** Sandelholz; **I** legno di sandalo; **S** sándalo.

Sesamum indicum: sesame; **F** sesame; **G** Sesam; **I** sesamo; **S** ajonjoli; **Arabic** tahina; **Chinese** chi mah; **Japanese** goma.

Tamarindus indica: tamarind; **F** tamarin; **G** Tamarine; **I** tamarindo; **S** tamarindo; **Indian** amyli; **Indonesian** asam.

Theobroma cacao: cocoa, chocolate, cacao; **F** cacao, chocolat; **G** Kakao, Schokolade; **I** cacao, cioccolata; **S** cacao, chocolate.

Trigonella foenum-graecum: fenugreek; **F** fenugrec Sénegré; **G** Bockshornklee; **I** fieno greco; **S** alholva, **Indian** methi.

Tropaeolum majus: nasturtium; **F** capucine, cresson d'Inde; **G** Kapuzinerkresse; **I** nasturzio; **S** capuchina.

Tuber magnatum/melanosporum: truffle; **F** truffe; **G** Trüffel; **I** tartufo; **S** trufa.

Vanilla fragrans: vanilla; **F** vanille; **G** Vanille; **I** vaniglia; **S** vainilla.

Xanthoxylum piperitum: anise pepper, Sichuan pepper, fagara, farchiew spice; **F** poivre anise; **G** Anispfeffer; **I** pepe d'anice; **S** pepe di anis; **Chinese** faah-jiu **Japanese** kinome, sansho.

Zingiber officinale: ginger; **F** gingembre; **G** Ingwer; **I** zenzero; **S** jengibre; **Indian** adruk; **Chinese** cheung; **Indonesian** aliah.

Flavours and uses

The following is a summary of the main characteristics of each spice, with its main applications in cooking.

Allspice: Mixture of nutmeg, cinnamon and clove.
Worldwide uses: pickles, stews; broths for meat and fish; in cakes, puddings, relishes and chutneys.

Aniseed: Flavour of liquorice.
Worldwide uses: cakes, biscuits, breads, confectionery; to flavour alcoholic drinks and cordials.

Anise pepper: Hot, peppery, citrus flavour.
Chinese cuisine: Particularly Sichuan, in pork, duck and chicken dishes; in spiced salt; in Japanese cookery, sansho (dried leaves) add fragrance and piquancy to soups, noodles and rice.

Asafoetida: Strong, unpleasant smell and flavour; in small quantities enhances other flavours with onion-like taste.
Indian cuisines: Principally vegetarian curries, pickles, lentils etc.

Bay leaf: Slightly bitter, resinous and pungent.
Worldwide uses: In stews, broths, marinades, pickles; ingredient in *bouquet garni*.

Caper: Aromatic, acidic, reminiscent of goats' cheese.
Worldwide uses: Particularly in Mediterranean, in sauces, salads, fish, pizzas, some cheeses.

Caraway: Strong liquorice flavour.
Worldwide uses: Principally northern Europe, in rye and other breads, cakes; pickles, sauerkraut; pork and duck; liqueurs eg Kümmel.

Cardamom: Warm, slightly pungent, 'spicy' flavour.
Middle Eastern and Indian cuisines: In curries, savoury rice dishes eg pilaus, in pickles, coffee; in Western cuisines in pastries, buns, punches.

Cayenne: Hot and pungent.
Western cuisines: To spice fish and shellfish, eggs, vegetables, cheese dishes, in devilled sauces, as condiment.

Celery seed: Distinctive warm, bitter flavour of fresh stalks.
Western cuisines: in celery salt, soups, sauces especially barbecue, in savoury baking; marinades; ingredient in Bloody Mary cocktail.

Chilli: Hot, fiery, burning flavour; varieties differ in hotness and pungency.
Worldwide: Notable in Mexican, Indian, south-east Asian and Chinese cuisines; in curries of all kinds, in Indonesian *sambals* (relishes); in Sichuan cooking of China; in Mexican tacos, sauces, meat and chicken dishes; in West Indian pepper sauces for meat, fish and poultry; in southern European cooking in sauces and in *harissa*, used to flavour *couscous* in north Africa.

Chocolate and cocoa: Warm, rich, slightly sweet flavour. Western and Mexican cuisines: Usually sweetened, as a drink, in cakes, puddings, creams, biscuits, confectionery; in Mexican cooking, flavours meat, fish, chicken and tomato dishes adding rich, interesting taste.

Cinnamon and cassia: Pungent, sweet, spicy flavour. Worldwide: In Western cookery, in cakes, buns, biscuits; with fruits, in punches, in desserts; in Middle East, flavours meat and vegetables; ingredient in many Arab and Indian spice mixtures.

Clove: Sharp, spicy and strongly aromatic.
Worldwide: In Western cuisines, for studding ham, boiling beef, with stewed fruits, in mulled wines and punches, in spiced cakes and biscuits; ingredient in many Middle Eastern and Indian spice mixtures.

Coffee: Full, highly aromatic, slightly bitter flavour.
Worldwide: As drink, sweetened in cakes, desserts, creams, biscuits, confectionery.

Coriander: Slightly sweet spicy flavour with hint of orange.
Middle Eastern and Indian cuisines: In Middle East and Mediterranean, flavours all kinds of meat and vegetables, stuffings and rich dishes; ingredient in most curry and Indian spice mixes; also flavours Eastern sweets and puddings.

Cumin: Strong, aromatic, slightly bitter flavour.
Middle Eastern, Indian and Mexican cuisines: For fish, meat, *couscous* and vegetables in Middle East; ingredient in most Indian curry powders: ingredient in Mexican chilli powder and used in sauces, with chicken, pork and *enchiladas*.

Curry Leaf: Warm, aromatic, faint capsicum flavour.
Indian and south-east Asian cuisines: In mildly spiced dishes, marinades, chutneys, relishes, with vegetables, pilaus and in some curries, especially in southern India and Malaysia.

Dill: Fresh, aromatic, slight anise flavour.
Western cuisines: Principally in pickles, sauces and marinades for fish, with grilled lamb and pork, vegetables eg cucumber and cabbage.

Fennel: Warm, sweet, slight anise flavour.
Western cuisines: Especially in fish stocks and sauces; as flavouring for salami in Italy; sometimes in cakes and breads; in China, ingredient in five-spice powder.

Fenugreek: Strong bitter flavour.
Indian cuisines: Notable ingredient in many commercial curry powders and in wide variety of Indian spice mixtures; especially used with fish and vegetables, in *dhals*, chutneys and pickles.

Garlic: Pungent, aromatic, powerful onion flavour.
Worldwide: In Europe, used in meat and fish stews, salads, French dressing, in sauces eg *aïoli*, with vegetables; essential in Indian and south-east Asian cuisines to flavour all types of curries and spiced dishes; also important in Chinese and Japanese cooking.

Ginger: Hot, strong spicy flavour.
Worldwide: In Western cuisines, in cakes, puddings, biscuits, jams, preserves and pickles and in beer and cordials; essential in Indian cuisines in curries, vegetables and almost every savoury dish; equally important in Chinese and, in Japanese cuisines, principally fish dishes.

Horseradish: Strong hot flavour like mustard.
Western cuisines: Principally in northern European cooking in sauces for fish, sausages, chicken and roast beef; also in dips and with vegetables such as beetroot, cabbage. In Japan, wasabi (Japanese horseradish) is used as a dipping sauce for fish.

Juniper: Strong, bitter-sweet, slightly pine flavour.
Western cuisines: With game, pork, bacon, in patés; in stuffings for poultry, duck and geese, with vegetables such as cabbage; commercially to flavour gin.

Lemon grass: Aromatic, ginger-lemon flavour.
South-east Asian cuisines: In fish dishes, in meat, vegetable and poultry curries, often with coconut; in marinades, pickles and relishes.

Liquorice: Aromatic, bitter-sweet flavour.
Western cuisines: In confectionery and drinks.

Mace: Sweet, nutmeg-like flavour but stronger.
Western and Middle Eastern cuisines: In West in fish and shellfish dishes, veal and chicken stews, sauces, cakes and pastries; in Middle East in meat and chicken casseroles, rice dishes, stuffings.

Mushrooms and fungi: Mild, delicate flavour.
Western and oriental cuisines: Many varieties with different flavours in sauces, stuffings, soups, as vegetables alone: in Orient with fish, meat and poultry; dried used as seasoning rather than vegetable.

Mustard: Strong, hot pungent flavour.
Western and Indian cuisines: In sauces, with meat, poultry, in devilled dishes, with eggs, in salad dressings; with cheese, in pickles and chutneys; in Indian cooking in curries, pickles, vegetarian dishes.

Nigella: Bitter, pungent, peppery flavour.
Indian cuisines: As *kalonji* or wild onion seed, ingredient in garam masalas, curry mixtures, in vegetable dishes and *dhals,* pickles and chutneys.

Nutmeg: Strong, sweet, spicy, aromatic flavour.
Worldwide: With vegetables eg spinach and sprouts, in sauces, puddings, custards, cakes, eggnogs; ingredient in many sweet spice mixtures.

Olives: Distinctive, slightly acidic flavour.
Western and Middle Eastern cuisines: Particularly in Mediterranean cooking as *hors d'oeuvres*, in salads, pasta sauces, pizzas, in robust meat and chicken dishes, with vegetables eg aubergines [eggplants], tomatoes; oil in cooking, salad dressings and sauces.

Onions: Sharp pungent flavour that mellows to slight sweetness in cooking.
Worldwide: Essential in soups, stocks, marinades, all types of meat and chicken dishes; in salads, pickles and chutneys; important in every cuisine worldwide.

Oregano: Pungent, peppery, herb flavour.
Western and Mexican cuisines: In fish, meat and poultry dishes, with aubergines [eggplants], tomatoes, cheese, in pizzas; in Mexico, ingredient in chilli powders, in chillied meat and beans.

Paprika: Warm, generally mild, sweet capsicum flavour.
Western cuisines: Principally eastern Europe, in goulashes, chicken dishes, with cheese, cream, in sausages, with eggs and shellfish, in sauces, with vegetables eg cucumber, cabbage, potatoes, for garnishing and colouring.

Pepper: Strong, hot pungent flavour; white milder, green peppers are refreshingly piquant.
Worldwide: As table condiment, in pickling mixtures, broths for beef, ham; seasons all types of savoury dishes, often as dominant ingredient eg steak *au poivre*; green peppers, mashed, in sauces for duck and chicken.

Poppy seed: Crunchy, nutty flavour.
Worldwide: In West, in breads, cakes, biscuits, pastries, with noodles; in Middle East, in breads, confectionery; in India in some curries and breads.

Saffron: Highly aromatic agreeably bitter, distinctive flavour.
Western, Middle Eastern and Indian cuisines: Principally in Mediterranean in chicken and rice dishes, *paella*, fish dishes, *bouillabaisse* and soups; in Middle East in *pilaffs*, meat dishes and sweetmeats; in Northern India in festive pilaus and delicately spiced dishes.

Salt: Salty.
Worldwide: As table condiment enhancing other flavours, as preservative in pickles and brines, to extract bitter juices from vegetables, in spice mixtures; essential in all types of savoury dishes.

Sesame seeds: Distinctive nutty flavour.
Middle Eastern and oriental cuisines: In Middle East, on breads, cakes, as *tahina* paste, ingredient in confection, *halva*; in Orient, frequently toasted or ground in Chinese, Japanese and Korean cooking, as condiment.

Soy: Salty, beefy flavour (sauce).
Oriental and south-east Asian cuisines: As sauces, pastes, bean curd, in all savoury dishes, marinades, to season dips and accompaniments; black bean, hoisin, miso are common soy-based sauces for rice, noodles, meat, fish and chicken dishes.

Star anise: Strong, harsh aniseed flavour.
Chinese cuisines: In long-cooked dishes of pork, duck and chicken, in stocks and soups, ingredient in Chinese five-spice powder.

Sugar: Powerfully sweet.
Worldwide: As sweetening agent in beverages, puddings, cakes, custards, pastries, creams, in fruit, jams, preserves; in home-made and commercial confectionery; occasionally in savoury glazed and sweet-sour dishes.

Sumac, Sicilian: Sour, astringent fruit flavour.
Middle Eastern cuisines: As souring agent and seasoning in marinades, meat, chicken and vegetable stews, sprinkled on kebabs and grilled meats.

Tamarind: Refreshing, sour flavour.
Middle Eastern and Indian cuisines: In drinks and as souring agent in Middle East; in India, in curries, chutneys, sometimes jams; ingredient in Worcestershire sauce.

Turmeric: Distinctive, warm, slightly bitter flavour.
Middle Eastern and Indian cuisines: As seasoning and colouring in meat, fish, rice dishes, sauces, vegetables; in India in many curry mixes, pickles and chutneys.

Vanilla: Sweet permeating aroma and flavour.
Western cuisines: In ice cream, desserts, cakes, confectionery, especially with coffee or chocolate, with fruits, milk and cream-based puddings and creams.

Selected spice mixes and pastes

Proportions are given so that readers can vary the quantities made as desired. Proportions can also be changed according to taste. *See also* pages 20-23 for additional curry and spice mixtures.

Apple pie spice mix: (Britain, USA): cinnamon, ground 4: clove, ground 1; nutmeg, ground ½.

Basic barbecue spice mix (Britain, USA): chilli powder 1; garlic powder 1; oregano, dried 2; cumin, crushed 1; onion powder 1; salt 1; celery seed, crushed 1; paprika 1; brown sugar 1.

Chicken seasoning (Britain, USA): garlic powder 1; salt ½; paprika ¼; cinnamon, ground ⅛; tarragon, dried ⅛.

Chilli powder (Mexico/worldwide): chilli powder 2; cumin, crushed 1; oregano, dried 1; garlic powder 1.

Gado-gado sauce paste (Indonesia): garlic, minced 2; chillies, chopped 2; shrimp paste ¼; laos powder ¼; brown sugar 1; peanut butter 6; coconut milk 2; lemon juice 1.

Goma (Japan): sesame seeds, crushed 4; soy 2; sugar 1; MSG ½.

Lamb seasoning (Britain, USA): oregano, dried 1; black pepper, crushed ½; bay leaf, crumbled ¼; basil, dried ½.

Malaysian garam masala (South-eastern Asia): cumin, ground 1; peppercorns, ground 1; clove, ground 1; cardamom, ground 1.

Mild curry powder (worldwide): coriander, ground 2; cumin, ground ½; turmeric 1; garam masala ½; fenugreek, ground ¼; cardamom, ground ¼; chilli powder ¼.

Mixed spice (Britain): allspice, ground 1; cinnamon, ground 1; clove, ground 1; ginger, ground 1; nutmeg, ground 1.

Nonya spice (Malaysian Chinese): onion powder 2; garlic powder 2; chilli powder 2; lemon grass powder/sereh 1; sugar 1.

Pickling spice (worldwide): allspice, whole 1; chilli, whole 1; cinnamon, whole 1; cloves, whole 1; ginger, diced 1; mustard seed, whole 1, black peppercorns, whole 1.

Pilau spice (India): cardamom, ground 2; coriander, ground 1, cinnamon, ground 1; cloves, whole 1; nutmeg ½; saffron for colouring.

Pumpkin pie spice (USA): nutmeg, grated 1; cloves, ground ½; ginger, ground ½; allspice, ground ½; cinnamon, ground ½.

Sambal ulek (Indonesia): chilli, crushed 4; salt ½; tamarind juice 2.

Sichuan spiced salt (China): salt 1; anise pepper ½.

Spiced salt (worldwide): per 500 g/1 lb salt: black peppercorns, ground 1; coriander seeds, ground 1; bay leaves, crushed ¼; cloves, ground ¼; chives, dried, crushed ¼.

Punch spice (Britain): orange peel 1; cloves, whole 6; cinnamon 1; cardamom seeds, whole 3; coriander, whole 3; ginger to taste.

Tika paste (India): chilli powder ½; garlic, minced ½; ginger, minced 1; turmeric 1; pepper, ground ½; coriander leaves, chopped 2.

Trinidad masala (West Indies): coriander, ground 8; chilli powder 3-4; black peppercorns, crushed 3; aniseed, crushed 2; cloves, ground 2; cumin, ground 2; mustard seed, crushed 1.

Books for further reading

The following list includes both reference and recipe books, listed by author.

Benghiat, Norma, *Traditional Jamaican Cookery*, Penguin 1985

Benghiat, Suzy, *Middle Eastern Cookery*, St Michael 1984

Bonar, Ann, *Herbs*, Hamlyn 1985
Vegetables, Hamlyn 1986

Brennan, Jennifer, *Thai Cooking*, Jill Norman and Hobhouse 1981

Carrier, Robert, *Robert Carrier's Kitchen Cookbook*, BCA 1987

Chapman, Pat, *The Little Curry Book*, Piatkus 1985

David, Elizabeth, *A Book of Mediterranean Food*, Penguin 1963
French Provincial Cooking, Penguin 1987
Spices, Salt and Aromatics in the English Kitchen, Penguin 1985

Davidson, Alan and Jane, *Dumas on Food*, OUP 1987

Edwards, John, *The Roman Cookery of Apicius*, Rider 1984

Fernandez, Rafi, *Malaysian Cookery*, Penguin 1985

Garland, Sarah, *The Herb and Spice Book*, Frances Lincoln 1979

Greenberg, Sheldon & Ortiz, Elizabeth Lambert, *The Spice of Life*, Mermaid Books 1984

Grigson, Jane, *Charcuterie and French Pork Cookery, Penguin* 1967
Fish Cookery, Penguin 1979
The Mushroom Feast, Penguin 1983

Heal, Carolyn & Allsop, Michael, *Cooking with Spices*, Panther 1983

Heath, Ambrose, *The Penguin Book of Sauces*, Penguin 1977

Jaffrey, Madhur, *An Invitation to Indian Cooking*, Penguin 1979

Larousse Gastronomique, Hamlyn 1964

Lo, Kenneth, *Chinese Provincial Cooking*, Sphere 1984
Complete Encyclopedia of Chinese Cooking, Octopus 1979

Mabey, David, *The Little Mustard Book*, Piatkus 1987

Marks, James F, *Barbecues*, Penguin 1979

Martin, Peter and Joan, *Japanese Cooking*, Penguin 1982

Médecin, Jacques, *Cuisine Niçoise*, Penguin 1983

Nichols, Lourdes, *Mexican Cookery*, Fontana 1986

Ortiz, Elizabeth Lambert, *Caribbean Cookery,* Penguin 1987

Reekie, Jennie, *The Little Chocolate Book*, Piatkus 1986

Richardson, Rosamund, *The Little Garlic Book*, Piatkus 1982
The Little Mushroom Book, Piatkus 1983
The Little Nut Book, Piatkus 1983

Roden, Claudia *Coffee*, Penguin 1981
A New Book of Middle Eastern Food, Penguin 1987

Rosengarten, F, *The Book of Spices*, Livingstone 1969

Salaman, Rena, *The Little Mediterranean Food Book*, Piatkus 1986

Simon, André and Howe, Robin, *Dictionary of Gastronomy*, Nelson 1970

Singh, Dharanjit, *Indian Cookery*, Penguin 1984

Walker, Jane, *Creative Cooking with Spices*, Quintet 1985

White, Florence, *Good Things in England*, Cape 1940

Wilson, C Anne, *Food and Drink in England*, Peregrine 1973

Suppliers and useful addresses

Spices and flavourings are widely available in supermarkets and grocery stores throughout the UK and USA. Indian and Chinese spices can be found in specialist [gourmet] shops in major cities and towns. The first two addresses are of the major spice suppliers in Britain; the others are listed by area and described in the entry.

UK
McCormick Foods
Dormer Road
Thame
Oxon OX9 3SL

Schwartz Spices
Wenman Road
Thame
Oxon OX9 3SL

London
Culpeper
21 Bruton Street
London W1X 7DA
Branches throughout London and other major cities and towns. Retailers of spices and herbs, as well as honeys, mustards, oils, condiments and scented waters.

Holland & Barrett Ltd
Branches in London and throughout the country.

Crabtree & Evelyn
6 Kensington Church Street
London W8 6HP
Branches in London and abroad with retail outlets in major cities and towns. Herbs and spices, chutneys, mustards, oils, honeys, preserves and scented waters.

The Curry Club
P.O. Box 7
Haslemere
Surrey GU27 1EP
Retail shop in Piazza, Covent Garden London; wide range of Indian, south-east Asian and Mexican spices by mail order for members.

Loon Fung Chinese Supermarket
31 Gerrard Street
London W1
Extensive range of Chinese and Indonesian spices, condiments and fresh foodstuffs.

Enco Products Ltd
71-75 Fortress Road
London NW5 1AU
Suppliers of West Indian and Caribbean spices, flavourings and condiments; they will advise on nearest stockists.

The Japan Centre
66-68 Brewer Street
London W1
Suppliers of Japanese spices

Aberdeen
Robert Mess and Co
29 Blackfriar Street

Ambrosia Wholefoods
169 King Street

Fresh Fields
13-15 St Andrew's Street

Nature's Larder
60 Holburn Street

Birmingham/Coventry
Herbs and Spices
1a Forman's Trading Estate
Forman's Road
Sparkhill
Birmingham B11

Northwood Spices Ltd
42 Barr Street
Hockley B19

Nuneaton Spiceland
72 Riversley Road
Nuneaton

Brighton
Sussex Herbs
Unit 6
Cliffe Arcade
Cliffe High Street

Country Store
88 Beaconsfield Road

Cambridge
Arjuna Wholefoods
Mill Road

Beamont's Health Store
Grafton Centre

Natural Selection
Regent Street

Cardiff
L'Epicure
40 High Street
Cowbridge
Nr Cardiff

Wally's Delicatessen
43 Royal Arcade
Cardiff

Berni's Delicatessen
57 Wellfield Road
Cardiff

Herby Spices
198 Whitchurch Road
Cardiff

Cheltenham
Gibby's Deli
274 High Street

The Shambles
The Courtyard
Montpellier Street

Edinburgh
Real Foods Ltd
14 Ashley Place
Edinburgh EH6

Exeter
Watty's Delicatessen
16 Catherine Street

Glasgow
Peckham's
Unit 100
Central Station
Glasgow 1

Epicure Delicatessen
46 West Nile Street
Glasgow

Fazzi Brothers
67 Cambridge Street
Glasgow

Leicester
Speciality Foods
29 Beaver Street

Peppers Wholefood
59a Queens Road

Manchester
Ihesaq Food Stores
89 Wilmslow Road M14

Happy Nut House
85 Deansgate M3

Weigh and Save
Arndale Centre

Plymouth
Continental Food Centre
48 Cornwall Street
Plymouth

Wah Lung
95 Mayflower Street
Plymouth

Southampton
Bedford Place Healthfood Centre
4a Bedford Place

Danaan Wholefoods
6 Onslow Road

Hasbeans
45 Oxford Street

Sheffield
Kung Eng
169 London Road
Sheffield 2

Tyne and Wear
Cumin and Caraway
7a Front Street
Shotley Bridge
Consett

Yarns and Spices
1 Station Terrace
East Boldon
Wearside

Brighton Oriental Food Store
16a Brighton Grove
Tyneside

Worcestershire
Ahimsa
249 Worcester Road
Malvern Link

USA

Chillies, Peppers, Garlic, Onions

Crinklaw Farms
Box 706
King City, CA 93930
Tel: 408-385-3261
408-385-6658
elephant garlic, chillies

The El Paso Chile Company™
100 Ruhlin Court
El Paso, TX 79922
Tel: 915-544-3434
chillies

Ili Ili Farms
Box 150-B
Kula, HI 96790
Tel: 800-367-8004
Maui onions

Willacrik Farm
PO Box 599
Templeton, CA 93465
Tel: 805-238-2776
elephant garlic

Coffees and Teas

Community Kitchens™
PO Box 3778
Baton Rouge, LA 70821-3778
Tel: 504-381-3900

Gillies Coffee Company
160 Bleeker Street
New York, NY 10012
Tel: 212-260-2130

Grace Tea Company Limited
50 West 17th Street
New York, NY 10011
Tel: 212-255-2935

Harney & Sons Limited Fine Teas
Salisbury, Connecticut 06068
Tel: 203-435-9218

Rainbow Tea & Spicery
PO Box 293
Clackamas, OR 97015-0293
Tel: 503-657-3055

Starbucks Coffee and Tea
2010 Airport Way South
Seattle, WA 98134
Tel: 206-447-1575

Flavourings and Extracts

Bickford Flavors
282 South Main Street
Akron, OH 44308
Tel: 216-762-4666
flavourings

Northwestern Coffee Mills
217 North Broadway
Milwaukee, W1 53202
Tel: 414-276-1031
extracts, herbs

Snow White and Rose Red
PO Box 275
Springville, UT 84663
Tel: 801-489-7982
powdered vanilla

Fruit

Hawaiian Plantations
1311 Kalakaua Avenue
Honolulu, HI 968126
Tel: 800-367-2177
808-955-8888
pineapples, stuffed dates

Pinnacle Orchards
441 South Fir
Medford, OR 97501
Tel: 800-547-0227
fruits

Sphinx Date Ranch Inc
4041 E Thomas Road
Phoenix, AZ 85008
Tel: 602-224-0195
stuffed dates

Herbs, Spices and Flavourings

Aspen Mulling Spices
c/o Wax & Wicks, Inc
PO Box 191
Aspen, CO 81612
Tel: 303-925-3984
mulling spices

Foxhill
Box 7
Parma, MI 49269
Tel: 517-531-3179
herbs

Rathdowney Herbs Limited
3 River Street
Bethel, VT 05032
Tel: 802-234-5157
herbs and spices

Select Origins Inc
Box N
Southampton, NY 11968
Tel: 516-288-1382
spices and dried mushrooms

Tsang and Ma
PO Box 294
Belmont, CA 94002
Tel: 415-595-2270
oriental seasonings

United Society of Shakers
Sabbathday Lake
Poland Spring, ME 04274
Tel: 207-926-4597
herbs and teas

Honeys and Syrups

American Spoon Foods
411 East Lake Street
Petoskey, MI 49770
Tel: 616-347-9030
preserves and honey

Moon Shine Trading Company
PO Box 896
Winters, CA 95694
Tel: 800-722-4844
honey

Mustards, Relishes, Ketchups, Chutneys

Beaverton Foods
4220 SW Cedar Hills Boulevard
Beaverton, OR 97005
Tel: 503-643-7634
mustards

Chalif, Inc.
RD 3, Box 27220
Wyndmoor, PA 19118
Tel: 215-233-2023
mustards

Groff's Farm Enterprises
RD 3, Box 912
Mount Joy, PA 19118
Tel: 717-653-2048
relishes

Jasmine & Bread
RR 2, Box 256
South Royalton, VT 05068
Tel: 802-763-7115
ketchups

The Silver Palate
274 Columbus Avenue
New York, NY 10023
Tel: 800-847-4747
chutneys, mustards, preserves, vinegars, sauces

Victorian Pantry
153 Utah Avenue
South San Francisco, CA 94080
Tel: 415-871-0340
chutneys

Vermont's Clearview Farms
RR 1
Enosburg Falls, VT 05450
Tel: 802-933-2537
relishes

Nuts

Ace Pecan Co
PO Box 65
Cordele, GA 31015
Tel: 800-323-9754
pecans, nut-of-the-month plan

Country Estate Pecans
L & C Gourmet Products, Inc
PO Box 12607
Tucson, AZ 85732
Tel: 602-791-2062
pecans

Durey-Libby
PO Box 345
Carlstadt, NJ 07072
Tel: 201-939-2775
nuts

Fiesta Nut Corporation
PO Box 366
75 Harbor Road
Port Washington, NY 11050
Tel: 516-853-1400
nuts, chocolate-covered nuts

Gourmet Nut Center
1430 Railroad Avenue
Orland, CA 95963
Tel: 916-865-5511
almonds, pistachios

Lindsay Farms
PO Box 81015
Chamblee, GA 30366
Tel: 404-454-6395
nuts, candies

Missouri Danday Pantry
212 Hammons Drive East
Stockton, MO 65785
Tel: 417-276-5121
nuts, candies

Nuts D'Vine
PO Box 589
Edenton, NC 27932
Tel: 800-334-0492
peanuts

The Peanut Patch
PO Box 186
Courtland, VA 23837
Tel: 804-653-2028
peanuts

Peanut Supply Company
114 North Houston
PO Box 860
Denison, TX 75020
Tel: 214-463-3161
peanuts

Road Runner Pecans
1985 Salopek Road
Las Cruces, NM 88005
Tel: 505-526-5949
pecans

Sunnyland Farms
Albany, GA 31703
Tel: 912-436-5654
pecans

Surry Shop Peanuts
10208 Ranger Road
Fairfax, VA 22030
Tel: 703-385-7368
peanuts

Westnut
PO Box 125
Dundee, OR 97115
Tel: 503-538-2161
hazelnuts

Specialty Foods

Balducci's
424 Avenue of the Americas
New York, NY 10011
Tel: 800-228-2028, ext. 72
212-673-2600

Dean & DeLuca
Mail-Order Department
110 Greene Street
Suite 304
New York, NY 10012
Tel: 800-221-7714
212-431-1691

Grandma Morgan's Gourmet Kitchen
PO Box 972
Lake Oswego, OR 97034
Tel: 503-761-4303

Mission Orchards
PO Box 6947
San Jose, CA 95150
Tel: 408-297-5056

Provender
3883 Main Road
Tiverton, RI 02878
Tel: 401-624-9991

SE Ryckoff & Company
PO Box 21467
Los Angeles, CA 90021
Tel: 213-622-4131

Williams-Sonoma
100 North Point Street
San Francisco CA 94133
Tel: 415-421-7900

Zabar's
2245 Broadway
New York, NY 10024
Tel: 800-221-3347
212-787-2000

Associations

American Herb Assn
PO Box 353
Rescue,CA 95672
Tel: 916-626-5046

American Herbal Products Assn
59-25 63rd Street
Maspeth, NY 11378
Tel: 718-894-8200

American Spice Trade Assn
PO Box 1267
Englewood Cliffs, NJ 07632
Tel: 201-568-2163

Flavor and Extract Manufacturers Assn of the US
900 17th Street NW
Suite 650
Washington, DC 20006
Tel: 202-293-5800

Herb Society of America
Two Independence Court
Concord, MA 01742
Tel: 617-371-1486

Honey Industry Council
13637 NW 39th Avenue
Gainesville, FL 32606
Tel: 904-332-0012

International Maple Syrup Institute
PO Box 715
Swanton, VT 05488
Tel: 802-868-7244

National Assn of Fruits, Flavors, and Syrups
PO Box 776
177 Main Street
Matawan, NJ 07747
Tel: 201-583-8188

North American Maple Syrup Council
c/o Lynn H Reynolds
Route 2, Box 326
Hortonville, WI 54944
Tel: 414-779-6672

Vanilla Bean Assn of America
c/o Fritzsche-DNO
76 Ninth Avenue
New York, NY 10011
Tel: 212-929-4100

Vermont Maple Syrup Industry Council
c/o Don McFeeters
Morrill Hall
University of Vermont
Burlington, VT 05405
Tel: 802-656-2990

Index

ACKNOWLEDGEMENTS
Rex Features 9; Bridgeman Art Library 10, 11; The Hutchison Library (Lyn Gambles) 12, 19; The Hutchison Library (Bernard Regent) 13; Mary Evans Picture Library 15; Tom Deas 16, 17b, 128, 129, 130 131a; A-Z Botanical Collection Ltd 17a; The Hutchison Library 14, 18, 20, 22, 23, 134; The Hutchison Library (Sarah Errington) 21a, (R Ian Lloyd) 21b, 132, 133; The Hutchison Library (Lesley Nelson) 131b; H J Heinz Co Ltd 135.